THE CAROLINA CORPORATION

THE
CAROLINA
CORPORATION

Inside Dean Smith and the Tar Heels

STEVE HOLSTROM

TAYLOR PUBLISHING COMPANY
Dallas, Texas

Copyright © 1988 by Steve Holstrom

All rights reserved

No part of this book may be reproduced in any form without
written permission from the publisher.

Published by
Taylor Publishing Company
1550 West Mockingbird Lane
Dallas, Texas 75235

Library of Congress Cataloging-In-Publication Data

Holstrom, Steve.
    The Carolina Corporation / Steve Holstrom
    p. cm.
    Includes index.
    ISBN 0-87833-654-0 : $16.95
    1. University of North Carolina at Chapel Hill -- Basketball.
2. Smith, Dean. 3. Basketball -- United States -- Coaches. I. Title.
GV885. 43. U54H65 1988
796.32 ' 363 ' 09756 -- dc19   88-24893
                                                        CIP

Printed in the United States of America

10 9 8 7 6 5 4 3 2 1

To my family,
Mom and Dad, Don, Pat, and Susan
for their support and understanding over many years;
to my wife, Madonna, and my daughter, Sarah, for their love;
and to Steven for the opportunity.

CONTENTS

FOREWORD

One of the first questions I get asked at speaking engagements is "Is it true that you and Dean really hate each other?" Well, we're not close socially, but we don't hate each other. We're competitors. And when you compete, you don't tell each other your shortcomings. Dean is a very good competitor. He's good at trying to get every psychological edge he can, and he doesn't give many edges away, either. Good coaches are that way and he's one of the best. Still, a lot of people think that we hate each other because we've had some misunderstandings and our teams have played a lot of close, great games against each other.

My relationship with Dean Smith really began about 25 years ago when I was coaching at Davidson. Dean was the new coach at North Carolina and our two teams competed against each other in practice scrimmages in the old Charlotte Coliseum. From the very beginning I knew he was a competitor. I also knew right away that he was a person who would never say anything that would hurt someone or reflect negatively on one of his players or the North Carolina basketball program. He might not always tell you the whole story or tell you exactly how he feels, but he'll tell you what he thinks is the proper response or what is best for North Carolina basketball.

He's the best at handling the media of anyone that I know. Everything he says is very guarded and very calculated. I admire that about him— he's always in control of the situation. But, I can't operate that way. I just say what I think and I lose my temper sometimes. I have never heard him put his foot in his mouth. Consequently, he's very good at public relations and obviously a very good basketball coach.

I had never seen any of his teams practice until the last couple of years when I was working in television. I was impressed with his enthusiasm and the way he teaches. And he knows how to get every psychological edge. Dean used to start on the officials during the preseason scrimmages. He would bring them down to Chapel Hill and put them up in a nice motel, feed them in a nice resturant, and pay them a couple hundred dollars to referee scrimmages. There was no rule against it then. Now the officials are assigned and you can't pay or entertain them.

Dean keeps up with the officials' records, too. He would go up to one before a game and say something like "Hey, we lost the last three times you officiated," and it puts pressure on the guy for that game. We're not supposed to talk to the officials before a game now. In recruiting, he would never come right out and say something negative about a competitor, but he will say things in a way that still gets the point across.

Dean's always the first to come up with a new edge. He was the one who started having basketball teams staying in all them fancy hotels. When I started coaching at Davidson, we had what we called "local entertainment." We would stay at the school we were playing and sleep in a room on campus. Davidson had a room off of the gymnasium with bunks in it for visiting teams. Dean started having his teams stay in motels. At Davidson after my team won a game we might go out and eat steaks, but if we lost we would eat hot dogs. Well, the word got around that Dean fed his team steak win or lose. So I had to start feeding my team steaks when they lost. I think he was one of the first coaches to put blazers on his players and buy them nice slacks. He wanted his team to look better than anyone else. I bought my players nice blazers and slacks, but he bought cashmere jackets and very expensive pants, shirts and ties. Of course, there was nothing wrong with doing that at the time. It was legal and it was an edge. It is illegal now.

UNC basketball has a wonderful image because of the way that Dean has been able to handle the press, radio, and TV people. If I had to pick the main reason why I wanted to read about Dean's program it would be because of the way they have dominated the ACC. I never liked playing against the Tar Heels because they were always so tough to beat, but when you beat them it meant a lot.

For 20 years or so, Dean's program has dominated the ACC and been a force nationally. For 16 of those years, I coached Maryland in the same league. We won more games (134) against ACC opponents (tournament included) than anyone except North Carolina (they won 183). However, we were a distant second. Reading *The Carolina Corporation* has given me an interesting look inside that program; maybe it'll give me an edge on ol' Dean.

Charles "Lefty" Driesell

INTRODUCTION

Three leading topics for discussion concerning the state of North Carolina are, depending on whom you are talking to, Jesse Helms, Tammy Faye and Jim Bakker, and Dean Smith and the Tar Heel basketball program.

Helms, a highly visible senator, has never been one to quietly go about his business of providing the nation with a role model for ultra- conservatism. "Love him or leave him" has always been the battle cry for those who support his views.

The Bakkers, the second most highly publicized couple in the world behind royal couple Charles and Diana, gave the globe still another reason to question television evangelism. Their trials and tribulations only prove how much they need the Lord's forgiveness themselves, however. "Love them or leave them" has been the battle cry for those who still believe in the part-time shepherds, part-time entertainers.

This book looks closely at the third entity — the North Carolina basketball program. And lest it be intimated that the Tar Heel organization is the only one of the three that is universally respected and admired, it can safely be said that one usually loves or hates the Tar Heels as well.

Like other large established companies, UNC has integrated some of the very tactics that have made IBM, AT&T, and GM the powerful trendsetters they are today.

This corporate consistency allows the program to win even in the so-called lean or rebuilding years. The 1987-88 edition was one such season. UNC had lost the services of five seniors, including All-America point guard Kenny Smith and stalwart front-line players Joe Wolf and Dave Popson. All three contributed greatly to the program, helping to compile a 115–20 record over four seasons, including an undefeated ACC regular season. All three were drafted by the NBA, Smith and Wolf in the first round.

The whole team would make up the loss. Back in uniform were academic casualty Kevin Madden and redshirt freshman Pete Chilcutt. They joined a nucleus of active returning players: Jeff Lebo, J.R. Reid, Scott Williams, Steve Bucknall, and Ranzino Smith. In addition, freshman recruits Rick Fox and King David Rice were expected to contribute. The nine combined to meet the challenge, winning the conference regular season and overachieving their way to the "Final Five." Such accomplishment is expected from the Tar Heel program.

Carolina's unique approach to basketball has provided a blueprint for success. And the man behind the company's prosperity is Dean Smith. It is Smith, the CEO if you will, who instills a sense of team sacrifice above individual honor. And although it's not vogue in the "Me" generation, the sense of cooperation and unity that Smith instills in his program is highly commendable in these selfish times. At the same time, his tendencies are inflexible and restraining, capable of suppressing highly talented superstars. To ensure consistency, Smith maintains a rigid and strongly disciplined program. The bottom line is not result-oriented for the sake of always winning, but for attaining excellence while competing against one's self. The individual is asked to take a back seat to the team player.

Entrepreneurs need not apply; North Carolina looks only for men that follow the company line.

I.
THE COMPANY

The Man

He works in a $33.8 million building built largely through the results of his successes. Though he does not own it, it is his building. It bears his name. Throughout the building, the walls reflect his signature stamped in photographs of his company's many accomplishments. A bust of the man prominently distinguishes a public entrance foyer. He doesn't use the entrance. He feels it is pretentious. His entrance is more remote and protected by an electronic security system.

The entire building is wired with state-of-the-art electronics. Video and audio cable run throughout the building. Scores of phone lines snake their way through predetermined portals. Satellite signals are received and can be transmitted from the two dishes permanently mounted on the roof of an adjacent annex.

In his suite of offices, one man sits at the controls. At his disposal is a vast array of equipment and information. His filing system covers years of surveillance, the fruits of the labor of a hundred or more attendants. A dozen or so newspapers are read and clipped from daily. The airwaves are monitored for data from around the country to be taped and referenced for future use. The muffled sounds of computer terminals and printers are present. Statistics are a way of life at his company and the numbers are updated constantly. Seldom is it completely quiet in the outer offices of his suite. His inner sanctum is different.

His immediate surroundings are in keeping with the tasteful selections that adorn the rest of the building, but are softer and appear more lived in. The twin couches and assorted side chairs look comfortable, not decorous. It is obviously the office of an important individual, but it also reflects his personality, not the position he holds. There is a faint odor of cigarette smoke, but the overriding smell is one of success.

Seated in a high-backed executive's chair behind a formidable desk, the man contemplates the numerous decisions that he alone can make. A stack of pink message slips signifies calls he will return; his executive secretary will handle an even greater amount, with his approval. Another batch of correspondence needs only his signature to be set into motion. Piles of newsprint, file folders, videotapes, and remote controls cover his desk. A human element is present in an assortment of family photographs, a large glass ashtray, coffee mugs, and both Diet and Classic Coke cans.

His time is the most precious commodity of all. His calendar is rigidly scheduled. In addition to the constant demands of running a multimillion dollar operation are numerous individual requests for his time. The media is a regular source of such queries. His opinion and advice are sought at many levels in his industry. There is little chance to escape the relentless demands placed upon him. Everyone's needs are met, every audience eventually granted. Priorities are maintained, flexibility tolerated only when a company man needs to see him. For his ultimate responsibility is to his company — to recruit and teach new men to carry on the success he began. It is a responsibility he doesn't take lightly.

The man is Dean Edwards Smith. His company is the University of North Carolina men's basketball program.

Though millions know of the man and his program, little is known about the inner workings of the business or its chief executive officer. Generally willing to share his professional knowledge with most who ask, Coach Smith chooses not to disclose his personal life to an inquisitive public. But to fully understand the complexities of the company, one must know a bit about its architect. Even his peers in the industry will admit to a lack of personal insight. Some venture a description by virtue of his chosen profession.

"If anyone was ever born to be a coach, it's Dean Smith," said Al McGuire. "He's the Jack Armstrong-type person."

The quotation has been printed in hundreds of thousands of North Carolina basketball media guides over the years. Many writers also cite McGuire's words, eager to quote someone as famous as the former Marquette basketball coach and current NBC color broadcaster. Other journalists are pleased that a credible source has been close enough to Smith to define what the esteemed coach is really like. Most are forced to repeat the description for lack of a personal vantage point from which to assess Smith's personality in their own right.

Although Smith is a household word whenever collegiate basketball is discussed, only a handful of close friends know his true personality. Many in his small inner circle choose not to divulge any personal interaction, keeping shared experiences to themselves. Others know of Smith's preference for privacy and agree to guard it well. When an insider does go on record about Dean Smith, the remarks are limited in scope and revelation.

"He's a rare combination of effectiveness," says Christopher Fordham, then UNC chancellor and one of Smith's golfing foursome. His description indicates the distance between the coach and his friends. "There's the human side, the technical side, and the spiritual side. We would all like to be as effective in our work as he is in his."

Of all the possible descriptive words he could select, Fordham, a knowledgeable academician as well as a close personal friend, chose to describe Dean Smith as being effective. The adjective is not out of line. Nondescript. Structured. Generic. Stubborn. Competitive. Bland. All are words similarly used to describe the coach. And without formulating descriptions from firsthand experience, the personal estimations are correct. However, the results Smith obtains with such consistency are anything but commonplace. Few college basketball fans would argue that Dean Smith isn't the game's best tactician and consummate innovator.

Perhaps it is only fitting to describe the man by his achievements. He is, after all, the game's winningest active coach. Still, many think his systematic approach to basketball is boring and constraining, compared to some of today's colorful contemporaries. "Give us the fire of a Bobby Knight, the bearish arrogance of a John Thompson, the outspokenness of a Billy Tubbs or the pizazz of a Jimmy Valvano," cries a public yearning for a more dynamic personality. Yet, in the same breath, the public also demands the accomplishments of a Dean Smith.

Describing Smith as a Jack Armstrong-type personality may be correct for both the coach and his program, but for different reasons than those expressed by McGuire. Jack Armstrong isn't real. The radio program, *Jack Armstrong, the All-American Boy*, featured a fictional character created by former journalist Robert Hardy Andrews in 1933. The character was portrayed as a super-athlete whose bottom-of-the-ninth, last-second efforts always saved the day for Hudson High School and thus stood for everything right and glorious in team athletics. Young Jack's skill and prowess were proclaimed later in the radio series theme song:

> *Wave the flag for Hudson High, boys,*
> *Show them how we stand;*
> *Ever shall our team be champions*
> *Known throughout the land!*

Armstrong's character was as wholesome as the program's sponsor, Wheaties, the "Breakfast of Champions." Overseen by Dr. Martin L. Reymert, a well-known child psychologist and director of a laboratory for childhood research, each script was checked for wholesomeness. And because of its lofty standards of moral character, the radio show was accepted with both wide-eyed innocence and narrow-minded cynicism. So too is the Carolina basketball program under Dean Smith. "He represents this institution so well that people can't quite believe it," Fordham says. "The negative feelings are largely the result of envy and jealousy, but nevertheless, they are strong feelings."

Smith and his basketball program have unconsciously attempted to parallel the early American radio program. For those who believe, the Carolina program stands for what is right in collegiate athletics — academics first, unselfish team play, and finally athletic excellence in competition. But like any team with heavenly expectations, perfection can only be attained in fiction. Though the Carolina basketball program strives to achieve the heights, and comes as close as any in the nation, the program that seems too good to be true *is*, in reality, too good to be true. What you see is not necessarily what you get. More important than any single component of the Carolina tradition is keeping its rarely tarnished image polished to a bright sheen. With the same "good" intentions as the huge corporations that proclaim concern for the public welfare while acting to increase their profits for select shareholders, the Carolina company is content to champion its belief in education before athletics, while spending millions to the contrary.

In an address to the NCAA Convention in January 1988, Fordham said, "We willingly pour countless millions of dollars into sports at all levels, while the poor do without medical care, people sleep in streets, and our schools and colleges are deprived of the support which they should have." While Fordham was making a plea to correct confused and distorted values in collegiate athletics, his school's basketball program was deep into spending a $1.2 million annual budget. Running the nation's showcase program isn't cheap.

The Carolina company has long since abandoned a schedule of intercollegiate basketball games among regional teams. The team bus has been replaced by a chartered jet. Regional matchups have given way to international play. College gymnasiums have become huge coliseums. Viewing the Carolina basketball program as an amateur varsity sport is, like Jack Armstrong, fiction. The truth, in this case, is not stranger than fiction, only more complicated.

A study of Smith's "corporation" is complex and simple at the same time. If his methods were reduced to a science, he builds and maintains his program with mathematics. It is no strange coincidence that both Smith and his chief assistant coach of 21 years, Bill Guthridge, are educated mathematicians. The required course for an insight into the x's and o's of the Carolina game plan would be Probability and Statistics 101. His game philosophy is straightforward. The team that scores the most points in a game wins. The team that makes the most shots wins. The team that shoots the highest-percentage shots usually makes the most shots and thus wins. In direct correlation, the team that forces its opponents to take and make fewer shots, and to take lower-percentage ones when they do shoot, wins.

Smith's formula for a consistent winning program is much more complex than the mere winning of a game. It takes an intelligent CEO to run the nation's premier basketball factory. And few, if any, can match Dean Smith.

"He's very smart and he's also a people person — he understands people," says Guthridge, the closest person to Smith on a professional level. "Those two traits stand out above everything else. He knows basketball and he's smart. He can remember what this or that coach did five years ago in a similar situation.

"Also, he has confidence and conveys that confidence to the players."

Knowledge and confidence are two good terms to describe how his players perform in Carolina blue. Smith's ability to instill his basketball savvy and philosophy of play into his young executives is uncanny. Belief in the system and the discipline to follow that system are critical to the continued success of his program — one that has evolved extensively in the 27 years since Smith took over the head coaching duties.

Though the University of North Carolina–Chapel Hill has enjoyed 78 years of winning basketball, the Tar Heel basketball program did not attain national distinction until 1956–57. That season, head coach Frank McGuire put the program into the record books with a perfect 32–0 record that resulted in the school's first NCAA championship. The day following the championship game, McGuire asked Dean Smith, then an assistant coach at the Air Force Academy, if he would be interested in an assistant coaching job at North Carolina. Though Smith didn't accept the position until it was offered the following year, hiring him proved to be one of McGuire's greatest achievements — at least in the minds of those who follow collegiate basketball.

Smith was a quick study. The young assistant coach learned about loyalty and concern from McGuire. "Imagine how good it made me feel in my first year as his assistant when — out of the clear blue — he called me into his office and said, 'I'm going to New York on a recruiting trip for several days, so you take practices while I'm gone. I think you're ready to do that.' Always gracious and kind to everyone from the teenage peanut vendor to the athletic director, Frank is a man who seems to sincerely believe that every person stands on the same level." It is a trait Smith incorporated into his own philosophy of life. Smith's loyalty to his staff, players, and former players is absolute.

After a brief stint as McGuire's assistant, Smith took over the reins of the program prior to the 1961–62 season. McGuire left Carolina for the professional coaching ranks, but not before he lobbied Smith into the head coaching position and not before leaving Carolina on NCAA probation. McGuire stated publicly that he wanted to coach Wilt Chamberlain and the Philadelphia Warriors, citing a lack of challenge in the collegiate game. In reality, the Irish coach had just concluded what he described as the worst year of his life.

In the course of one year, the North Carolina program underwent a lifetime of trauma and scandal. The list of problems began surfacing in the spring of 1960. UNC was put under investigation by the NCAA for alleged illegal recruiting; Atlantic Coast Conference Commissioner James Weaver put freshman standout Billy Gallantai of Brooklyn, New York, on athletic probation for a year for misrepresenting a fact on his eligibility statement; the NCAA found UNC guilty of "excessive entertainment" of athletes and "insufficient accounting of athletic funds" for basketball recruiting, and placed Carolina on a one-year probation with sanctions that made the Tar Heels ineligible to compete in any postseason tournaments. North Carolina then withdrew from the ACC basketball tournament that season; Tar Heel Ken McComb of Ardsley, New York, was declared ineligible after the first semester for scholastic deficiencies; the team was involved in a brawl against Duke on February 4 that ended the game and resulted in the suspension of two Tar Heel players. Most damaging of all these events was the implication of Tar Heels Lou Brown and Doug Moe in a nationwide basketball scandal.

To make matters worse, the basketball budget, already far below what McGuire thought it should be, was cut even further. Sources close to then-Chancellor William Aycock have since said Aycock chose to fire McGuire, giving him six months to find another job. Dean Smith was then picked to be the "de-emphasis" coach because of his youth, character, and role in helping Aycock deal with the earlier NCAA investigations and resulting trials. It was hoped Smith would repair the damage and put together an honest, and perhaps less visible, program.

No doubt reluctantly at first, Dean Smith, a relative newcomer to collegiate coaching at the tender age of 30, took over the position of head coach. He had only three years under his belt as the Tar Heel assistant coach, and many North Carolina supporters weren't sure the young man from Kansas could continue UNC's winning ways. In addition to the stigma of the NCAA and ACC probations, Smith needed to get out from under the shadow of Frank McGuire's earlier success and forge his own program. Following in the footsteps of a proven NCAA championship winner was no easy task.

McGuire himself gave his protege advice on how to modify the program. "He told me to do something different, to make a change of some kind," Smith said. "Change the uniforms or change the bench, just do something to let people know I was the coach and not Frank McGuire. I didn't, but I should have."

It takes more than changing uniforms to become a winning head coach, especially when the school is in the process of de-emphasizing the varsity sport. Smith's first few seasons were not fun. Dean Smith didn't start his coaching career with towering centers and forwards, a trademark he has developed over the years. All-American York Larese had graduated. Doug Moe, Carolina's other All-American and a frequent baby-sitter for Smith's children, was kicked out of school for accepting $75 in expense money from a man later arrested and convicted of rigging collegiate basketball games. (Smith didn't give up on Moe even after he was no longer a member of the program. The new head coach was instrumental in getting Moe into Elon College, onto a team in Italy after graduation, and then into the ABA. After years of coaching pro ball, Doug Moe was selected this past year as Coach of the Year in the NBA for his handling of the Denver Nuggets.) Only four players returned for the 1961-62 Tar Heel season, including premier guard Larry Brown, who went on to play and coach in the ABA before becoming one of the country's better basketball coaches. As a result of the scandal, the university cut the working budget for the basketball program to the minimum. Smith and company finished the year with a dismal 8–9 record. It turned out to be the only losing season of Smith's head coaching career.

Due to the circumstances, the fans and the administration were understanding. Aycock went out of his way to assure the new coach that winning was not the primary concern. The chancellor told the young coach that he had a job as long as there were no NCAA probations, no gambling, and no fights. Smith kept his job. In addition to keeping Aycock's three golden rules, Smith improved the program's record to 15–6 the next year, on the strength of wily Billy Cunningham, a great collegiate star and later a standout NBA player, coach, and broadcaster. But the third year turned out to be the charm. A snake charm.

Instead of building on his success, Smith began to doubt and second-guess himself. He began to juggle his lineup, causing inconsistent results. Looking back in the late '70s, Smith noted the mixed messages he gave to his players. "I couldn't make up my mind which players to play," Smith said. "I kept shuffling players and changing my lineup; I'd say it was the worst coaching of my career." The lesson was not lost on the coach and he filed away the unpleasant memories, determined not to commit the error again. "Athletes are secure when they are playing regularly," he continued. "Any time you have a guy looking over his shoulder, saying 'Hey, if I make a mistake, somebody else is going to start the next game,' it does something to that player so that he can't concentrate on his job."

Smith no longer feels the same way. While the company chooses to stress that a starting role is not important, playing time is. Carolina basketball players must constantly look over their shoulders after making a mistake. In the '80s, the coach is quick to pull players off of the floor.

But during the 1963-64 season, Smith was too close to the problem to stand back and notice his mistakes. With a woeful 6–6 record, the Tar Heels returned to Chapel Hill on the evening of January 9 after a trouncing by the Demon Deacons of Wake Forest. The scene that greeted Smith and company adds historically to the legend of Dean Smith and no account of his program is complete without it. As the chartered bus rolled through campus toward Woolen Gym, then the Tar Heel home court, a mob of angry students gathered to demonstrate their displeasure. Hanging from a large oak tree outside the gym was a burning dummy representing Coach Smith. As the bus braked to a stop, members of the team angrily prepared to rush out and defend their coach's honor. Smith remained calm and instructed his team to behave like gentlemen and ignore the mob and the burning effigy. In this instance, Billy Cunningham and some teammates didn't listen to their coach and broke through the student protesters to pull down the dummy. The players were defensive about their coach and felt he had done well with a mediocre team.

Smith, bruised mentally by the experience, has tried over the years to overcome the nightmare. In an authorized biography, *The Dean Smith Story: More Than a Coach* by Thad Mumau, Smith spoke about the students and the motivation behind their actions. "It could have been just a group of students who felt the way those did who participated in that thing; or it could have been that everyone felt that way, I don't know. Anyway, two days later we went over to Duke for our next game and upset Duke, which was going great in its heyday. So, I'm glad those students did what they did because what happened certainly gave us an emotional edge for the Duke game."

True, the Tar Heels won by three points. But the real reason Smith chose to place the accent on the following game was for piece of mind — his piece of mind. Smith constructed a positive scenario to mask his former embarrassment. Few negative instances have occurred since to match such a stormy beginning. But even after 25 years the coach is still defensive about anything said that is less than flattering about himself or his program.

So much for ancient history. Though the initial years of transition from junior executive to chairman of the board were rocky, Smith persevered to achieve living-legend status. His teams flourished so much that the Tar Heels outgrew two gymnasiums en route to the 21,444-seat Smith Center. Through 27 years, Dean Smith developed his systematic approach to winning basketball. His results are a matter of record. With a lifetime tally of 638 wins to 182 losses, Smith is by far the winningest active collegiate coach in the game today. His consistency is equally amazing. In the '80s, no other program has come close to matching the company's accomplishments. For eight consecutive seasons the Tar Heels have won at least 27 games and finished the season ranked in the Top 10 by both the Associated Press and United Press International. His results are obtained by a combination of mathematics, intelligence, attention to detail, repetition, innovation, loyalty, astute business practices, and the stubbornness not to change any of these. As Smith would be first to acknowledge, his players have won a great many basketball games. Though he would be the first to disagree, the overwhelming success of the program is due to Dean Smith.

True, the players Smith and company groomed over the years would most likely have achieved success at other schools. But it is less likely they would have learned the strong fundamental aspects of the game or grown to their full potential without the coaching imprint Smith stamps deep into his players. "I think you cannot do your job and say, 'Here's the ball, gang,' or the players will go out and they won't live up to their potential," says Smith. "A coach is supposed to bring them together as a team. What we do is discipline them first and then say, 'Now you're free.'"

Freedom is not gained easily in the company. Smith's system breaks down the self and builds a team player out of each member — recruit and walk-on — both on and off the gym floor. Many observers feel Coach Smith's discipline inhibits those who play for him. Others note that Smith creates cloned players as easily as McDonald's makes hamburgers. The players begin to walk, talk, and look alike, displaying what Smith deems appropriate behavior. Smith reminds the public continually that "we do things the right way here." And the right way at North Carolina is his way. Off the court, team members are required to be polite, wear coats and ties to games, and never detour from the company line. On the floor, players are expected to hustle, display good sportsmanship, and pass up personal glory for the well-being of the team. Individuals can score, but only in the context of the offense — and then only with Smith's blessing.

Former UNC standouts Walter Davis, James Worthy, and Michael Jordan all exploded as offensive scoring machines upon entering the NBA. They were definitely held in check in college. Marty Blake, an oft-quoted

NBA scouting guru, speaks of Smith as the only person to hold Walter Davis to 15 points a game. The same can be said for many current and former Tar Heels. Jordan, who sets new standards for scoring each year he plays in the NBA, holds no scoring records at Carolina. His career scoring average at Carolina was a mere 17.7 points per game. "Most people think Coach Smith put a leash on us and wouldn't let us just go out and play," says James Worthy, now starring with the 1988 World Champion Los Angeles Lakers. "That's not true. He has a team-oriented system, but he didn't put any restraints on me." Worthy's best collegiate game was his last in a blue and white uniform when he literally took control of the 1982 NCAA tournament final in New Orleans, scoring a career-high 28 points. Had it not been the championship game, Smith might have removed Worthy from the game for such demonstrative heroics. The power forward left Carolina following his junior year to translate his blossoming skills into dollar bills — and succeeded.

As any player will *publicly* testify, *who* scores for the company isn't important. Players learn quickly to downplay the numbers they put on the scoreboard. Points are merely the result of a "great" assist from a teammate. "We never think in terms of who's going to get the points," Smith says. "We're worried about North Carolina getting the points." Stat sheets provided by the Carolina sports information staff, recently renamed the UNC sports publicity staff, list the players alphabetically as opposed to "number of points scored" or "minutes played," unlike the majority of publicity departments at other schools.

Smith's underlying concern is that all players play within their capabilities. There is no ceiling set on displaying talent, only that the talent be achieved and built upon through repetition in practice. Showtime moves or dunks are considered inappropriate in most cases, and are tolerated only if the player has demonstrated such a play beforehand. Former players now in the NBA often eschew a spectacular dunk when a simple layup will suffice. Playing time, the only reward other than a scholarship, is given to those who perform to consistently high standards. The most gifted athletes are not always the ones Smith puts on the floor. "He's very truthful to his players; truthful enough to tell you your limitations — what you can and don't do, what you're good at and what you're not good at," says Michael Jordan of the Chicago Bulls. "And he expects you to work on them and he can tell if you didn't."

Players who don't toe the line shouldn't expect their coach to scream and holler. Discipline takes a different route with the company. Smith is grounded in a personal philosophy of Christian theology and modern teaching methodology. With a Baptist upbringing and later study of such theologians as Dietrich Bonhoffer, Soren Kierkegaard, and Paul Tillich, Smith utilizes peer pressure and guilt to carry the weight when it comes to reprimanding his athletes or motivating them to achieve excellence. "He makes you feel everyone on the team is sacrificing for you," says Phil Ford, a legendary Tar Heel, former NBA Rookie of the Year, and recently named UNC assistant coach, "and that you should be doing the same for them." The individual is not just letting himself down, but he disappoints the entire program if he fails to perform to the best of his ability. Such a philosophy is the essence of self-sacrifice. It also encourages team play.

"If a rule is broken," Smith says, "we punish as a team. We believe in group punishment for an individual infraction. We have found this peer-pressure method far more effective in building team morale than motivation created by fear, reward, or any other means." Punishment usually takes the form of the whole team running wind sprints. "The coaching staff gives a great deal of attention to being fair in its criticism as well as in administering punishment when it is necessary. We criticize the act rather than the person."

Once this sense of duty is instilled, the player can be taught how to play the game. Better yet, he can be taught how to play the game according to Dean Smith. "I knew going there that it was a team-oriented basketball style that he coached," says Brad Daugherty, another ex-Tar Heel turned NBA All-Star, "but I didn't realize how much so until I got there. The game was 'we' basketball. And team basketball is a challenge because you have to discipline yourself to play in rhythm with other individuals, because if you're not [in rhythm], you throw off the whole scheme of things.

"When you play for Coach Smith, you learn to play a game you don't really know. You may think you know the game of basketball, but you don't until you have played for him." To play for him is to have learned from him.

More so than any other gift he possesses, Smith is a teacher. A master teacher. And if Smith makes any demands on his students, it's that they study his lessons unequivocally. "The only thing I tell my players is, if you decide basketball is important, then do it well," Smith says. "If you decide. Only you can decide that. Because we're talking about real artists by the time they get to this level. That means hours and hours of practice." Self-sacrifice. Team play. Discipline.

"Years ago," Smith explained, "Dr.[Robert] Seymour [his church's pastor] gave a sermon that made so much sense to me. It was called 'The Paradox of Discipline,' and I had it mimeographed. He made the point that the disciplined person is the one that's truly free. The student who says, 'I could make A's if I tried,' but who doesn't have the discipline to sit down and do it, is the one who's shackled. The disciplined student is free: he has the choice of making an A or D."

If the student athlete has the motivation and desire to succeed, he would be hard-pressed to find a better prepared teacher. Dean Smith brings a wealth of experience to his pupils. Systematically, every player receives equal doses of fundamentals, strategies, skills, and confidence that can be put to use in basketball and life. Each player also learns he can count on his teammates, and more importantly, Smith himself, for the rest of his days. Though teaching may be God's greatest gift to Smith, Smith's greatest gift to his players is the knowledge that he will always be there for them. It is both a strength and a weakness.

"It must have been very difficult for him to tough it out with me when I had a serious personal problem after my seventh year in the NBA," says Phil Ford. "After all, didn't he have enough to take care of in Chapel Hill without having to call me every day to see how I was coming along with my recovery? That in itself was a lesson to me in what true friendship is all about.

"I could tell from watching and listening to him during my years at Carolina that Coach Smith is a deeply spiritual man, but never did he force that side of his life on any of us players. He practiced it instead of preaching it, but we all knew it was there. When I started my life over again at age 29, I sought out the spiritual side of Coach Smith and found him to be an even sturdier rock than I thought he was."

To know that Dean Smith is always available is a great relief. His knowledge, care, and contacts have helped many a former player in need. Such compassion takes its toll on Smith, for he doesn't take the responsibility lightly. Over the years his "family" has grown into triple digits and many of those members have enlarged the clan with families of their own. Christmas cards and letters are exchanged with former players and their families. Personal visits and phone calls occur frequently. It has been documented that the coach still corresponds with a house painter who encouraged Dennis Wuycik to attend Carolina 20 years ago. Smith is consulted for everything from marriage counseling to job changes. His advice requires thought and effort. His burden increases continually.

Family members see him as a counselor — the man who has the answer to their problems. Outsiders and interviewers see him as a man who seeks to control each circumstance, changing the subject or asking questions to steer the conversation. Overall, Smith's imperfections are rarely revealed. "I'd say his flaw is that he gets caught up sometimes in the masculine image of being the supplier of everyone's needs, the one in control of every situation," said Linnea Smith, the coach's wife and closest friend. "The thing that's missing [from portrayals of Smith] is the vulnerability. He has affectional needs. He is very sensitive and sentimental, and he can express deep emotions intimately even better than I."

Interested parties will have to take her word for it. Smith's feelings are seldom available for public consumption. Though a skillful public speaker with a memory for names and faces that is astounding, the man's personal life is not for sale. Dean Smith could be elected to any political office in North Carolina, and he could easily make a million dollars in commercial endorsements. Instead, he chooses to pass up additional fame and fortune to further develop and maintain the nation's showcase collegiate basketball program.

Keeping his program the best in the land requires the services of a great many support people. It also takes money. A great deal of money. In fact, the company makes and spends more money than any other collegiate basketball program in the country.

North Carolina, like most dominating athletic programs in either football or basketball, relies heavily on rich tradition and the revenues generated by radio, television, and gate receipts to maintain its status. North Carolina athletics command an annual budget of over $12 million. Prior to the season, UNC Athletic Director John Swofford projected that the 1987-88 basketball program would add a cool $4.1 million to the athletic department coffers. The figure didn't include nearly another million dollars received from 1988 NCAA tournament winnings or nearly a quarter of a million dollars from the school's share of concessions. Against budgeted expenses of $1.2 million, basketball at North Carolina is a very profitable business.

Success breeds success. Three ways in which the company's success is measured are results, revenue, and public relations. Without a good product (results) there are no sales (revenue), and eventually there will be no interest and no need for communication (public relations). At North Carolina, all three are stellar, with only occasional problems in the publicity department. Though the overall athletic program at North Carolina is one of the nation's best, dealing with its sports information/publicity staff for access and information is often constraining and fruitless. Any fast-breaking negative news concerning Tar Heel athletics is stonewalled and not willingly shared with the media. As any successful business is apt to do, less-than-shining examples of corporate enterprise are carefully screened from the public eye until the crisis subsides and a suitable strategy for a "harmless" press release has been developed.

In the '80s, the company is riding the peak of its basketball prowess. No other program is able to consistently stay within shouting distance of the nation's premier program. While programs at such universities as Indiana, Kentucky, Louisville, and Georgetown have all demonstrated their proficiency over the years, none has sustained such greatness year after year. The 1988 NCAA tournament is a good example. Indiana, then the reigning national champion, lost to the University of Richmond in the first round of the tourney. Georgetown lost in the second round. Kentucky and Louisville each advanced one game further, but fell short of reaching the regional finals. Only North Carolina, in what was supposed to be a rebuilding year, got within five minutes of the Final Four to reach what Smith referred to as "the Final Five."

What is it that sets North Carolina apart from the rest? Why do so many of the nation's premier student athletes choose to attend UNC to play for Dean Smith? Why are the Tar Heels always *the* team to beat?

Recruiting

You can't have a great program without great teams. You can't have a great team without great players. Great players have to commit to the program with regularity before the program becomes great. A player chooses a program for its coach, its previous players, the results those players produced, and the players currently enrolled. At North Carolina, all four reasons are a given. And with the possible exception of the past two years, large-scale recruiting has long since given way to quantified selection.

In Smith's case, the young coach began learning the recruiting ropes from the ever-smooth Frank McGuire. McGuire already had a firm hold on recruiting from New York, long a breeding ground for talented players. His contacts provided the program with a continuous flow of excellent players to supplement those who hailed from North Carolina and the surrounding states. The regularity of New York recruits on what was called the "Underground Railroad" gave the Southern university its first national recognition. McGuire recruited talent first, and then adjusted his program to the talent on hand. He allowed the team to establish its own style of basketball, adapting to whatever strengths developed among the players. McGuire left the strategy to his assistant coach, turning energies to pacing the game and providing his team with psychological counseling. His style of letting his players play was in direct contrast to the later coaching style of Dean Smith. Still, the young coach observed and cultivated McGuire's skill at recruiting highly talented athletes. Former assistant coach Roy Williams did most of the legwork involved in recruiting, with chief assistant coach Guthridge logging almost as many hours. (Williams has since left UNC to become the head coach of the Kansas basketball program.) Personal correspondence from the coaching staff to young recruits and their parents includes newspaper clippings, magazine articles about the program, and current media guides, but such communication usually comes after the prospect has been carefully scrutinized. Smith is the ultimate decision maker and normally assumes the role of "closer." The coach often spends time with the recruit talking about anything except basketball. Phil Ford says Smith met with him and his parents in Rocky Mount, North Carolina, and discussed studying and graduating and larger issues such as world hunger and race relations. Talking hoops wasn't necessary. By the time Dean Smith visits a prospect's home, a scholarship offer is in mind if not in hand. No recruits are asked to visit the Carolina campus, unless the company is extending a scholarship.

As his program grew in stature, Smith later improved on McGuire's recruiting concepts by adding qualifications to the selection process. North Carolina is always in the market for the best the country has to offer in terms of basketball talent, but not without reservations. If Smith has his way, his athletes are seen but not heard. While exceptional athletes receive encouragement to attend UNC, it is vitally important the athlete be able to fit into the overall scheme of the program. The recruited athlete will receive a scholarship, learn basketball skills, and hopefully graduate from the sound academic university. Any personal laurels or professional fame are sacrificed or at least postponed until graduation. The team, and ultimately the program, comes first.

Gradually, in order to be considered, highly sought prospects around the globe must evolve into highly sought prospects who can also fit into the mold of what a good student athlete should be. The ideal candidate would not only be an exceptional basketball player, but also a student athlete who would present the public with the appropriate Carolina image. The prospect need not be a pre-med or English lit major with combined SAT scores in the teens, but to suit up with the team he must be able to maintain a higher standard of education than even the NCAA requires. Kevin Madden, a junior swingman this season, still has two years of eligibility left due to sitting out his sophomore year to improve his academic standing. According to the official company line, after Madden completed a so-so rookie season the coaching staff critiqued his academic year. Though he met the requirements of the NCAA, they felt he needed to study more books than hoops. Madden was then officially "suspended" from playing in 1986-87.

Many outside the program felt there were other reasons. Tom Solomon, a sports writer in Greensboro, felt strongly enough to write a commentary in the November 14, 1986, issue of *The Sports Page* entitled "Is Kevin Madden Dean's Point to Prove?" The article questioned the team's true motivation behind the action to bench the sophomore. "Beneath all the self-serving hype about academic priorities, what Madden's suspension appears to be is, quite simply, a disciplinary action on the part of Dean Smith and his staff," wrote Solomon. The writer went on to say that in his freshman year, Madden showed little of the talent and promise that had made him one of the nation's top recruits.

"Madden's history at Carolina, though short, is an interesting one. Before his first practice session, and as a result of the investigation into [N.C. State] Chris Washburn's 470 SAT score, it was revealed that the Carolina basketball coaches had recruited a player whose SAT scores were also below the anemic 500 level. With [fellow incoming freshmen] Jeff Lebo's and Marty Hensley's SAT scores already a matter of public record, and with Steve Bucknall having attended an exclusive private academy in Massachusetts, the onus of suspicion fell squarely upon Madden's young shoulders."

Solomon then reported that Madden had made "decent academic progress" and had even scored three B's and a C in summer school. "No," Solomon continued. "Rather than academic maturity, it appears Madden is sitting out this year to work on developing a personal maturity. His practice habits, his unwillingness to play in the traditional summer pickup games prior to his freshman season, his frustration at being the low man on the totem pole in Dean Smith's seniority system — these appear to be the true reasons why Madden will not play this season ... but why cloak it in the guise of 'academic insufficiency?'

"No doubt a year spent ordering his priorities will do Kevin Madden some good, but I can't stop asking myself if he would have played this season if the Carolina team really needed him ... so Madden's suspension looks to be more than a little convenient. If convenience had decreed that Madden play, however, how willing do you suppose Dean Smith would have been to 'do what's best for Kevin Madden?'"

Regardless, Smith and company take academics seriously. So seriously, in fact, that they budgeted an additional $42,000 solely for "academic support" for the 1987-88 school year. Madden's sabbatical proved so successful that Smith says Madden now enjoys studying so much that the staff has a hard time getting the young would-be scholar away from the books in order to pursue his basketball degree. Additional monies may need to be budgeted for "basketball support" in the future.

Only a few North Carolina basketball players need such attention. Smith maintains his program will only chance, at most, one exception per year when it comes to recruiting an athlete who falls short of regular admission requirements. Madden was one such exception in 1985. For the most part,

Smith chooses to turn down marginally qualified hoopsters. "You wouldn't believe the guys we turned down for academics," Smith told members of the UNC Educational Foundation at an annual meeting in 1987, "or maybe they're flakes — but they can play.

"When I retire, I'm going to write a book — and make some of you mad — about the players we could have had and chose not to take." Smith's book may contain a chapter on players that UNC should have had, chose to take, but never attended. For the 1988–89 season, Smith recruited Kenny Williams, a player who has been described as a combination of James Worthy and Dominique Wilkins. His formidable skills weren't enough. Williams, easily one of the top prospects in the country, couldn't meet UNC admission requirements when he failed to graduate with his high school class. He subsequently reported an SAT score of 690, 10 points shy of the minimum score the NCAA requires for freshmen to be eligible. With such a high profile concerning academics and its relationship with athletics at North Carolina, Smith regretfully had little choice but to advise the recruit to apply elsewhere for admission, to a junior college or another four-year school.

For the past two years, North Carolina's selection/recruiting process came up well short of its established norm. Starting the recruiting battles with a list of approximately 30 prospects, the company would make do with an incoming class of one. Hubert Davis, an unheralded guard from Burke, Virginia, would represent the UNC basketball class of '92.

Besides flakes and non-scholars, Smith also avoids young men with swelled heads to match their bulging skills. If Smith had his way there would be no publicly acknowledged stars in the North Carolina program. Recruits are never told they will start or be given playing time should they decide to attend UNC. Even J.R. Reid, one of the nation's most heavily recruited prep players of all time, wasn't promised a starting role on the team. He was promised the world at other schools.

"Nothing more outrageous was said to me than when some coaches told me they would win the national championship next season if I went to their school," says Reid. Make no mistake, Reid knew he would start right away at North Carolina. With the commitment from Scott Williams, a center/forward, to attend UNC, Reid knew he would see action at his preferred position of power forward. Reid had done his homework on Smith-instilled Tar Heel etiquette. If Reid was overconfident or cocky about joining the Tar Heels with more acclaim than James Worthy or Michael Jordan, he wasn't obvious about it. "Initially he acted like he was blending in before he had a chance to blend in," said Kenny Smith, a senior Tar Heel at the time of Reid's arrival. "And that was before school even started."

In two years of North Carolina stardom Reid never strayed from the company line. As journalists flocked to his side after UNC games, the future NBA superstar answered questions directed his way with Smith's editorial *we* instead of a more self-serving *I*. Away from Smith and the media, Reid is more brash. His Virginia license plate reads "I Dunk 2."

Obviously, there are many ways to let blue-chip recruits know they will be valuable assets to the program. It is common knowledge North Carolina players are not bribed with hot cars, fancy clothes, available coeds, or a pocketful of cash. Prospects looking only for a short term gain don't even think of North Carolina. Consequently, attending UNC is a gamble, albeit a calculated gamble, for most high school recruits. If the player is skilled and coachable — and it's unlikely he would have been asked to attend the school if he wasn't — he will receive the best hoops degree awarded. One has only to look to the professional ranks to see the fruits of Smith's efforts over the years. Currently 10 former players are playing in the NBA, many others ply their skills in European professional leagues, and another group has joined the coaching ranks. Still, it is a gamble that the "prospect" will be able to earn consistent playing time on the talent-laden team. Often players are imported despite inferior credentials.

"Doug Elstun just came to school," Smith said. "He didn't come on scholarship. I know his dad, but I mean — I am guilty of this — the guy comes to camp and you get to know him pretty good. If someone says they're dying to come, I really like them a lot better." Elstun, a freshman walk-on in 1987, made the journey from Kansas. It is doubtful Elstun could have played on many Division I teams. For the 1987-88 season he played a total of 16 minutes. (His father, Gene Elstun, played on Dick Harp's Kansas team that lost to North Carolina in the finals of the NCAA in 1957. Harp is an assistant coach with the company.)

There are no guarantees a player will have four full years of a scholarship provided when he signs a letter of intent. North Carolina, like most programs, controls a player's destiny while he attends the school. Smith does have an excellent track record concerning scholarships, however. "The NCAA rules don't allow players to sign for all four years," Smith says. "I can't understand that, but I can say that I've never taken a scholarship away and that tells any family that he [Smith] isn't going to change now.

"I also had one young man try to give up a scholarship in the '60s. He wasn't playing that much and he wanted to devote more time to his studies. I said, 'No way, you go back to your studies, but you keep the scholarship.'"

For the most part, and to Smith and company's credit, athletes who attend Carolina on a basketball scholarship do graduate. Not all graduate from UNC, however, and not all finish in four years. Some students pick up their degrees at other schools. Others need more than four years and a few summer sessions to complete their degrees, and a few declare hardship and postpone a year's worth of studies to jump to quick success in the pros. Walter Davis, the NBA Rookie of the Year in 1978, received his associate's degree in parks and recreation 10 years after leaving North Carolina. "I missed several credits because of the Olympics in 1976 and didn't get my degree," Davis says. "I went back to school after my rookie year, but I still didn't finish. I didn't go back again because my priorities weren't straight." One of Davis' priorities — a severe cocaine addiction — has since been straightened out, as well. Still, the vast majority of company men and all of the female managers graduate on time.

Like any business that screens prospective employees only to be disappointed after one doesn't work out, Carolina hires some recruits who look better on paper than in person. Some athletes can't cut the mustard in the classroom or on the floor. Some players suffer drug or alcohol problems. Some are faced with a basketball career on the bench due to stiff competition for playing time. Others clash with the program or its coach. Some are injury prone and spend much of their collegiate career in street clothes. A few know from the outset that they will become scrimmage fodder for their "playing" teammates, but are disillusioned after months or years of hard practice without ample reward. These players must choose between being a little man on a big campus or a big man on a little campus. Some of these student athletes stick it out, refusing to acknowledge publicly that their collegiate basketball experience at North Carolina soured. A few recruits opt to transfer, feeling that it's better to make their basketball fortune at another school where more playing time would exist and an NBA dream might still become reality. Only starters in college have a real chance of making it to the pros.

"Most of them come here with the idea that it will be difficult for them to play here," Smith says. "With [center] John Brownlee — I knew his dad really well. That's the only reason we were out there. We [Brownlee's father and Smith] went to school together and played on the same freshman team together. I told John how difficult it would be for him to play here, but his dad later told me that it only challenged him to come." Brownlee came to UNC as a member of the class of 1986, but later transferred to Texas. "He did the right thing in transferring," Smith continued. "Be sure you play at the school you transfer to, and Texas was last in its league the year before he went." Brownlee became a valuable asset in the Lone Star State. It's also doubtful Smith would want a player to transfer to a school where he might face the company squad during his career.

The young bright-eyed and bushy-tailed hoopsters who sign on the dotted line at North Carolina may not know that all they are getting in return for their signature is a chance to have a chance of playing for the nation's best collegiate basketball program. The opportunity to get a free education at a great university and to study hoops under one of the country's greatest teaching coaches doesn't sink in right away. It's well and good to state publicly that a degree is the main reason for attending North Carolina, but a crack at the NBA three or four years later is the real carrot at the end of the stick — at least for the talented recruit.

Also on each year's roster are role players for whom the opportunity to attend the university as a member of the basketball program is a dream come true. These are the players who add credibility to the program as one with the student athlete in mind. Without any false expectations, these designated role players work hard at studying on and off the court, realizing the sheepskin and a trunk full of memories will more than make up for any struggle along the way.

Visibility

The program is usually not brand new to prospects when they first arrive in Chapel Hill. Television exposure provides the nation's basketball youth with many glimpses of the team that travels the world in search of a good amateur game. With most broadcasters and color analysts proclaiming Dean Smith and his program to be one of, if not *the,* classiest of programs, the Tar Heels have become America's team. Wherever the team plays, the stands are dotted with folks clad in sweatshirts and jackets displaying the UNC logo or simply "Carolina" in white against a powder blue background.

According to Ruth Boyce, director of alumni records at UNC, in 1988 there were 168,917 living UNC alumni — 90,453 in North Carolina. Even if all were true-blue basketball fans, the totals would represent only a fraction of the company's followers. Hundreds of thousands of fans who claim North Carolina as their team are not alumni. Some have never been within a thousand miles of the Tar Heel State. Somewhere along the line, the self-adopted fans swear an allegiance to the program and its coach. Everybody loves a winner, and Carolina is a proven testament to winning.

But a winning tradition does have its drawbacks among sports fans in this country. Americans also have an affinity with underdogs for a variety of reasons. Often, fans choose to root for the team with the lesser chance of winning. The public prefers an upset to a yawner. Fans would rather see a closely contested game than a one-sided clinic. With Carolina constantly in the limelight as the favorite, there are often as many fans pulling against the team as there are cheering for it. In the ACC, fans of the seven "other" schools take great pride in rooting against North Carolina. At the annual ACC tournament in March, thousands of fans quickly ally to harmonize vocal power against the team to beat. And most often, the team to beat is North Carolina.

Regardless of team preference, the average college basketball fan knows about the North Carolina Tar Heels. In a nation connected by cable and satellite, blue chip "infants" are well aware of the program before Smith and his network of contacts know about them. Exposing the program to junior and senior high school basketball players is not necessary. Nationwide, the Tar Heels logged more television airtime than any other collegiate team during the 1987–88 season. Excluding ACC and NCAA tournament appearances, Carolina graced the national airwaves 16 times, four more times than either Georgetown or Syracuse. In 1988 alone, the Tar Heels were televised regionally in 18 of their 21 games prior to the NCAAs. And the exposure is not limited to television. The Tar Heel Sports Network broadcasts every game to an estimated half-million listeners over 62 radio stations. The radio figures don't take into account fans such as Steve Wright, who once wrote to the network from Bogota, Colombia, to say that he listened to a broadcast on a snow-capped mountaintop on the equator, and the thousands who listen overseas via the Armed Forces Radio Network. Still, radio and television broadcasts are just one aspect of self-promotion.

Another way the company sells interest in its product is its basketball camp. Most schools have a summer camp or a series of clinics designed to showcase the school's coaching staff and favorite player alumni. These camps provide intensive skill-building outlets for area youth and put some serious change in the pockets of the coaching staff. Obviously, the better the school's basketball program, the more prestigious the summer camp. Getting into the North Carolina basketball camp is almost as hard as getting into the program. No advertising or publicity is necessary, and in fact, is actually discouraged. Prospective campers must be referred by Educational Foundation members, and space is so limited in the coveted camp that attendees practically need to be signed up at birth. Entrance to one of the three summer sessions is gained by returning a completed application mailed exclusively from the basketball office in late winter. The 1988 camp was filled within two weeks. Still, the camp could be a remote way for a 10- to 18-year- old to earn a crack at playing for the company.

Ranzino Smith, as a young local hoopster, played his heart out in many a UNC basketball camp and literally caught the eyes of the coaches. It eventually helped him obtain a scholarship and a starting position at North Carolina. Many of the campers bring that same dream each year. They also bring a substantial check to pay for the privilege. To his credit, Smith ensures a limited number of "scholarships" are made available to the local school systems for kids with limited resources. Lucky attendees during the summer of 1988 were treated to mini-clinics from the likes of Michael Jordan and Dudley Bradley, another distinguished company alumnus. Also in attendance to work the camp were such former Tar Heel greats as Sam Perkins, Kenny Smith, Joe Wolf, Phil Ford, and Walter Davis.

The basketball camp is low-profile compared to the bright lights that surround the rest of the program. North Carolina, like most big-time sports programs, attracts numerous private and school-sponsored publications to spout the company line. In addition to game programs, which contain many student- and sports publicity staff-written articles, the annual UNC Basketball media guide is the single most visible recruiting tool for the program. The guide, put together by members of the sports information department, has won awards for excellence. Averaging just under 100 pages, the guide's stated purpose is to provide members of the media with an accurate copy of past and present statistics along with information about the program and its members. In reality, the guide has evolved into a glittering promotional piece. "It really has three purposes," says UNC Athletic Director John Swofford, whose office oversees the distribution of tens of thousands of the annuals. "One is to provide a yearbook. It's also used for recruiting and it's used to give to contributors to the program. They're also for sale." Swofford makes no mention of the guide as a tool for the media, its professed purpose.

Long gone are the mimeographed stat sheets held together by a single staple. In their place is a corporate annual report — only a financial outlook is missing. The "state-of-the-program" guide contains biographical sketches of the coaching staff and athletic director; historical information; the season's outlook; an outlook on the Tar Heel's opponents, including each team's schedule, returning lettermen, current personnel, and past records; information about the university; all-time scoring and coaching records; and many other facts and figures about the program. Adorning most of the glossy pages are high-quality action photos of present and past players and cheerleaders, gleaned from professional photographers who flock to North Carolina ball games.

There is also a directory of Smith's lettermen. It contains the whereabouts and the occupations of each former player or manager. Prior to the 1987-88 season, 158 of 164 lettermen, including those who transferred to other schools, graduated from a college or university. The directory is further documentation for parents of potential recruits as it distinctly proves the company's commitment to education.

As an established program, North Carolina no longer needs to lace its media guide with enticement. Pictures of shapely coeds or bosomy cheer-leaders, like those seen in the 1974–75 media guide, have since given way to more serious historical prints. Prior to 1987, many of the inside photos were in color. The NCAA has since restricted the use of color to the covers of the guides, to ensure that the richer programs don't purchase an unfair recruiting advantage. "Brochures, and especially the media guides, had gotten out of hand," says Dave Lohse, an assistant sports information director (SID) and the current editor of the basketball media guide. "I've seen brochures where 125-member football teams have run every player's mug shot in four-color. That's an abuse of the privilege. In our old books, and this is not to be critical of Rick [Brewer, sports information director], but in our old books, the 16 pages of color pictures that were in the middle without any copy were wasted space. Those pictures were in there strictly for the fans." And the recruits. With today's sophisticated printing and publishing methods, the loss of color will be negligible, and offset by fancy screens and diecuts. The programs with money to burn on glossy publica-tions will still outspend and outshine those that don't. The NCAA doesn't restrict the number of copies a school can print.

There are other publications that promote the Tar Heel cause. The best-known is *Carolina Blue*, a colorful tabloid devoted strictly to UNC athletics. In its eighth year of publication, *Carolina Blue* devotes an average of 40 pages to mainly football and basketball coverage for 9,000 subscribers. Though the mini-newspaper is unashamedly biased, it is a comprehensive record of the positive side of Tar Heel athletics. Publisher John Kilgo uses great care to ensure nothing is printed that might raise the eyebrows of a UNC administrator or an ardent Educational Foundation member. The bias goes much further than simply overstating the company line or using overzealous adjectives to describe UNC victories. Well-publicized inci-dents depicting UNC athletes in a less than flattering context are usually either completely omitted or politely buried deep in later issues. "It was frustrating as hell," says Scott Smith, a former writer for *Carolina Blue* and currently the sports editor for the *Charlotte Leader*. "You couldn't write about everything you knew or what came out in player interviews. I had a great interview with Kevin Anthony [former Academic All-America quar-terback, who resigned from the Carolina football program] where he was very open about his [negative] relationship with Dick Crum [head football coach who was later forced to resign]. It would have made some very interesting reading, but it never got into the paper. The specific things he said about Crum were edited out. The paper should give both sides of an issue. Instead, you were just a PR guy."

Dave Lohse, in addition to his publicity duties at UNC, is a writer for

Carolina Blue. Neither Lohse nor Rick Brewer is listed in the masthead of the publication, yet both are paid as contributing writers for articles they submit. Despite his proximity to the Tar Heel program, Lohse maintains that the tabloid doesn't receive any preferential treatment from his office when it comes to access to the university. "No, they're treated just like anyone else," he says. "They don't get any special treatment."

Athletic Director John Swofford sees the relationship in a different light. "The actual idea [of having a publication devoted exclusively to UNC athletics] started prior to *Carolina Blue*. A magazine came out in the late '70s, but it wasn't successful and after a year it was not able to continue. But it was a good idea and we thought there was a market out there. What evolved is *Carolina Blue*. It's really a joint venture between Jefferson Pilot [Communications Company] and the North Carolina athletic department. We support it promotionally and try to work with them and provide access to the programs." Scott Smith agrees with Swofford. "With football players we have more access, we didn't have to go through the SID (sports information director's) office," he says. "We could just catch them at the training table before dinner. It was understood that *Carolina Blue* writers could do that, nobody else could. If anybody else did that, they could get in trouble. It's harder to get close to the basketball players, they keep them in their own little environment."

Members of the basketball office are also known to closely scrutinize the tabloid for anything that might cast the wrong light on a player or coach. One former *Carolina Blue* writer quoted a Carolina player as using the word "ain't" — only to receive a personal phone call from Dean Smith encouraging the journalist not to do it again. Barry Jacobs, author of the annual *Fan's Guide to ACC Basketball* , feels he knows the best way to keep from incurring Smith's wrath. "Dean Smith is one of the few basketball coaches you'll meet who differentiates among writers depending on whether or not they quote him saying who or whom," Jacobs says.

In recent years, a new publication has emerged concerned exclusively with North Carolina basketball. Three annual volumes of *Carolina Court, Inside Tar Heel Basketball* have been printed since 1986. Published by Four Corners Press in Chapel Hill, the oversized softcover book is also biased toward the UNC fan, but in a much more informative and entertaining way than *Carolina Blue*. With many full-color photos and statistical charts, the magazine provides a pictorial overview of the past season and a brief insight into future players. National and regional advertisements and a hefty price tag help defray the editorial costs.

Publishers Art Chansky and Alfred T. Hamilton Jr. compile and write about all facets of the program. Chansky's longtime relationship with

Coach Smith and former assistant coach and fraternity brother Eddie Fogler, now head coach at Wichita State, enabled him to get closer to the UNC basketball family than most outsiders. At one point in the early '80s, Chansky and Fogler were business partners in a bar and restaurant called Four Corners. In 1987, Four Corners Press joined the Village Companies corporate group, a highly successful Chapel Hill-based firm that also produces the Tar Heel Sports Network as a joint business enterprise with the university.

Chansky's stance has not always been visibly pro-UNC. In 1976, he and Dennis Wuycik, a former Tar Heel basketball star and Academic All-American, co-founded *The Poop Sheet*, a speculative publication whose content is based primarily on opinion and rumor concerning the inside scoop on the region's football and basketball programs. For years, ACC coaches and fans felt *The Poop Sheet* slanted its conference "rumors and insights" in favor of North Carolina. At one point the prejudice may have existed. When Chansky left *The Poop Sheet* a few years later, publisher Wuycik attempted to deliver objective critiques and speculation in the newsletter. Following the 1987 basketball season, Wuycik published a scorching opinion criticizing Dean Smith, his coaching style, and the company's failure to win the big games — most notably the 1987 regional final against Syracuse. The piece went so far as to claim that Smith was the most overrated coach in the game. Calling the coach predictable and inflexible, the story echoed the feelings of many frustrated Carolina fans. When an impromptu meeting took place between the coach and his former player about a month later, Wuycik prepared for the worst.

"He said he had read the article," says the smiling Wuycik, remembering the mild confrontation. "Then he told me he didn't think it was a well-written piece." Considering the inflammatory remarks printed, Smith was overly gracious. Wuycik never publishes bylines with the articles and blurbs that appear in his pages. Though he said he didn't write the actual published piece, he claimed the ultimate responsibility as editor and publisher of the publication. It wasn't the first time — and probably not the last — Smith voiced displeasure at content appearing on *The Poop Sheet*'s pages. Wuycik, the company's registered outlaw, remembers a time Smith likened his newsletter's recruiting news to a scenario where a man has two girlfriends. Everything is fine until one girlfriend finds out about the other. Coaches — especially those in the ACC — like to keep recruiting news out of the public eye.

Smith went on record against *The Poop Sheet* years ago because of its recruiting insights. "Speculative reporting is not very journalistic," he said. "I guess I can base that on Bob Woodward's quote from his lecture in

Durham where he said that it was absolutely irresponsible for there to be any sort of speculative reporting in journalism. To take that a step further, I would say that any writer who is writing recruiting in newspapers based on speculation ... that is not very good ... I know other coaches who have planted rumors in recruiting to have them picked up. I don't think it's helpful to the player being recruited or the schools recruiting him."

Throughout the years, its regional audience has determined that it is all right for *The Poop Sheet* to maintain a different set of standards. More often than not it proves to be prophetic. Wuycik doesn't just publish hard facts. He feels that his 5,000 subscribers look at his publication as an entertainingly fresh perspective on sports. If interested fans want objective news, they should buy newspapers — though not necessarily the local one.

The Chapel Hill Newspaper, a weekly turned daily in 1972, has long been considered a pro-UNC news organ. Due in part to its proximity to the university, its former longtime publisher and North Carolina grad, Orville B. Campbell, and an endless supply of UNC journalism students, the paper provided the company with a positive mouthpiece for over 34 years. Many a regional sportswriter got his or her start covering the Tar Heels in Chapel Hill before moving to a larger newspaper. From newsprint to the television screen, the company covers all the angles.

One way to see highlights of the basketball team is to watch *The Dean Smith Show*. During the season, the weekly television show provides Carolina fans with a chance to see and hear Smith analyze video highlights of recent UNC games. Again, only the positive aspects (mostly offensive plays) are shown, with host John Kilgo providing little in the way of insight into the program or its members. *Richmond Times-Dispatch* sportswriter Jerry Lindquist compared the North Carolina and Virginia coaches' shows and their hosts in a column published in November 1987. "Coaches' shows are, as a rule, worse than awful, but a round of applause for Tom Dulaney, host of Virginia's football and basketball half-hour commercials. He doesn't fawn all over the coaches and isn't necessarily predictable. Why he's actually professional." Lindquist then jokingly told Dulaney to watch his step as he would set a bad example for the rest of the broadcasters doing similar shows. "The least Tom could do is kiss Terry Holland's ring every now and then. For proper technique, see John Kilgo on the North Carolina coaches' show."

UNC Athletic Director John Swofford hosts a weekly national cable program entitled *Carolina SportsWeek*. The 30-minute show highlights many varsity sports and sports figures from past UNC glories. Seen in most markets on Tempo Cable Network, the program potentially reaches over 15 million homes throughout the country. It also serves as a half-hour commercial and recruiting tool for North Carolina.

The Tar Heel Sports Network earns considerable revenue from an exclusive arrangement with the North Carolina athletic department. The cost for the radio rights to broadcast North Carolina's basketball games is no longer the drop in the bucket it once was. Jim Heavner, the president of Village Sports Inc., watches over the numbers involved in airing one of the country's best collegiate sports networks. "It's up to the school if they want to release what we pay for the rights to produce the network," Heavner says. "I can tell you that it's a hell of a lot more than what it was in Bill Curry's (the former producer of the network broadcasts) day around 18 years ago. The school was getting something like $30,000 for football and $10,000 for the rights to the basketball games then." It's believed that the rights cost well over 10 times that amount today. "The advertising costs have changed dramatically as well," he continues. "I don't know what the costs were back then, but its about $1,000 per [network] spot now and that's about the price of a spot on national CBS radio."

Sales were up 24 percent for Village Sports in 1987-88. Sales projections for 1988-89 are around $1 million, with 70 percent of the ad sales sold prior to the end of the 1987-88 season. Carolina success translates into serious revenue for those who carry the company line.

The publications, television and radio shows, and national game exposure all go a long way toward building a positive image of the company for young potential hoopsters. Other big-time college programs have similar high-recognition factors, but with the possible exception of Indiana, which is still riding the waves of a national best seller, *A Season on the Brink*, and a 1987 national championship, no other collegiate basketball program is more visible than North Carolina during this decade.

The Environment

As if the national attention North Carolina receives isn't enough, players who aren't swayed by Tar Heel recognition are often convinced by the environment. It doesn't hurt that the university's home rests in the center of "one of the 20 nicest places to live in the United States," according to *Time* magazine. The combination of a beautiful campus and state-of-the-art basketball facilities is often hard to resist. Carolina players are not asked to practice or perform their basketball skills in a cold drafty gymnasium that is poorly lit and smells of stale sweat. Instead, the building where the players will spend the majority of their waking hours is a monument to collegiate basketball. The Dean E. Smith Student Activities Center, in use since early 1986 and since renamed by the UNC athletics department the Smith Center, is everything a basketball player could hope for, and then some.

The Smith Center is the best arena money can buy. Lots of money. Fundraising to build a new arena began in 1980, and with the help of a 25-person steering committee and the Educational Foundation Inc., the campaign got under way in hopes of raising about $30 million. When the deadline for donations was reached in August 1984, $38 million in gifts and pledges was on the books. After just under four years of construction, the resulting $33.8 million, 300,000-square-foot facility stood without equal. The Smith Center was then given to the university and the state of North Carolina.

Naming the building was even easier. "It's been an overwhelming consensus since I've been around," said Moyer Smith, executive vice president of the Educational Foundation. "It was a given that this facility should be named for Dean Smith." Smith was originally uncomfortable with the decision, but after realizing that the donors wanted his name over the doors, has accepted it.

Starting with a high-tech floor and rising 150 feet to the fiberglass translucent dome, the building doesn't resemble a typical gym or field house. Built into a natural valley, the earth-toned structure rises out of tall Southern pines to make a unique statement. Outside, the building is awe-inspiring. Inside, it is equally breathtaking as the first-time visitor is treated to a sea of Carolina blue. Still, the most fascinating facets of the arena are hidden from view. The extraordinary playing surface is more than a glossy hardwood basketball court. Underneath the maple planks and a one-inch plywood sub-floor are hundreds of metal springs bolted to four-by-four wooden beams. The entire floor is capable of giving up to one-eighth inch when several players are in one area. The patented Spring-Aire court system was designed to cut down on the wear and tear to the legs of the high-flying basketball players. Parents of potential NBA multimillionaires must be pleased with the additional safety feature.

There are no bleachers in the Smith Center. Instead, there are only different degrees of theater-style seats. From the VIP courtside seats that resemble the width and comfort of Concorde seats, to smaller, fully upholstered seats that reach to the top rows of the upper level, all 21,444 chair seats reflect school colors. No seat is more than 150 feet from the floor and no seat, except a few behind the baskets, have an obstructed view.

A single switch controls the computer-assisted lighting system. The electrical lighting is enhanced during daylight hours by streams of natural light shining through the 15,000-square-foot, Teflon-coated fiberglass roof. The natural lighting gives the facility an openness that warms the arena even during the coldest of winter days.

The sound in the Smith Center wasn't overlooked, but is definitely overheard. Sporting what has been called a "personal speaker" system, the arena has a main speaker cluster hanging from the roof, 14 satellite clusters, and 146 small speakers underneath the upper level. The resulting sound is crisp and clean without blistering the ears of those sitting near a speaker. Rounding out the space-age electronics are four wall-mounted scoreboards and two digital message boards, designed for four-color advertising and athletic program promos. (The message boards are also ineffectively used to encourage collective cheers throughout basketball games.) By placing the scoreboards on the sides of the arena, the view of the entire area is without obstruction.

The Smith Center also houses many other niceties, out of sight from the mainstream crowd. Fans can take a hidden escalator from courtside to a donor's "memorabilia" room. Filled with glass-enclosed artifacts from Carolina's sporting past, the 3,000-square-foot room can be used for pre- and postgame social gatherings. Designed by Jerry Goodman, who also designed the Pro Football Hall of Fame in Canton, Ohio, the room holds exhibits from all Carolina sports.

Randy Mews, a staff writer for *Carolina Blue*, once described it as "a modest room, distinctly Carolina, yet there is not an abundance of Carolina blue. In a way, it's much like the Smith Center itself. No expense was spared to make it state-of-the-art, and no other college has anything like it."

The walls hold oil portraits of important UNC athletic administrators and of course, a painting of Dean Smith. The floor is covered with a specially woven beige carpet emblazoned with a UNC logo. Far and away the most popular feature is a running videotape of Carolina's two national championship games and a come-from-behind win over a Ralph Sampson-led Virginia team. One artifact, a vertical lightbox designed to resemble a stained-glass memorial, contains an almost caricatured photo of Smith. Completely out of place, its tacky, maudlin appeal is in high contrast to the rest of the room.

Still another gathering place is available for the building fund contributors and Donor's Club card holders. Formally named the Hargrove "Skipper" Bowles Hall in honor of the late state senator and former president of the Educational Foundation, the room in the attached Maurice Koury Natatorium annex is also a convenient place to meet alumni and friends around game time. Depending on the time of the game, the Educational Foundation provides meals or snacks for the privileged. No alcohol is served except prior to the annual banquets.

After the game, selected guests, players, parents, recruits and coaches gather in the coaches' suite of offices to unwind and informally chat. The 3,000 square feet of offices, nicknamed "Mahogany Row," are not like the former institutional afterthoughts where physical education instructors-slash-coaches had a desk, a few textbooks, and a stack of boxes containing basketball shoes.

The company goes for the Wall Street corporate look. The entrance reception area is parquet-floored in dark hardwood. An oriental rug and recessed lighting add a dramatic effect. With a wall of glass, the foyer is spacious with high ceilings to accommodate seven-foot-tall visitors. Current team trophies line the top of a credenza. A custom-made sectional couch molds with a curved wall. Both are covered with suede-like fabric. Off the entrance is Smith's office. Few executives have working quarters that rival these. From traditional rich hardwood cabinetry and a generous seating area to modern electronic touches, the office is efficient and first-class without being ostentatious. The only obvious giveaway that the office belongs to a coach is a built-in wall rack housing rows of game basketballs. Looks can be deceiving. Glenn Corley, one of the designers of the Smith Center, may have unlocked a secret when he said, "Coach Smith will be able to use a single button to lower a six-by-eight screen out of his office ceiling, close his doors, dim the lights, draw his curtains and start a preprogrammed tape." Few executives enjoy such convenience.

Assistant coaches Bill Guthridge and Phil Ford, head junior varsity coach Randy Weil, and administrative assistant Dick Harp all have space in the suite. Most offices contain video playback and computer equipment. Across from Smith's office, Linda Woods, Smith's executive secretary for nine years, has a small office and down the hall another secretary, Kay Thomas, has work space. The hallway wall showcases seven neatly matted and framed *Sports Illustrated* cover pages radiating past company glory. Considering Smith frequently disputes *SI* policies and the attention it gives his underclassmen (a taboo in Smith's seniority-dominated structure), it's surprising to see the covers receive such prominence. The offices also contains mail slots for the players, a media room, and a well-stocked kitchen.

Beneath the offices and the sports information department suite, lies the team dressing room, team lounge, training room, and weight room. All four are well-designed and furnished according to the needs of the six- to seven-foot players. The interior doors are secured with push-button combination lock systems with codes known by players, trainers, and managers. Should a player want to shoot baskets at a time other than normal working hours, he needs to call one of the coaches for entry. Student athletes are not privy to the outer door combination. It is the only door that isn't automatically unlocked for members of the team.

The weight room contains the latest in strength training and maintaining equipment and is run by Harley Dartt, the team's notorious strength and fitness coach. Dartt is the object of many player-related horror stories because of the way he intimidates new recruits. Marc Davis, head basketball trainer, plies his craft in a state-of-the-art training room. Davis is responsible for ensuring the athletes' day-to-day well-being.

North Carolina players don't suit up for games in a drafty, wet-floored locker room. The company dressing room is a cozy yet spacious configuration that is carpeted and spotless. Each player has his own independently lit and electrically wired dressing area that is comparable to a theater makeup cubicle. The living space comes complete with a custom-made locker adorned with an engraved placard proclaiming the player's name and number. Instead of the usual planks of worn pine are individual designer chairs appointed with casters and pneumatic pedestal bases. The dressing room can be seen after games, but the actual changing area is off-limits to the press. This way, the players can shower and dress at their leisure before speaking with members of the media in an adjoining area. The reporters and broadcasters are restrained by a human wall comprised of managers and sports information assistants. On occasion, players manage to disappear into the showers hidden from view to effectively duck questions concerning a loss or a poor performance. With the millions of dollars poured into the facility, it's highly unlikely the hot water could ever run out.

To the team's credit, a few players of consequence, usually upperclassmen known for espousing the company line, graciously wait to shower until the media has a chance for a 15-minute postgame exchange. These precious few stay in uniform and answer questions from the swarming herd of journalists covering the program. It is a standing UNC policy that the locker room is closed quickly, after both wins and losses, and many a reporter on deadline must reluctantly give up a chance to speak to uncooperative players who feel the need to scrub diligently behind their ears rather than entertain repetitious scribes.

Most regular meals are enjoyed in the dining room of the nearby Granville Towers, home to the Tar Heel underclassmen. "Our players eat with all the other students," Coach Smith says. "We don't have the training table that all the other sports, like football, have." The players don't suffer. Like training tables at most Division I schools, the program embraces rigid nutritional standards for its athletes. The days of 20-ounce cuts of beef have given way to lighter portions of baked chicken or fish — except for pregame meals, where the company voted to stand by the traditional steak. Salads, numerous carbohydrates, and vegetables have become the mainstay. Fruit juices and lowfat milk have replaced carbonated soft drinks. In fact, trainer Marc Davis, who also monitors some nutritional aspects of the program, requires players to forego any carbonated soft drinks prior to games and insists that no caffeine-containing beverages be consumed on road trips. Not only does the caffeine cause sleeplessness, but according to Davis it can trigger a positive result in a drug test. (It's a good thing coaches and sports journalists aren't tested.)

In-town games often involve a postgame or pregame meal at a nearby restaurant. "We do eat our pregame meals in restaurants," Smith says. "Postgame meals are what the ACC allows, which is $10 or something." In-town games usually mean a trip to the nearby Slugs restaurant, a place where very little is available for under ten dollars. Out-of-town games can mean a chance to dine in some of the world's better restaurants. "We do stay at the best places and eat at the best places," Smith says, "but it's something we do for them [the players] legally. We could go out and stay somewhere else or eat somewhere else and give the rest of the money to the poor. If the junior class came to me and said, 'Let's use that money to give to the least empowered people in the world' — I think it would be marvelous — but the NCAA would probably say that's illegal. So ..."

Smith is an important representative to the collegiate governing body. Over the years, his thoughts and insights have carried more than one coach's weight. With new blood currently running the NCAA, Smith's experience and acumen may take on even greater significance in policy-making. Freshman athletes may one day again find themselves ineligible to compete on varsity levels if Smith and followers of his philosophy ever decide to press for legislation. On October 2, 1983, *The New York Times* ran a 40-column-inch piece written by Dean Smith entitled "Why Freshmen Should Not Play." Smith wrote that the reason for his stance was the need to make a strong statement to incoming athletes that their academic work comes first in time and importance. "Almost all of the problems of intercollegiate athletics — excessive commercialism, compulsion to win (albeit illegally) and the whole success-failure ethos — impinge directly upon the talented freshman student athlete," Smith concluded. "If we are serious about wanting to minimize these adverse factors and place our primary concern on the student athlete, we should eliminate freshman eligibility." Until then, freshman athletes on the company's roster will continue to carry the team's video equipment and chase down all the loose balls in practice.

Only the freshmen are closely monitored as far as lifestyle and choice of living accommodations are concerned. All freshmen must live and eat in Granville Towers student housing. Upperclassmen can, and most often do, choose to live off-campus in a quieter setting. Though not mandatory, most of the basketball players also choose to not list their phone numbers. Jeff Lebo, a current member of the team, made a huge miscue his sophomore year. "I made the mistake of publishing it my second year. I got some Duke fans calling me the night before a game over there. And then after we lost I got a call from some students saying, 'Duke, Duke, Duke,' — it wasn't fun.

"But overall, it's only your freshman year when you don't know what to expect. You learn year to year from the other players, but it's up to you individually to handle living in a glass house. You can live a normal life, but in the back of your mind you know that everything you do is being watched because people know who you are."

Practice

The coaches do most of their watching during practice.

Dean Smith doesn't allow the public to view varsity basketball practice — with exceptions. Occasionally, interested fans or members of the media receive permission to attend a one- to two-hour session. The permission, of course, comes from the coach. It also comes with strict reservations. And so it should. Practice is the cornerstone of the company's foundation.

As with all areas of the program, visitors, like the players, managers and even the coaches, must adhere to a stringent set of rules during practice. After receiving the okay from Smith in advance, a visitor finds out the particulars from Linda Woods, the program's executive secretary. Woods verifies the permission with the coach and instructs you to stop by the basketball office to pick up a permit to attend practice. Practice is a serious event at North Carolina, and permission to attend a practice is not given lightly.

"Here's your permit," she says, handing you an official-looking Carolina blue pass with your name written on it. "Practice viewing is allowed from the upper decks only."

"I guess Coach Smith doesn't want what he says to the players to be overheard," you kid, trying to hide your displeasure at having to sit so far away.

"That's the idea," she says with a smile. "You know they're closed practices, he doesn't have to let you in."

"No problem."

"Practice begins today promptly at five."

Hearing any coaching wisdom would be next to impossible from the second tier of seats, but at least the visitor gets a bird's-eye view of the entire practice. Within minutes you find your way from Smith's outer office to the upper decks of the center and take your seat in section 217, intent on seeing how the Tar Heels prepare for a big game.

Most of the seats that normally line the court are gone, disassembled into retractable sections surrounding the floor. The resulting wall of seats gives the practice area even more of a fishbowl look. From high above the court the team and staff look like gladiators trapped in a coliseum. The two "game day" basketball standards are in place, but in addition, eight more baskets are available for individuals and pairs to work on shooting. Well before the scheduled 5:00 p.m. start, the players are busy shooting and playing one on one. The atmosphere is very businesslike.

The only sounds come from the pounding of the leather and rubber against wood and fiberglass. If any players are talking, they are doing so in very soft voices. Every player has a ball and a place to shoot. Six managers, clad alike in dark blue shorts and white T-shirts, scurry around the floor assisting shooters by rebounding and feeding the ball back with deft bounce passes. The coaches work the floor, making corrections in form and stopping action to give advice. Assistant coach Roy Williams bounces passes to Scott Williams for turnaround jumpers. Randy Weil, another assistant coach whose official title is head junior varsity coach, talks with Steve Bucknall about using the backboard. Dean Smith, an average-sized man with an oversized midsection, strides around the floor, smiling and making short observations to freshman King Rice who is playing one-on-one with junior walk-on Rodney Hyatt.

Compared to his corporate suits, the head coach looks more relaxed in warm-ups and running shoes. He is not. Practice at Carolina is strictly business. Nothing is left to chance.

Your observations are interrupted when a young manager appears from nowhere and asks for your permit to attend practice. You show it to the polite assistant and begin to return it to your shirt pocket.

"I need to have the permit," the manager whispers, still out of breath from sprinting up to where you're perched. "Coach Smith wants to know who is watching practice. Also, would you move over to the far half-court seats over there? It would be less of a distraction." He points to where two people are sitting across the center. "He likes for anybody watching to sit in the same area."

You comply, trying to comprehend how you could be a distraction for anybody so far below. You choose a new seat a couple of rows from the other visitors and again are caught up with the action on the court. Though the color and pageantry of a Carolina game isn't present, the chance to see a "closed" practice lends electricity to the occasion. The unstructured shooting warm-up appears serious, but it is casual compared to the 124 minutes that follow.

With a glance at his Rolex, Smith blows his whistle on the stroke of 5:00. He doesn't have to blow it twice. Within seconds the entire team assembles at the center circle on the floor. Business begins with a brief comment from the coach that includes a tally of who on the team has gained "plus points" since the last game. Plus points, as manager Michael Burch later explains, are legal brownie points. The players earn plus points as a reward for practice and game performance. "For example," he says, "If a guy takes a charge during practice he gets a plus point. When the coaches grade a film [videotape] the players get points. During practice a coach may shout out points for a player. All of the stats are tabulated and the first-, second-, and third-place winners in each category get points ranging from two points to a half a point.

"At the end of practice, a player can use some of his plus points instead of running. Every plus point equals 10 seconds of running."

Smith then quizzes the team, asking sophomore reserve guard Jeff Denny a question from the day's practice schedule sheet. The sheets, posted in the locker room before each day's practice, contain the schedule of the practice, the intent of the day's work, and an inspirational message. "They each have to memorize it or the whole team runs," Smith says. "The inspirational messages are taken from all major religions — I don't always agree with the ones I choose — but it's hoped the players can draw on them for strength some day. The emphasis of the day might be something simple like catching the ball with two hands."

Denny gives the right answer and evokes a round of applause from his teammates. Sophomore Scott Williams and freshman redshirt Pete Chilcutt answer follow-up questions. Before disbanding the group, Smith makes a few comments concerning the upcoming game on the following evening. After consulting a copy of the day's schedule pulled from his hip pocket, Smith blows his whistle and practice continues with full-court defensive drills.

It's easy to be impressed with the organization and execution of a Carolina practice session. Nothing is left to chance. Every detail has been worked out and everybody connected to the program dutifully performs his responsibilities. The managers work the hardest. Throughout the session and without direction, the managers set up and break down various elements necessary to the day's overall practice plan.

During drills on the court, three managers run the clock and keep track of various stats at the scorer's table. "We keep stats for any scrimmage situation," Burch says. "We keep shots taken and made, turnovers, and then we break it down into points per possession. And we have a percentage loss of ball. We give them [the stats] to the coaches after each practice and they get posted for the team to see. We also keep accumulative stats for the year — shooting percentage from two- and three-point range, assists, rebounds, fumbles, bad passes — it all goes onto a chart and every two weeks Coach Smith gets that from us and we go over it in meetings."

At North Carolina, managers routinely carry briefcases to work. Company managers are not volunteers. Like other university employees, some managers are salaried. Guthridge interviews 30 to 40 applicants each year. The ranks are cut down to 10 who sign on to work with the junior varsity and the basketball camp in the summer. The best managers go on to the varsity the following year. In addition to performing the day-to-day chores of keeping soap and fresh towels in the locker room, the managers need to possess a solid background in arithmetic. North Carolina plays, practices, and wins by the numbers.

Overhead scoreboards are used throughout practice to time different segments and to record the score between the white (first team) and the blue (second team). All four scoreboards are prepared for practice by replacing the acetate gels where the team names are usually placed. Instead of "Carolina" and an opponent's name are the words "Blue" and "White." The attention to detail is overwhelming. So is the willingness to serve. Should a player fall to the floor in practice, one of the managers sitting at the scorer's table will sprint to the spot to towel-dry the sweat-stained hardwood. Another manager sits courtside near the action with a clipboard to record stats and notes vocalized by the coach. Another manager stays busy moving chairs, toss-backs (a tightly netted apparatus that allows the players to rebound their own practice passes), and various pieces around the gym floor. A cooler of Gatorade is prepared and stored on a table at the far side of the center, though no players go near it. Next to the "watering place" is a row of blue folding chairs, exactly one seat for each member of the team.

At a point midway through the practice, the clock is set at two minutes and started when Smith blows his whistle. Seniors can visit the watering place to replenish fluids and take a seat. In timed intervals, the juniors and underclassmen are allowed to join their upperclass teammates to cool off and take a drink. At the 30-second mark a manager calls out the time remaining. At 10 seconds, another warning is shouted. When time has expired, the horn sounds and practice resumes immediately. No time is wasted. No players are tardy. The players are back on the floor and the managers are busy cleaning up the "rest" area, moving the chairs about 10 feet toward the court into another line. The chairs are not used again until after practice, when the coach will say a few words to the team, but moving the seats as little as 10 feet means three less strides for the tired players to take. Refilled cups of Gatorade sit underneath each chair in readiness.

Meanwhile the action on the court is changing every 10 to 15 minutes as the Tar Heels go through a program of game-situation scrimmages. Former players swear they never came across a situation in a game that they hadn't experienced in practice. All work is aimed at improving the white team's play. The white team is actually made up of the players who are expected to play in the next game. In 1987–88, as many as nine players were adorned with white jerseys. Should a player not be expected to play due to injury or demotion, he will wear a blue jersey until notified. There are times when a player is asked to reverse his jersey because he is not hustling, but such an occasion is very infrequent. There are also times when players wear blue solely for scrimmage situations. Conversely, strong play can earn a player the opportunity to join the "good" guys in white. The UNC program prides itself on treating all players equally. The color of a jersey, like the color of a player's skin, makes no difference to the quick eyes of the coaching staff. All players are under constant scrutiny from both the coaches and the managers, who dutifully chart every shot, rebound, and turnover in every practice. In the past, even summer pickup games were monitored and charted by managers.

It is in practice where a player earns the right to play. Players must prove their skills in rehearsal before being allowed to act on game day. Center Scott Williams earned the right to shoot open three-pointers after he consistently hit a high percentage of the jumpers after months of practice. Reserve Pete Chilcutt developed a jump hook shot and was then given the right to take it. Coach Smith doesn't like surprises. If a player wants to showcase a skill, he must first display his wares over a period of time. If the percentage of made shots isn't what Smith and company demands, the shot is used only in practice scrimmages. Even the managers are tested on their skills in practice.

"Most drills in practice are competition between the blue and white teams," Burch says. "I keep track of what goes on in each possession. Coach may ask how one team got ahead of the other and I can answer him with what happened on each possession. Once he does that a couple of times in the first couple of weeks of the season, he knows that you're on the ball. The coach gives you a little test and if you pass, he feels a little more confident with you."

A third group of students are also hard at work. Enough can't be said about the dedication of the remaining "practice" players. Their rewards are few and mostly consist of the appreciation of the coaches and teammates and the stories they will one day tell their children. They hustle throughout practice, throwing themselves into roles as specific opponents. Most of the practice players are very good athletes, though most are clearly not in the same league as their better-known teammates. All work hard and take the workouts seriously. Occasionally, the practice players outshine the starters. Even Coach Smith has said he wishes his first team could shoot as well as his blue team does in practice. Without the pressure of competing for playing time or looking to improve standing on the team's shot chart, the practice players fill the basket with good shots and take charges on defense, a gutsy, sometimes dangerous act that can result in injury.

When a player has a question, the action stops and Smith fields the question in a loud voice so that all can hear. This is a positive change from Smith's previous philosophy of not wanting to disrupt practice to answer player queries. Usually, the questions are asked by underclassmen and the coach is quick to give a clear answer for everybody on the floor. Of all of his many skills, teaching is unquestionably the coach's greatest gift. Smith, a true educator, is, for the most part, a positive reinforcer. Good plays are noticed audibly. Bad plays or mistakes usually warrant only a scowl, a disapproving glance, or are ignored completely. Occasionally, Smith loses patience and lets loose an outburst that gets the attention of all of the athletes. Those who play for and work with the head coach rarely, if ever, see or hear a loss of control. One of Smith's primary strengths is his restrained, no-nonsense manner. Keeping a cool head is one more skill that is developed through intense, well-organized practices. Though Smith's emotions are immediate and vocal — ask any referee within earshot during a game — his calm confidence is reflected in the heat of highly contested games and scrimmages. The coach realizes that winning games is not the sole reason his program is the best in the nation. Day-to-day consistency and constant improvement is what Smith and company strive to achieve. What transpires in practice, and later develops in game situations, becomes the basis for a career as a company representative — a career that often translates into fame, wealth, and respect.

II.
WARM-UPS

The annual sports banquet that follows every basketball season from junior high to the professional ranks usually marks the end of a team's involvement as a whole. It is most often a happy event, a time when players and coaches join together to break bread and break the more formal teacher–student relationship to don a more fraternal demeanor. The wins and losses that provided the season's highs and lows are forgotten. The team tables the memories of hours of practice, long trips, and missed opportunities in order to remember the good experiences one last time.

North Carolina basketball banquets signify something different.

On April 13, 1987, in addition to the traditional awards dinner, a torch was passed. Like the spring season that is just beginning, the program regenerates itself and begins afresh with its annual basketball banquet. The seniors, the only specially treated members of the team, are free to personally acknowledge what their experiences have been like. Each, in turn, takes the chance to briefly reminisce about his recent past, and give one last parting bit of advice for the team he leaves behind. It is also a time of liberation for the select few who would soon leave the shelter of the country's premier basketball family. Smith, the father of the clan, will be available to a player for the rest of his life should he be needed, but his presence and control will never again be the same.

Soon the players who were once "all for one and one for all" would be divided into fractions, going their own ways. The two best players headed for the NBA to attempt a career in professional basketball. Two others would try foreign professional leagues in the hopes of eventually making it to the NBA. One went directly into business. All were free to begin life on the outside. The only rules that would govern their lives would be self-imposed. Each would experience one last night as a Tar Heel basketball player. Each of the five departing seniors in the Class of '87 left with a different impression from his four-year swim in the UNC fishbowl.

For most of the former North Carolina players, the memories would only be good ones. For a few, the recollections would also remind them of what might have been.

"It was a struggle," senior Dave Popson said of his four years at Carolina. Popson, a much-heralded player out of high school, never quite reached the level of expectations many held for him. "But with the help of my teammates, I persevered. It will help me not only in basketball, but in the bigger game of life." Still in the presence of his coach, Popson chose his words carefully, but a month later, in a relaxed interview away from the university, he revealed his frustrations more intimately.

"My junior year was a nightmare," he says. "It might be that the control Coach exerts has a strangling effect. But that's just the way the system is. I mean, when the system is kicking, and we're going full-strength, we're tough to beat. But then for the past four years we come down to the end of the season and the bottom just falls out.

"Coach will stress being regimented. He tells you to be creative out there and don't go with the set play all of the time — to go out on your own a little bit. But that's tough to do when you're trying to do all the regimented stuff and run the play through. And that freedom is limited to an extent. And there is so much competition for playing time. If you do mess up, you're coming out, and you know you might not go back in."

Another senior, reserve utilityman Curtis Hunter, fell short of the national basketball gurus' predictions as well. Early on, following on the heels of UNC's all-time great Michael Jordan, Hunter's style of play was compared to the NBA superstar. But no one would ever see those skills develop. Hunter spent five years as a Tar Heel, but he missed all of 1984 and an additional 21 games due to injuries. His role diminished gradually throughout his stay in Chapel Hill. In the end, after a tryout with the Denver Nuggets and a brief stint in Great Britain in a European League, Hunter returned to his hometown of Durham, North Carolina, and took a part-time job coaching a high school girls' basketball team.

Practice player Michael Norwood, one of a long line of "walk-on" players at UNC, enrolled for an education. Trying out for the junior varsity as a freshman was something he planned on. Winning a scholarship his junior year was an unexpected thrill. "Walk-ons are very important to the team," Norwood stated prior to his senior season. "If schools only had 13 or 14 McDonald's All-Americans, the guys who didn't get much playing time might not hustle as much in practice. Guys like me go to practice and play hard — which makes everyone practice and play hard. I know that I won't see a lot of playing time, and probably the only time I'll start is my last home game."

At his farewell banquet Norwood displayed a solid sense of humor to go along with his role-playing sense of duty.

"It was exciting being asked to pose for pictures and sign autographs because I was on the Carolina basketball team," he said. "One time a kid asked me if I was on the team and before I could answer he asked me if I was Curtis Hunter." While the banquet crowd of 1,500 roared with laughter, Norwood added, "So, I signed your name, Curtis."

The final two seniors were destined for the professional ranks. Each would distinguish the school as two of only four former McDonald's All-Americans chosen in the first round of the NBA draft. Forward Joe Wolf and point guard Kenny Smith both fit the mold of Dean Smith's ideal players, but for different reasons. Wolf played hard-nosed, hustling basketball in the paint. His numbers were consistent and his defense was steady. Kenny Smith ran the point with intelligence. With legendary speed and impressive shot-making abilities, only Coach Smith could hold down Kenny's scoring statistics. The high-flying speedster was showy at times, but he was able to read his coach's wishes and restrain himself.

Smith and Wolf knew the score on and off the court. When it came to toeing the company line with the media, both were well versed and rehearsed. But, off the record, both were candid and full of mirth. Wolf was always ready to give the correct *Carolina* answer to the media, but he did so with a twinkle in his eye. The 6–10 forward was also the most emotional senior on the team.

Wolf spoke first on the night of the banquet. "I have no special stories to tell tonight," he said. "Every moment was special to me." Twice he tried to thank his coach and his family, but couldn't, as he was overcome with tears and emotion. "When you live eleven hundred miles from home and your family tries to come to every game that they can in your senior year — this is what happens to you."

Rick Brewer, the UNC sports information director, introduced Kenny Smith, noting that the senior had received numerous awards that year. Among them were All-ACC, All-America, and the *Basketball Times* National Player of the Year recognition. "All of those awards were easy to get when you play with these guys," Smith said. "I remember the first time I played with some of the team when I first got here. I stepped out on the court and was facing Phil Ford. The guy's a legend in his own time and I'm on the same floor with him. But then, as we played, I thought 'Michael [Jordan] is on my left and Sam [Perkins] is on my right — it's not that hard.'"

It wasn't that hard to note that the graduating class was an outstanding one, combining an overall win–loss record of 115–20. In 1986-87, the Tar Heels had finished the season 32–4. The team amassed a perfect 14–0 ACC regular season record. It was the program's 23rd straight finish in the league's first, second, or third spot. For a UNC class, however, it was labeled a failure. None of the seniors had enjoyed an ACC tournament championship or a trip to the NCAA Final Four. Expectations for Carolina teams are always high and the Tar Heel Class of 1987 had not delivered. The disappointment wouldn't last long. A season had just ended, but a new season was beginning. Kenny Smith continued the cycle and renewed the expectations, saying, "I hate to say this, coach, but I think you're going to win the national championship next year."

Everyone in the audience wanted to believe the handsome point guard. In the backs of their minds, the remaining players felt it was possible. The team and its supporters were ready to put the recent past behind them and look optimistically to the future. As always, a strong nucleus of players would return, and quality recruits anxiously awaited their chance to fill in any holes. But the players and fans would not appreciate the skills Joe Wolf, Dave Popson, Curtis Hunter, and especially, Kenny Smith, took with them until well into the next season. Only one senior, Ranzino Smith, would be a regular on a team faced with a tough non-conference and conference schedule. The Tar Heels would face Syracuse in the season opener, Vanderbilt in Nashville, Southern Methodist at home, Illinois in Champaign, UCLA in Los Angeles, and 10 other warm-up games (including an exhibition with the Soviet National team) prior to any conference action. Then in addition to 14 ACC contests, UNC would squeeze in Temple University, a highly ranked powerhouse, in the Smith Center less than 24 hours after playing Maryland.

North Carolina would take on some of the best the country had to offer without a tested point guard and with two rusty reserves. Jeff Lebo would move to the point from the second guard position, with sharpshooting guard Ranzino Smith riding shotgun. King Rice would spell Lebo when he learned the system. Steve Bucknall and J.R. Reid would divide forward responsibilities and Scott Williams would start at center. Sixth man Kevin Madden could swing between guard and forward, while Pete Chilcutt and Rick Fox could back up the front line. The team was young and inexperienced.

The future, if the near future held another national championship, was realistically two years down the road.

•   •   •

The future was now for the latest five company graduates. Even before their sheepskins were inked, the squad joined forces with seniors from rival ACC schools for an ACC All-Star Classic Circuit barnstorming tour. The annual tour normally encompassed the entire state of North Carolina with occasional forays into surrounding areas. It was a perfect chance for the players to cash in on recently gained non-amateur status. Former Duke Coach Neill McGeachy promotes one of the better known and attended tours through Sugar Creek Enterprises Inc. Instead of taking on local All-Star teams, the Classic Circuit divided seniors from six ACC teams and Davidson into two fairly balanced teams that would play each other.

Balance wasn't important, however. Neither was the game played in Winston-Salem on April 15th. The evening showcased two dozen ineligible ACC players in a no-holds-barred, shoot'em-up skirmish. The only real competition came in the pregame warm-ups. Players vied to see who could make the most spectacular dunk. At halftime, the show continued with a three-point contest and a local player dunk display. A good time was had by all, with the best part for the players being the check they would get for their troubles. (Sizable crowds would appear at each stop on the tour, paying $6 to $8 for a viewing and a crack at getting an autograph. Kenny Smith, Joe Wolf, and Tyrone "Muggsy" Bogues spent more time signing their names than they did filling the hoop.)

UNC fans always look forward to the first chance of seeing ex-Tar Heels freed from their program's strong discipline. The game was an offensive extravaganza. Only token efforts were made on defense. The rest of the game was pure showtime. Dunks, alley-oops, double-pumps, and pro-distance three-pointers were the order of the night. Smith looked like he was in true heaven, as opposed to the blue heaven he had just vacated. His passes became more flamboyant, rivaling those of the late Pete Maravich. His dunks were spectacular.

In North Carolina, a state devoted to collegiate sport, sports journalists were on hand to cover even such an "entertainment" event. With the four-year season over, the postgame player quotes were more colorful. Answers couldn't affect playing time or risk the wrath of a coach this time.

●　　●　　●

On May 7, 1987, with one year in the pros under his belt, former Tar Heel Brad Daugherty was named to the NBA All-Rookie team. It shouldn't have been a surprise. Daugherty had been chosen first in the NBA draft a year earlier. More importantly, he was a solid contributor to the UNC program for four years, coming into its ranks at the ripe old age of 16. He said he owed his success to his former collegiate coach.

"You may think you know the game of basketball," Daugherty said, "but you don't know the game of basketball until you've played for Coach Smith. You learn to play at another level. It's a different game, totally. Playing for Carolina means the individual is going to be fundamentally sound, number one. Number two, he's going to be a disciplined basketball player. And number three, he's going to have an unselfish style.

"Without him, there is no way I'd be sitting here right now with everything I have and everything in front of me. So I really am appreciative. You can only tell him so many times, but I think he knows how much all of us appreciate him."

Daugherty would further distinguish himself in his second NBA year when the 7-0 center was named to the East All-Star team.

•   •   •

The next day, forward Henrik Rodl left Chapel Hill for his home in Germany. He'd be back. Rodl "conveniently" attended Chapel Hill High School for a year to further his studies. He left the high school and the United States with North Carolina Player of the Year honors after leading the Tigers to the state 4A basketball championship in March at the Smith Center. After completing two more years of academic work in Germany, it was hoped he would return to the same gym to complete a basketball degree at UNC.

Due to his notoriety, the team's best-kept secret import was noticed by other schools in the ACC, but his adopted hometown and its university retained the inside track for recruitment. Rodl's chances of return were further enhanced when his American high school sweetheart chose to attend UNC.

•   •   •

Three weeks later, UNC released the news that two NBA exhibition games had been scheduled in the Smith Center for consecutive weekends in October. The Los Angeles Lakers would take on the Cleveland Cavaliers one week before the Chicago Bulls would face the Dallas Mavericks.

UNC fans would be entertained by former Tar Heels and their professional teams. The list of alumni was impressive. Pictures of Michael Jordan, James Worthy, Brad Daugherty, and Sam Perkins, all starters on their respective teams, graced the cover of the program, and Mitch Kupchak and Al Wood, two longtime NBA players (and UNC stars), were scheduled to be on hand as well.

Most of the players would be playing in pickup games throughout the summer, anyway. Many team alumni men return to Chapel Hill year after year to hone skills and groom the future generation of Tar Heel greats. In addition to "working" the UNC basketball camp sessions, many of them find time to participate in daily summer games on the North Carolina campus. Most current undergraduate players remember going to preschool practice to learn Carolina tradition at the hands of current professionals.

"You're in awe at your first pickup game," says Jeff Lebo. "My first one was with Michael Jordan, James Worthy, Sam Perkins, and Walter Davis, to name a few. You're in dreamland. And they play pretty hard because they don't want anybody to show them up. They want you to know what it's like in the pros. Those games are pretty serious — no joking around."

• • •

On June 19, 1987, Dean Smith released the upcoming basketball schedule for his team through the athletic department's office, causing thousands of fans' mouths to salivate in anticipation. He stated the schedule would be tough on his inexperienced team. Few believed him. (*USA Today* pollster Jeff Sagarin did. In Sagarin's Final College Basketball Computer Ratings published on April 19, 1988, the company was rated as playing the second toughest schedule at 82.54. North Carolina would eventually finish the season with a 92.42 rating and an overall ranking of seven. Sagarin's poll is arguably the most scientific poll conducted as it takes into account schedule strength and the scores of all Division I games played. The computer assessment picked Kansas, the eventual 1987-88 champion, as the team with the toughest schedule strength. Still, the Jayhawks finished below the Tar Heels in overall ranking. Arizona, the team that would defeat Carolina in the West Regional, topped the rankings with a 98.96 rating but with a strength of schedule value of only 78.80.)

• • •

"It was the UCLA-North Carolina game of a lifetime," wrote Mike Downey of the *Los Angeles Times*. "There were guys with long hair, short hair, gray hair, almost no hair. There were guys with guts like beach balls and guys as hard-bellied as lifeguards. There were funky dunks and two-handed set shots, rainmaker jumpers from Lynn Shackleford and loose balls pounced upon by Phil Ford, power moves by Curtis Rowe and twists and shouts by Dudley Bradley. Even Gail Goodrich did a walk-on. It was time capsule basketball. Only thing missing was Lew Alcindor in an Afro."

It was a vivid description of the dream matchup of all time. Downey was writing of the Collegiate Legends Classic, the ultimate pick-up game of the '80s. Alumni games are not usually as vibrant. But when the UCLA dynasty met the UNC sovereignty, the air was indeed majestic. Each program had fostered over 20 first-team All-Americans. Each program had sent nearly 30 players to the NBA. Each program made 13 consecutive trips to the NCAA tournament. Each program is legendary.

The list of attending Tar Heel players was incredible. For North Carolina, 23 collegiate and professional stars suited up to play. Lennie Rosenbluth, Mike Pepper, Phil Ford, Dick Grubar, Steve Previs, John Kuester, Bob McAdoo, Mitch Kupchak, Dudley Bradley, Michael Jordan, Joe Wolf, Al Wood, Bill Bunting, Charlie Scott, Bill Chamberlain, Kenny

Smith, Tommy Kearns, Sam Perkins, Matt Doherty, Rusty Clark, Rich Yonaker, James Worthy, and Tommy LaGarde all saw action.

The actual game wasn't important; it was the command performance that mattered. The Tar Heels beat the Bruins, 116–111, but only the final few minutes were competitive. Carolina won the game in typical come-from-behind Tar Heel fashion. Down by as many as 18 points in the second half, Worthy, Jordan, Smith, Wood, and Wolf awakened from semi-slumber to reopen the eyes of the national television audience. UCLA was still in the game, but the majority of the Bruin superstars were well past their prime, and no match for their younger counterparts in a game where condition and speed are all-important. Without Kareem or Bill Walton to hold down the middle, UCLA's dynasty faltered.

The Classic was the first of its kind and maybe the last. What program could follow such a historical matchup? Dean Smith, the honorary coach of the North Carolina contingent, hoped it would be repeated. John Wooden, the honorary coach of the Bruins clan, was disappointed with the attendance (only 4,828) but optimistic about the future. "I know if they did this sort of thing in North Carolina next year, they'd fill that 25,000-seat building of theirs." But no one would find out the following year, for no rematch was scheduled.

●   ●   ●

A Tar Heel recruit gave the first indication the upcoming year would prove to be exciting for those who follow the Carolina basketball program. It was not positive.

The latest addition to the team, freshman prospect King David Rice, was involved in a knock'em, sock'em brawl in his hometown of Binghamton, New York, on August 8. In downtown Binghamton around 1:00 a.m., an altercation broke out between police officers and a number of youths outside a bar after two women were arrested for disorderly conduct. Though the confrontation began between the two women, police reported as many as 40 people were involved. The *Binghamton Press-Sun* printed that as many as 250 people took part in the brawl.

Chief of Police James O'Neil denied the paper's reported figure. "There was a scuffle of fairly good size, yes," he told *The Chapel Hill Newspaper*, "But it has gotten blown out of proportion. It happened in a section of town that's very active at night. There are a number of establishments that are half juice bars — for non-drinking-age customers — and half bars. It [the brawl] happened at a time when a lot of people were leaving the bars and milling around in the street."

Rice said he got involved when one of his friends, Eric Coleman, jumped into the fray to protest how one of Coleman's friends, John Harris, was being treated by the police. When police then focused their attention on Coleman, Rice began shouting at police to leave him alone. "I was yelling because of the way they slammed 'Ric [Coleman], and while I was yelling I got slammed myself," Rice told the *Binghamton Press-Sun.*

"They [the police] were telling everybody to leave," Rice continued. "And when people didn't leave, they started hitting people. Some of the cops wanted to make it a better situation, while others only wanted to make it worse. They were too rough."

Rice may have felt the police were using too much force, but the tally of those hospitalized indicated the contrary. Of the five people hospitalized, three were police officers. The future Tar Heel was one of 12 people arrested in connection with the disturbance, nine of whom were members of either the Binghamton High School 1986 state championship basketball or football teams. Rice was booked on charges of disorderly conduct and resisting arrest, both misdemeanors, after being arrested on the Monday following the incident. The police did not catch up to Rice until Monday, according to O'Neil, because of processing and issuing of warrants. In his comments to newspaper reporter Paul Ensslin, the police chief sounded almost apologetic that the promising freshman was involved. "It was just one of those things where he felt he had to help out a friend of his when he should have said, 'I better get my butt out of here,'" he said via a phone interview. "It was really a minor thing, but we've got to do what we've got to do."

The *Binghamton Press-Sun* reported that Rice had filed a complaint saying the police used excessive force in quelling the disturbance. O'Neil stated at the time he wasn't sure if Rice would press charges and that the teenager wouldn't be given any serious punishment as he had no previous record. "He's a fine young man and we wish him no ill will," O'Neil said. "But we had no choice but to bring him in. Athletically, he's the best thing to come out of our community and we're proud of him."

It was obvious the police chief wished Rice wasn't involved. The community was proud of the young man it had produced and its police chief was reluctant to speak negatively about him. It was the kind of news item that wouldn't be appreciated by UNC and its followers, either. When *The Chapel Hill Newspaper* publisher Orville B. Campbell saw the story headline his sports page, he was enraged. Negative news concerning the Tar Heels was no news as far as the aged alumnus was concerned. Sports editor Lee Roberts shouldered the "blame" and later resigned to take a reporting job with the *Wilmington Star-News.*

On October 15, fall basketball practice began for the upcoming season.

For incoming freshmen Rick Fox and King Rice, the day would be favorably remembered as the beginning of their collegiate careers at UNC. Sophomore Scott Williams will never forget the day, either. Just hours after the Tar Heels' first official practice, a practice Williams couldn't participate in because of a nagging back injury, a family tragedy struck the Williams' household.

Across the continent, just outside of her apartment in east Los Angeles, Williams' father shot and killed his mother and then shot himself. Rita and Al Williams had separated six months earlier at her insistence. In a brief note found later in his car, Al Williams wrote that he could no longer live without his wife. His solution was to take both of their lives.

Dean Smith informed Williams, who immediately left for California to be with his brother, Al Junior, and to help with funeral arrangements. On the day Smith was to attend the funeral, the coach experienced a serious nosebleed in Atlanta. Against the advice of the emergency doctors, the coach and his wife flew on to Los Angeles and attended the funeral. Upon returning to North Carolina, Smith was confined to bed for four days. "The doctor said it could have been psychosomatic," Smith said, acknowledging that he had been forced to miss practice. A press release pointed out that the head coach has only missed two practice sessions in 27 years at Carolina, both to attend funerals.

"I felt fine," Smith said to Barry Jacobs for a *Newsday* article. "It's just pretty hard to move around with blood coming out of your nose. It must happen to people with big noses or something."

Former Tar Heels Mitch Kupchak and James Worthy attended the funeral to offer support. Assistant coach Bill Guthridge, also present in Los Angeles, traveled with the sophomore back to Chapel Hill. Smith and Williams later discussed the possibility of the sophomore sitting out the season, but Williams decided to play through his grief. Williams would not discuss the tragedy with the press or his roommate, Jeff Denny, a sophomore reserve. Smith also said little about the incident, respecting Williams' request for privacy. "It was the most traumatic thing that ever happened to me," Smith said later to a *Los Angeles Times* writer. "Obviously, it has an effect on him. Nobody could ever be the same after something like that."

It was only the beginning of a series of preseason woes.

"We have been lucky that in my 27 years as a head coach that this is the first time I've had to deal with a matter such as this," Dean Smith said in a November 1 press release. Though Carolina fans looked at the upcoming 1987-88 season as a rebuilding one, no one had expected the growing pains to mount so quickly.

The matter Smith spoke of was not the tragic loss that Scott Williams suffered weeks earlier. It was an altercation between J.R. Reid, Steve Bucknall, and a North Carolina State student a week earlier — one that added an element missing in the intrastate rivalry for many years. It was an element the team could do without.

Reid and Bucknall were charged with simple assault after a fight at a nightclub in nearby Raleigh, not far from the campus of N.C. State. Paul James Doherty filed a warrant with the Wake County clerk of court in the early hours of October 24, 1987. In the warrant, Doherty said Bucknall hit him "with a clenched fist to the right eye" and Reid spat in his face. If true, years of squeaky-clean player reputations and positive North Carolina PR would be compromised. There had been a few incidents in the past involving team members. The ones that made the news were harmless. Brad Daugherty once threw some candy at a car. Phil Ford was involved in a brief scuffle at the beach during his playing days, and Mike O'Koren surprised a few people when it was made public he was seeking a divorce when no one knew he was married. Most media personnel and fans dismissed the affairs as less than noteworthy. Assault however, was a different matter.

Smith would later remark that if spitting was assault, then he had been assaulted many times in N.C. State's Reynolds Coliseum over the years. Though humorous, the coach's attempt to belittle the incident was uncharacteristic of the high standards the coach set and demanded from his players.

In this case, spittle was only part of the injury. The blow by Bucknall knocked Doherty to the floor, where his head hit a support column. Doherty suffered a chipped tooth and went to Rex Hospital in Raleigh, where he received nine stitches for cuts on his eyebrow and nose. The 21-year-old student said Reid "confronted me and started to ask me if I was talking about them or trying to start a fight with them.

"I tried to tell them I had no idea what they were talking about. They left again and then one minute later they returned all over again. I tried to explain that I didn't know what was going on. This time Reid became more vocal again and more violent."

Then, according to Doherty, Reid began to curse and spit in Doherty's face. "I put my hand up and I can't say that I even touched him," he said. "As I put my hand up I was just punched. I was blindsided."

Coach Smith was out of direct touch with the media concerning the incident until a week later when he was present at the ACC's 26th Annual Operation Basketball media day in Greensboro, North Carolina. Through the UNC sports information office, Smith announced disciplinary action would take place regardless of any legal decisions.

"Although the players were verbally harassed and pushed in an effort to provoke some kind of response, I am taking disciplinary steps against them for not getting out when the harassment started," Smith said in a released statement. "This is a team matter and will be handled internally. However, since the suspensions will be obvious, I am going ahead and announcing that part of my action."

Both Reid and Bucknall were suspended from making the trip to Springfield, Massachusetts, for the Tar Heels' season opener. The Hall of Fame Tip-Off Classic and the nation's college hoops fans would, then, pay part of the price for the two players' ill-advised journey to the appropriately named Shooters II nightclub in Raleigh. Though both Reid and Bucknall would state publicly that they had let down their teammates by not being available for the game with Syracuse, neither was too upset. A sports reporter for *The Chapel Hill Newspaper* not scheduled to cover the game in Syracuse said he saw the two "punished" roommates leaving a local supermarket on the day of the game armed with a case of beer. The dynamic duo apparently found a way to drown their sorrows. As Reid was underage in North Carolina, it must be presumed he was just along to help carry the heavy load.

"We have no curfew rule during preseason practice or rule against dancing in clubs, as long as the players are of legal age," Smith's statement read. "This particular club is open to 18-year-olds. It's my understanding the N.C. State students were 21. (Reid was 19 and Bucknall was 21 at the time of the incident.) As authorities have reported, our players were not and had not been drinking.

"The players should have left when the verbal abuse began. The fact they did not walk away even though pushed and poked is the reason for the action I am taking. I haven't had to deal with a situation like this in the past.

"While I don't believe physical action should ever settle any confrontation," Smith continued, "I realize incidents like this are common occurrences across the country. But we have been lucky that in my 27 years as a head coach that this is the first time I've had to deal with a matter such as this."

The altercation turned out to be the least of his problems.

Smith added to the preseason woes by becoming ill and missing four days of practice due to excessive nasal bleeding and contributing to his weakened condition by continuing to smoke. Smith told various news media he was limiting himself to eight cigarettes a day.

Steve Mann, sports editor for the *Durham Morning Herald*, noted in an article that "Smith also admitted that, like he does on the basketball court, he's using the rules to his advantage. Instead of smoking a cigarette completely, he puts it out before finishing it and lights up what remains later in the day."

Members of the media who followed the coach and many an interested bystander secretly wanted to confront the dean of collegiate coaches and demand (read: gently request) he give up smoking altogether. It was doubtful anyone including his family could make such a request. Smith is seriously addicted to the habit. A year earlier, after a cliffhanger in Durham against close rival Duke, Smith found himself out of smokes prior to the postgame press conference. Noting a familiar fellow smoker in the audience, Smith bummed a cigarette. "I got a long ride back to Chapel Hill," Smith said nervously, "make that three if you can spare them."

Showing the importance Smith places on such a request, the very next time the coach saw the journalist — a press conference three days later — Smith handed exactly three cigarettes to the writer with another "thank you" before beginning his remarks.

Later in the 1987-88 season, Temple Coach John Chaney made a plea to the coach to "stop killing himself" with cigarettes. After his team blew out the hosting Tar Heels in front of a national television audience, Chaney was still in the press room when Smith arrived. Smith was not used to being the second coach interviewed in the Smith Center's makeshift interview area. The winning coach is the first to speak and only three coaches other than Smith had ever won that honor — Lefty Driesell in 1986, Mike Krzyzewski in 1988, and now Chaney.

"What did I tell you about those cigarettes," Chaney shouted as Smith walked in. "Stop it!" It's likely the well-intentioned words from Chaney fell on deaf ears. Smith has clung to his severe habit even though to do so belies his intelligence. Partly through a sense of guilt and partly through wanting to set a good example as a role model, Smith tries to not be seen in public smoking a cigarette. (The same is said about his drinking alcohol in front of minors or his parents.)

Jeff Lebo developed a groin injury, limiting his involvement in the first public appearance of the 1987-88 Tar Heels. UNC's first Blue and White interteam scrimmage for the faithful fell on November 7, in the Smith Center. The center was only half full, due in part to a rescheduled meeting between the North Carolina and Clemson football teams earlier that day.

ESPN offered to show the football game to the nation, much to the chagrin of the thousands of Tar Heel and Tiger fans who would miss seeing the game. The football matchup was originally scheduled to be broadcast on the Raycom Jefferson Pilot Television Network but because the game could ultimately determine the conference champion, it was chosen by ESPN to become the first game of a double header on its network. Thousands of cable-less viewers would suffer the loss, but the conference would receive greater exposure and monetary renumeration. Money talks.

The basketball scrimmage was in turn postponed until after the football game, but the North Carolina gridiron loss to Clemson put a damper on the day for the UNC faithful. Those who would have normally stayed in town for a chance to see the team that most represents the university departed. Smith went so far as to remark that the football team's loss affected the play of his players. Unlikely.

"It was better than the Wednesday night [inner-squad] scrimmage," Smith said after the game, "That [scrimmage] had to be the worst I can remember since being coach, so consequently I'm happier tonight. But, still, we've got a long way to go and only two weeks in which to do it.

"Of course, the competition with all of the jayvees and walk-ons isn't what it's like when we play against recruited athletes at other schools. We had a lot of non-recruited athletes on the floor tonight and it was a letdown, especially after the football team played so well and so hard and lost to Clemson."

When asked later about the calamitous Carolina preseason at a press conference prior to the game against Syracuse, Smith could only recite from the long list of occurrences and shake his head.

"And I've never been about run over at Duke before," he added.

Smith was referring to a near miss in Durham. The coach was attending services at the Duke Chapel with his family, including his visiting parents. After the service, while the Smiths were entering their car, a Duke Transit bus trailer crashed into the open front door on the passenger side of the loaned 1988 Cadillac Smith was using, narrowly missing his father.

"My mom doesn't walk that well, so a policeman let me drive up to the chapel after the service so I could let her in the car," Smith said. "My dad had just gotten in when the second part of the bus [a second bus trailer] squashed the back of the door against the front of the car. If I had been nice and opened the door for my dad, I probably would have been crushed to death." Smith's feelings toward the bus driver were forgiving.

"I felt kind of sorry for the lady who was driving the bus," he said. "She couldn't see the trailing bus in her rear-view mirror because it was on the curve when it hit my car." The Cadillac was provided by the UNC athletic department. He might have felt differently if the car was his own. Smith obtains his late-model BMW sedan from Joe Youngblood, a former UNC basketball team manager and current CEO of the Fletcher Auto Agency in Asheville, North Carolina.

Smith, who had previously, and jokingly, insisted Reid and Bucknall travel to Raleigh only when the Tar Heels play at N.C. State in order to circumvent trouble, may have thought about restricting his own travel to other ACC cities as well.

Later that month, Coach Smith made a radio appearance with Sally Sather, a Carolina sports photographer who had just published her first book of Carolina basketball photographs. The appearance was to help WUNC, the Chapel Hill public radio station, raise money during its annual fund-raising drive. Smith and Sather offered autographed copies of *Images of Excellence* for $100.

Smith, an avid follower of jazz and other programming found on the station, sat in to field telephone questions and make remarks about *Sports Illustrated* writer and television commentator Frank Deford's involvement with National Public Radio. Smith chose his words carefully, as the two were not the best of friends.

Deford had approached Smith five years earlier about doing a story on the coach. Smith wanted him to do the story on UNC and the basketball program instead. When Deford chose to write about the coach in an article entitled "Long Ago, He Won the Big One," the dean of coaches began a mini-feud that has lasted ever since. In his profile of the coach, Deford wrote of Smith's personal life, including his divorce from his first wife in 1973 and the devastating Tar Heel loss to Marquette in the 1977 NCAA final — both considered closed subjects to Smith. "Smith came from a family, from a whole culture, in which people didn't get divorced. Divorce was failure. Divorce was shame. By best accounts, Smith all but drove himself to the brink of madness, wrestling with his conscience, his morality, as he realized that his marriage had collapsed. Compulsively he immersed himself in his basketball family... Between the breakup of his first marriage and the start of his second, Smith was something of a lady's man, and much of the criticism of his being holier-than-thou, dates to that period."

Smith still reads Deford's work. For an off-the-floor assignment the following month, Smith ordered his players to produce a book report of sorts. "I made them read the *Sports Illustrated* story [prefaced] by Deford on the eight sportsmen of the year," Smith said. "They had to read it over Christmas and report which one they thought was the most sincere as a test question."

• • •

November 17 was a busy day for the UNC Athletic Department .

Head football coach Dick Crum was on the firing line at his regularly scheduled Tuesday press luncheon. Simply stated, Crum lost too many games to inferior football teams and it finally caught up with him. Though his first 65 games at Carolina brought the school a 48–16–1 record, his last 50 resulted in a dismal 24–24–2. Against Top 20 teams, the coach and his team were 2–21–1 since 1983. The Carolina fans and the media were restless. The coach was in line to be replaced the week following the last game of the season. It was an awkward day for those present.

Just that morning the *Raleigh News and Observer* proclaimed on the top of its front page that Crum was history. "Dick Crum's tenure as the University of North Carolina's head football coach is expected to end after Saturday's game against Duke, top UNC officials said Monday.

"Two high-ranking school officials, who declined to be identified, told *The News and Observer* Crum would be out as coach after the game in Chapel Hill. The officials would not specify whether Crum would resign or be fired," read the opening two paragraphs of the lead story by Caulton Tudor and Chip Alexander. The ball was rolling, but the official Carolina line was to hold off any questions in public until the remaining game was completed.

Then Chancellor Christopher C. Fordham and Athletic Director John Swofford dismissed the reports as "rumors" and said further comments would be delayed until after the season. Swofford did go on record to Charles Chandler of the *Durham Morning Herald*. "I will say that all athletic personnel matters will be handled through the proper channels, through the office of the athletic director and the chancellor. If any further comment is necessary, it will come at the end of the season."

Chandler noted that it was a different stance from Swofford's previous defense of Crum two years prior. Swofford quieted any speculation concerning Crum's job status on November 4, 1985. At that point, UNC had a 4–4 record in what turned out to be a 5–6 season. "In my eyes, Dick Crum has excellent job security," Swofford said at the time. "Our whole approach to our athletic program has been one of stability, continuity, and commitment to our people. And building a sound foundation that can weather periods when you don't win as much as you'd like to, or as your fans would like you to."

But that was then and this was now. In the world of collegiate athletics, words like stability, continuity, and commitment sounded nice but mean little. The bottom line was winning, and the fans and athletic department supporters determined how many games were necessary to be termed a winner. Though the Carolina athletic and academic system claimed the school was above pressure from its boosters and alumni, when it came down to push and shove it was the Educational Foundation Inc., who helped set policy. The Foundation later provided $800,000 to buy out Crum's contract.

The ouster of Crum had been expected for some time. The coaching profession is not often one that treats its members fairly. It isn't enough to be a good leader and an honest, hard-working teacher. The pupils, especially the handpicked and highly recruited student athletes, needed to produce wins. With Dean Smith on campus, the standard was firmly established for the rest of the athletic department.

Maybe another UNC company man, head women's and men's soccer coach Anson Dorrance, said it best earlier that day. Dorrance was also on hand to speak to the press about his two teams making it to the final four and final sixteen, respectively, earlier that week. A writer commented about Dorrance's success with his five-time national champion women's team, but added he thought the coach's men's teams hadn't arrived at the same level of play just yet. "Too often coaches are given too much credit when their teams win and too much blame when they lose," said Dorrance in reply to the joint praise and criticism.

Though he wasn't, Dorrance could have been speaking about Crum, or even Smith. And perhaps Crum wouldn't have been in the predicament if he possessed the public speaking and personality of an Anson Dorrance. Crum didn't have a gift for speaking to the public. No matter how hard he tried, he was too dry and humorless when it came to answering questions about his coaching or team strategies. Had his manner been less reserved and more relaxed and spontaneous, he might have weathered the criticism and still been the head football coach of the university. Personality plays a big part in job security.

At the press conference, Crum avoided any comment concerning his future with the university. It was the largest attendance of the media that fall and it may have been the shortest question and answer period elicited from the coach. Mum was the word.

During the luncheon that followed, a luncheon that Crum decided to miss, many of the writers present queried each other about the state of affairs at North Carolina's athletic department. The overriding question among several sports journalists was whether or not North Carolina cared if it had the best football team in the conference. After all, basketball reigned supreme in the ACC, and the overall crown seemed to be based in Chapel Hill.

"It's a business, " offered Frank Dacenzo, sports editor of the *Durham Sun*. "And the bottom line is winning. Coaches have to produce winning teams." Dwayne Ballen, a sports broadcaster at WTVD in Durham, was quick to point out how clean Crum's program was and that it graduated a great many of its players. "How could Carolina have their cake and eat it too?" he asked.

Joe Tiede, a longtime sports editor for the *Raleigh News and Observer*, remembered a line Crum had used a couple of years earlier. Crum had said, "North Carolina wants to be like Harvard from Monday through Friday, but like Oklahoma on Saturday." Crum knew realistically UNC would prefer to be more like the Sooners on the playing field.

After the press luncheon that followed Crum's terse remarks, Dean Smith arrived to speak about the basketball team's upcoming game with Syracuse. Smith wouldn't normally have addressed the media so far in advance of his team's first game, but the sports information department hoped the esteemed coach's remarks would take some of the headlines away from the Crum situation. The plan didn't succeed. Crum's ouster, and the way it was handled by the UNC athletic department, was hard news, and the entire university would feel repercussions throughout the year.

But the football season was almost over and the first basketball game would sweep away all conflicts. The real season, as far as North Carolina fans were concerned, was about to begin.

III.
FIRST HALF

UNC 96, SYRACUSE 83

The afternoon of November 21, 1987, was a chance for Dean Smith and company to don a role they never seem to get enough of.

North Carolina, preseason ranked as low as ninth in the nation (*Sports Illustrated*) and as high as second (UPI), would have one of its few chances at going into a game as the underdog. Syracuse was preseason ranked number one.

"I think we have a chance," Smith said earlier in the week, setting the stage. "We have six recruited athletes available, so David May (a non-recruited jayvee turned varsity player) may play more than he thinks. I shouldn't tell the press, he'd be so nervous. He was nervous about coming to varsity practice. I'm not going to tell him it's on national television."

The Orangemen of Syracuse, the last team to have beaten the Tar Heels (79–75 in the 1987 NCAA East Regional Finals), were poised and waiting for the chance to show a national television audience they should be ranked in the top spot. The Hall of Fame Tip-Off Classic in Springfield, Massachusetts, would be the scene of the contest, though many believed it would be no contest. In a piece entitled "Back From the Future," Curry Kirkpatrick, a UNC alumnus and sports journalist for *Sports Illustrated*, wrote that Syracuse, with Rony Seikaly, Derrick Coleman, and Sherman Douglas, would "pound the Tar Heels and then challenge gold-medal winner Brazil for the amateur championship of the universe." So much for alumni prejudice.

The Tar Heels were slight underdogs due to the preseason rankings. But added to the ranking hype was the news that UNC's Reid and Bucknall would not make the trip. The duo's punishment for straying into the altercation in Raleigh a few weeks earlier stacked the odds even higher against the inexperienced Heels.

"We have the psychological advantage," Smith said earlier in the week. "I think that's the biggest thing in our favor." Many of the fans felt it was the only thing in the team's favor. The faithful already wished the Heels would get another chance later in the season to play the Orangemen at full strength. Many of the media in attendance in Springfield also wished Reid, Carolina's future All-American, had made the trip to challenge Syracuse's All-America hopeful, Rony Seikaly. After all, it was the Tip-Off Classic, and everyone wanted to get the season started with a bang.

It was more of an explosion.

The game showcased the powerful offense and quickness of Syracuse, all right. But it also illuminated the strength of UNC's overall program. Smith prides himself on sacrifice for team honor. His team did not disappoint him, as it rose to the task to win one against the odds. Inexperience was tempered by exuberance and belief from within. Players new to the complex North Carolina system learned enough, most of it the hard way, to pluck a victory from the hands of a seasoned and skilled opponent. It wasn't easy.

Carolina warmed up only briefly, uncharacteristically emerging from the locker room just six seconds prior to the tip-off. Syracuse took the opening tap and drove directly to the hoop for the first score. The Heels recovered though, and the game seesawed through all but the final four minutes of the first half. The Orangemen built an 11-point lead, 50-39, and went into the locker room on the strength of two awesome dunks by Seikaly and two three-pointers by guard Matt Roe.

Syracuse looked formidable with strong drives from guard Sherman Douglas and power moves from Seikaly. Their halftime totals, 17 and 14 respectively, led the scoring by eight Orangemen.

Carolina also used eight players in the half, but only six put points on the board. Jeff Lebo's 10 points didn't surprise anyone, but freshman Rick Fox's 12 did. The 6-7 forward from the Bahamas started the game instead of sophomore Kevin Madden because Madden had missed three minutes of a team meeting the day before. Both played 16 minutes in the first half, but Fox contributed 12 points and six rebounds to Madden's five points and two rebounds. Fox joined an elite crew of just seven freshmen to start in their first games at North Carolina. Though his playing time would diminish considerably during the season, Fox would continue to be a strong contributor to the program.

"I wasn't nervous," said Fox. "When I went out there, it was just like high school." He shouldn't have been nervous. No one expected the youngsters in blue and white to win, or even play very well against what the pollsters considered to be the nation's best amateur team, especially without the services of two starters.

The second half began much like the first, as Carolina didn't emerge from the locker room until just seconds before play was to begin. But, in spite of making the first basket, the Heels increased their deficit to 14 points within five minutes.

If North Carolina were to get back into the game, it would have to make a move soon.

Enter center Scott Williams. The team called on its big man to start the big push. His answer was UNC's next seven points. And he carried the load while plugging up the middle on defense. Re-enter guard Ranzino Smith and the team began throwing fours. After scoring just four first-half points, he added four more before Williams' surge and after a Madden jumper, Smith added four more to cut the lead to four points.

Timeout, Syracuse.

"I said yesterday they would be more ready," said Seikaly after the game. "These people want to prove they can play. They weren't going to lose anything by losing to us. They were supposed to. The only thing they could do was win. If they win, they get all the credit." And if they lost, even the hard-to-please UNC fans wouldn't be too upset.

The momentum had definitely changed in favor of the Tar Heels, but the game was far from over. North Carolina went to a three-guard lineup after the timeout. It was a critical time in the game. The Orangemen and the Tar Heels traded baskets, with Syracuse maintaining a four-point lead. UNC packed its defense in, using both a zone and a thinly disguised sagging man-to-man. Williams kept the Heels in the game, and Seikaly ran the show for Syracuse.

After a Tar Heel steal, Lebo and Smith converted a two-on-one fast break to bring UNC within one point with 3:27 left to play in regulation. Senior Ranzino Smith had scored his 17th point, but in doing so he violated the team concept of passing the ball to the open man closest to the basket. Lebo was forgiving, giving Smith a pat on the behind and a gentle reminder that he had been open. Coach Smith was not so gracious. Slapping his hands in displeasure, the coach pulled Ranzino from the game.

The senior did get back into the game a minute or so later with the score tied at 81. Lebo quickly fed his returning backcourt partner with a backdoor pass and the team in a spread offense. Smith's layup was good. For the moment, Ranzino's earlier selfishness was forgotten.

Meanwhile, Syracuse may have been thinking choke with just 31 seconds left on the clock, but the Orangemen didn't show it. Seikaly went to the line with two chances to tie the game. He was three of eight from the charity stripe prior to these last two attempts. This time he made them both.

The next play was controversial. Syracuse's Derrick Coleman, or so the record books will say, stole the inbounds pass from Pete Chilcutt. Both Chilcutt and Coach Smith would later state that the ball was taken out of Chilcutt's hands while he was out of bounds, which is a technical foul. "I can say that I definitely thought he hit it," Chilcutt said in his postgame remarks, sounding like a politician. "I can't tell if he did or not, but when I was about to release it I thought he hit the ball."

Regardless, the officials didn't see it the way Smith and Chilcutt did.

Coleman, fouled by Williams, still managed to connect on an off-balance jumper. It was Williams' fifth foul, and as he walked off the court, it seemed the Orangemen would regain the lead with around 10 seconds left. Coleman, who was strangely silent while the Tar Heels made their second-half comeback, made up for his absence by drilling both free throws to give the nation's number one team a two-point advantage.

Lebo took the ensuing inbounds pass and raced to the other end of the floor. He kept dribbling, looking for a shot. But the Orangemen swarmed all over him to prevent the launching of a three-point attempt. The clock was down to about three seconds when he found Chilcutt inside. Picking up the bounce pass from Lebo, Chilcutt wheeled and lofted a short jump shot. It hit the back of the rim and bounced nearly straight up before falling through the basket as the buzzer sounded.

Overtime.

"I was kind of shocked," Chilcutt said of the last shot. "It was a lucky shot, I'll admit. But it fell." The hopes of the Orangemen could have, also. They didn't.

The overtime began with Syracuse scoring the first two baskets on layups. But North Carolina withstood the pressure as each remaining UNC player on the floor scored in the final three minutes to beat Syracuse. Ranzino Smith ended his 21-point MVP performance with two free throws, Chilcutt scored a layup, Fox contributed a free throw, Madden added two more from the line, Lebo canned two more from the line, and Fox ended the game with a breakaway dunk.

Final score — UNC 96, Syracuse 93.

"When we were beaten the last two years, everybody had a celebration," Dean Smith said after the game. "We did the celebrating today.

"I really do think we had the psychological edge, and that always helps. But more than that, it helps to have players like these — that just came through when they had to."

The coach was pleased. His team had responded to the challenge and the instructor in him was proud of his students. The players "like these" were the whole team. But the unexpected treat for both the coach and the fans was the freshmen. Redshirt freshman Pete Chilcutt was playing in his first college basketball game, not to mention against the nation's top-ranked team and its number-one performer, Ron Seikaly. Chilcutt contributed 14 points, and more importantly, 13 rebounds in the effort.

"I've never seen Pete play like that and I've watched him for two years in practice," said Smith about Chilcutt's performance. "He really rose to the occasion replacing J.R. Maybe he'll beat J.R. out now." Reid, listening and watching the national telecast, was back in Chapel Hill raising a toast to Chilcutt's extra effort. He wasn't worried. There was little possibility of the redshirt freshman replacing the All-America skills of Reid.

Fox was no slouch, either. His debut in a blue and white uniform included a seven of eight shooting performance and seven rebounds. Though he didn't score, freshman King Rice also did some nice things with the basketball in the 19 minutes he ran the offense. "I thought King was sensational defensively," said a beaming Dean Smith. "He would make some mistakes and then make up for it. I was very happy for King. Ranzino and Lebo are veteran guards, but I didn't hesitate to put King in there and I was happy with . . . hey, with the seven or eight guys that played. Everyone contributed."

In a year that was supposed to be only a rebuilding one, it seemed the foundation had been well laid.

UNC 73, USSR 71

Next on the agenda was an exhibition game with the Soviet National team. In a weak attempt at humor, the ads that appeared in the local newspapers ran with a headline of THE RUSSIANS ARE COMING. The ad could have been overlooked had it not gone on to use the verb *invade* in describing the upcoming meeting. Still, advertising a UNC basketball game is not important to the overall financial success of the program. Most games are sold out before going on sale. This game was different.

Luckily, both the two teams and the 14,098 in attendance in the Smith Center were present to participate in an athletic contest, even if it was one that would not count in either team's overall record. The Tar Heels squeezed out a win, 73-71. The inexperienced Carolina squad was fortunate in beating the Soviet's answer to the NBA. Two of the three centers from Russia were out of action that night, and the rest of the team was tired from too many games in too short an exhibition tour.

"My team shoot very bad in first period," Soviet head coach Aleksandr Gomelsky said in a press conference after the game. "(Aleksandr) Volkov not play good. He shoot many times and not make many."

Most of the Soviets "shoot many times." In fact, the Russian team shot 67 times to 54 from the floor for the home team. Their style of putting up shots as quickly as possible forced the Tar Heels to scamper on defense for most of the evening. UNC stayed with the poor-shooting Soviets, but looked ragged doing so. J.R. Reid tied both his teammate, Scott Williams, and Sergey Tarakanov of the Soviet team for high-scoring honors with 15. His points were the result of a four-of-13 field goal shooting performance, however.

"It was sort of ugly, but we'll take it," Reid said after the game.

It may have also been the most physical game the Heels played in 1987. Swingman Kevin Madden was quoted as saying he felt like he'd been in the ring with Mike Tyson. "I think it's the most physical game I've ever played since I've been at Carolina," he said. "Look at this," he added, while pointing to an injury over one eye.

Chalk up the physical nature of the game as one more "experience" for a team short of playing time against stronger and more physical players. Reid, who fouled out of the game, said he and his teammates didn't mind the contact. "It was a physical game, but that's the way that I like to play," Reid said, smiling. "I like it. Pete [Chilcutt] likes it. Kevin likes it. Scott [Williams] likes it." Coach Smith didn't particularly like the way Reid and Williams got into foul trouble as a result of the physical play.

"I liked our last three minutes," Coach Smith said. "I didn't like the way we turned the ball over in the second half against a zone defense that was passive. Chilcutt hit me with a beautiful pass for which I thanked him, you know, for the pass — but, actually Pete played pretty well.

"Ranzino and Jeff weren't sharp shooting the ball, and of course that's why we're an inconsistent team. We're not a good basketball team yet. I hope we become one."

UNC 82, USC 77

"I'm probably too impatient with the team and consequently I'm not doing a very good job," Dean Smith said November 27 after the Tar Heels narrowly avoided a loss to Southern California in Richmond, Virginia, site of the Central Fidelity Holiday Classic.

Those were sentiments only a very secure coach would admit in public. In most cases, Smith, ever the pessimist when it comes to describing his teams' chances against collegiate opponents, would have been taken with a grain of salt. After the Tar Heels' performance that night, the assembled media was quick to take note.

The team struggled throughout most of the evening, barely holding a lead against a team that sported 10 new members. The Trojans had finished in last place in the Pac-10 the previous year and were picked to finish only slightly higher in 1987-88. It wasn't until Ranzino Smith canned two free throws with just five seconds remaining that UNC could claim the victory and a chance to compete the next evening in the finals.

Ranzino led Carolina's scoring with 19 and backcourt mate Jeff Lebo added another 15. Together they shot seven of 13 from three-point distance.

Anthony Pendleton of USC nearly matched their efforts, hitting six of 14 attempts from downtown in his game-high 20 points. The Trojans totaled 39 points from beyond the three-point stripe and almost pulled off a major upset. The third-ranked Tar Heels looked nothing like a Top 10 team. "It's difficult [winning] right now 'cause we're such a young team," Lebo said, trying to supply the answer to a group of questioning reporters. "We have talent, but we're not playing as capably as we're capable of playing."

The answer to the problem was on most of the players' lips, but the solution would take time to solidify. The team needed chemistry, and Smith, the master chemist, would need to come up with the correct formula. "I think it's just the fact we've got to get our chemistry down and once we do we'll play a lot better," Kevin Madden said. "We were uptight tonight and I hope we can loosen up tomorrow."

Madden went on to offer his views on how to acquire the much-needed science. "We can't worry about who gets the credit. With J.R. and Jeff, you know, they're in the public eye more than the rest of the guys, and with the other guys we do what we can to hold up — it's like a support in a house. If you knock down one main beam, then the whole house goes down. We don't want to do that, so we want to support those guys. The further that they go, the further we go as a team."

Steve Bucknall agreed. "I think the biggest reason is that most of the guys haven't played a lot of minutes — a lot of important minutes. The rest of the guys are trying to learn each other's plays and work together as a unit."

Bucknall and Pete Chilcutt were the only two replacements who saw quality time. Freshmen King Rice and Rick Fox, who saw considerable action in the game against Syracuse, played only a few minutes in the game.

"It's going to take a while," Lebo acknowledged. "The young players are a little shaky on where to go and what to do right now, but it's still early in the year. Once we have more time to play together — the last two years we had five seniors who had played together and we really don't have that this year."

• • •

For the time being, however, Smith was setting the stage for an early season loss and preparing his team for the worst. He barely fielded the reporters' questions concerning the team's development, remarking that the earlier game between Richmond and Boston University was the best game of the evening.

"It seems like the first game was a lot more interesting and the two better teams played in the first game," Smith reiterated. "I honestly think that Richmond and B.U. was a much better game to watch — at least people got half their money's worth."

When asked about his thoughts on playing the host team, the University of Richmond, the following evening, Smith quickly regained his coaching stance. "It would be amazing for me if we could beat Richmond right now at Richmond. Basketball has always been a home-court game and always will be. I really will be surprised, but that's all right — we can go on from there."

UNC 87, RICHMOND 76

It was the first tournament trophy for the young team. Tar Heel fans hoped it would not be the last.

The hosting Spiders of Richmond led by three points with eight minutes remaining in the first half. But when Jeff Lebo tied the game with two free throws less than a minute later, the Spiders' lead was lost for good. North Carolina won the Central Fidelity Holiday Classic with relative ease, 87-76. The elusive "chemistry" was beginning to work — the players were becoming a team.

The Tar Heels mixed up a different formula from the night before. Gone from the starting lineup was outside bomber Ranzino Smith. In his place was the taller 6–5 swingman, Kevin Madden. Both contributed almost equally. J.R. Reid, Scott Williams, and Steve Bucknall held down the inside, picking up 34 points and 26 rebounds among them.

Game honors, and ultimately the tournament's MVP laurels, went to the team's floor leader and resident sharpshooter, Jeff Lebo. Lebo rolled the dice for UNC for 35 minutes and threw nothing but sevens. The junior guard from Carlisle tossed in seven of 11 shots from the floor, all from the bonus side of the three-point stripe. He added seven more points from the charity line and ended up with 28 points, his career high, and an MVP trophy. Lebo was "pleased" with his play. Dean Smith was quick to downplay Lebo's performance.

"Those of you who follow us know that I never like one player to come out and say, 'I'm going to take the game over,'" Smith said. "But I felt that his leadership, and J.R.'s too, [was important]. I challenged them as our starters to exhibit that leadership. I think Jeff was in control, but not necessarily trying to take all the shots. Some people think that a guy's supposed to come in and take over and shoot every time.

"I was a little unhappy with him in the first half with a couple of bad passes," Smith noted. "I said something to him and he promptly came down and shot a three-pointer and [then] made a great defensive play. So I guess I'll have to stay mad at him all year."

Lebo not only appreciated the show of discipline, but said he felt

Smith's criticism turned his game around. "I made some passes on the fast break that were marginal," Lebo remembered after the game, "and I really got frustrated with myself for throwing them. He [Smith] got on me and said, 'You know you've got better judgment than that.' In the second half I tried not to force things and it worked out for me."

It's not often a collegiate player, especially a legitimate All-America candidate, encourages criticism from anybody, much less his coach. A reporter asked Lebo if he'd like to see a little more of Bobby Knight, a coach infamous for his severe player criticism, in Dean Smith.

"I hope not Bobby Knight," Lebo grinned, "but maybe just a harsher Coach Smith."

Larry Brown, currently the highest-paid professional basketball coach and one of only a few North Carolina players who played for both Frank McGuire and Dean Smith, once told a writer that Smith got his points across in a unique way. "He was so different from Coach McGuire. Until you knew Coach Smith well, he could give you a very uncomfortable feeling. Why, he could give you a compliment and still make you wonder. Coach McGuire would get mad and call me a Jew bastard, and it rolled off my back. He called everybody something. But Coach Smith would just say, 'Larry, I think you could have fought over that screen,' and it would hurt me much more. It would go through me like a knife."

Lebo's lighthearted remarks were also laced with a grain of truth. Smith, ever the intelligent instructor, demonstrates his coaching ability and affection for his players with constructive criticism. Rather than sacrifice a player's learning experience by reacting solely for the moment, Smith imparts wisdom for future use by forcing the student athletes to think for themselves. Instead of berating Lebo for his poor passing with an offhand comment, Smith chose to praise him for past performance. Lebo knew he was being reprimanded, but he also knew his coach's criticism helped him to play better.

Lebo was acknowledging that a "harsher" Smith would be one way to force himself and his teammates to strive for even better performance. The mediocre-to-average execution the inexperienced team had demonstrated so far in the young season would not be enough against strong NCAA competition.

Lebo may have known that although you may get more with sugar than with vinegar, there was nothing wrong with stirring up the taste buds every now and then with an appropriate spice.

On November 29, the Associated Press released a story dealing with the stress ACC coaches face. The article noted that coaches are subject to "long-term pressures of recruiting, the stream of preseason interviews and the worry about players and performance in the classroom."

In addition, the public is now privy to the coaches' every nuance due to the media's close scrutiny. No coach is safe from the camera, microphone, or sportswriter's keyboard. "Our job is entirely in the public eye, every aspect of it," Duke's Mike Krzyzewski said. "There are a whole set of pressures to go along with that."

Dean Smith pinpointed the moment when the coach's visibility increased. "A change took place when we [the coaches] became prime time. The cameras chose to show the coaches sometimes instead of the game." With good reason. One of the major differences between professional and college basketball is the tight control the collegiate coaches have on their players. College players must respect their coach's wishes if they want to play ball, something that doesn't happen in the NBA where a player may earn millions more than his coach.

Most college games are decided by the coaching preparation, strategy, and skills. Obviously, the player's skills do come into play, but not without prior approval from the coaches. It also doesn't hurt visibility that colorful coaches such as N.C. State's Jim Valvano put on a visual display of contortions rivaling the athletic moves of Michael Jordan.

The article also noted that the coaches receive high salaries and thus are expected to produce wins on the court, which in turn produces more stress. Though they average $100,000 for actual coaching duties, the highly visible sports figures can raise their incomes and add to their stress with TV and radio shows, camps, endorsements, and other benefits. Valvano has a total income estimated between $500,000 to $1 million annually. Smith, who shuns the commercial limelight and turns down commercial endorsements, manages to earn an estimated $300,000 per annum.

Even with the high compensation, coaches find little time to relax and spend their money. Coaching is a full-time job that continues year-round and the pressure to succeed is enormous.

＊   ●   ●   ●

A few days later, on December 1, the *Durham Morning Herald* devoted five of its six top sports stories to Tar Heel-related matters. Only one could be considered positive PR by the North Carolina contingent.

Besides two lead stories dealing with the Crum resignation, one staff and wire report about the dropping of murder charges against Derrick Fenner (a former star tailback on the UNC football team), and an Associated Press story on the Heels rolling into the top position in the first AP regular-season college basketball poll, there was another AP wire story on the sentencing of Carolina's J.R. Reid and Steve Bucknall. The two players had appeared in the Wake County District Courthouse the day before.

Reid was placed in a deferred prosecution program by Wake County District Court Judge Stafford Brown, according to attorney Roger Smith. The 6–9 sophomore was ordered to perform 100 hours of community service under a project called Attitude Improvement Dialogue Program. He would also have to report to an Orange County probation officer once a month. His case was postponed until August 30, 1988, when the court would review his community service record and drop the misdemeanor assault charges if the work was performed satisfactorily.

Bucknall didn't get off as easily. The junior hoopster received a 30-day suspended sentence after pleading no contest to a misdemeanor charge. Bucknall had to pay a $25 fine in addition to $40 in court costs.

Apparently another Tar Heel had been involved in the altercation on that night in October. Assistant Wake County District Attorney Lori Fuller said in court on Monday that UNC freshman guard King Rice began arguing with the complainant, State student Paul James Doherty, accusing him of making derogatory statements toward the group, which included Reid and Bucknall. It was the second time in less than three months that Rice had been involved in a barroom scuffle.

Reid and Bucknall then mixed it up with Doherty. Doherty consequently filed charges, saying in a police report that Bucknall hit him "with a clenched fist to the right eye" after Reid spat in his face. Reid and Bucknall had paid for Doherty's medical expenses prior to their court appearances.

When the final judgment was handed down that day, "the incident" was over and done with as far as those involved were concerned. No further punishment would be doled out by Smith or the university. The matter would, with luck, be quickly forgotten. It would most likely remain that way until the Duke fans brought it up when the Heels visited Cameron Indoor Stadium in Durham for the regular season finale. The "Zoo," as NBC commentator Al McGuire fondly refers to the inhabitants of Duke's famed gymnasium, would never pass up a chance to needle young men in UNC uniforms.

UNC 86, STETSON 74

Carolina rolled into the regular season and its home opener ranked number one by the Associated Press. Coach Smith said his team was overrated as far as the rankings were concerned. Andrew Woodward, a 6–8 senior on the Stetson team, said he felt North Carolina and its strongman, J.R. Reid, were overrated. Both were right.

Though the Tar Heels beat the Hatters, 86–74, in front of a less-than-sellout crowd of 18,732 blue-and-white-clad fans, the home team didn't come close to playing like the nation's best. And Reid, whom former Maryland coach and then broadcaster "Lefty" Driesell called the best big man to ever play in the ACC, turned in a mediocre 12-point, six-rebound performance.

The win, UNC's fourth in as many games, did have a few good moments. There were some nice scoring spurts by Scott Williams, and Jeff Lebo contributed a season-high five steals. Neither was happy with the team's play. "I'd rather win by one and play great than win by 40 and not play well," Lebo said. "There's no question we're not satisfied with how we played."

Part of the reason for the Tar Heels' displeasure was embarrassment. They had amassed a 29-point lead with just over seven minutes to play when Smith decided to give his starters the rest of the night off, substituting deep into his bench. After Stetson scored the next 17 points, Smith called a rare timeout to re-insert his starters. "This is a good learning experience for them [the team]," Smith said. "I was tempted not to replace them [the substitutes] with three minutes to play as I thought it might have been a good lesson, but I think they learned their lesson anyway."

Williams shared what the team learned. "This just shows that each team we play is going to try their best to push us," he said. "No one will quit against us — Stetson certainly didn't. We got a big lead, and they caught us napping." The stat sheet woke up the young team.

Stetson, playing with front-line players averaging just 6–7, out-re-bounded the much taller North Carolina team 37–28, including a 20–8 margin in offensive rebounding. It was the one area Smith thought his team had mastered in the young season. "That was the one thing that I bragged about before the game," Smith said. "I said that's the one thing that I thought we were doing a good job on this year. We were consistently getting good position inside on the offensive board and boxing out real well on the defensive board."

Still, learning experiences aside, the Tar Heels preserved their top ranking. Even though they would lose it following the next game, the younger members of the squad were able to experience firsthand the intensity that every team brought to the task of upsetting the nationally respected UNC team.

"Coming into the game we felt we had a good chance to give them a very good game," said Stetson forward Martin Jenkins. "We had everything to win and nothing to lose. If we upset them it would be a great thing for us. Deep down we just wanted to come in and play hard and see how we fared against a team like UNC." Jenkins' thoughts mirrored those of most players facing the strength and tradition of North Carolina. Most non-Top 20 teams are loose against the Tar Heels. The pressure to win is off of the underdogs and placed squarely on the shoulders of the "favored" team.

• • •

While the first team played well enough to gain an adequate margin, the Carolina substitutes had let down their coach. The coach took out his frustration on a member of the media a few minutes later, prior to his postgame remarks, in an uncharacteristic confrontation.

Like the careful politician most successful people are forced to become, Smith is usually in full command whenever he appears in public. He knows what he says will be read or heard by thousands of curious fans and he cares deeply about how the public perceives the program. Smith's knowledge of the people who write or broadcast news of him and his program is astonishing, and he uses his abilities to influence media coverage. His quick eye catches and notes who is and who isn't present for his comments. Dean Smith rarely forgets a face and often prefaces his answers to questions with the first names of the questioner.

The initial reaction from most sports journalists is flattery at being recognized, even when the recognition is made to point out an error or a difference of opinion from the head coach. Once a writer takes on Dean Smith or his program, the coach is unlikely to forget. Upon winning the NCAA championship in 1982, Smith's first words were to remind a certain writer that he had just been proven wrong. Years earlier, Frank Barrows, then a staff sportswriter for *The Charlotte Observer*, wrote a revealing feature story on Smith. In his profile, Barrows theorized that Smith's strengths were also his weaknesses. He wrote that while the coach molded teams that were disciplined and talented, Smith left little room for flamboyant and instinctive basketball that is necessary to win a championship. And while Smith's list of accomplishments were laudatory, the prominent coach had never won the NCAA title. Barrows reached the conclusion that Smith would never change his style and thus would never win it all. The young writer's prose stayed on Smith's mind until years later. In a postgame interview with CBS sports commentator Brent Musburger minutes after his team beat the Georgetown Hoyas in New Orleans, Smith took the time to answer Barrows' theory with a verbal *touché*.

Smith obviously prepares his postgame comments in the hopes that he will one day be able to answer his critics. On other occasions, the coach forgets to keep himself in check and lashes out without thinking. His opening remarks after the Stetson game were a good example.

"You got a press pass, huh?" Smith interrupted his postgame comments as he noticed a young black reporter sitting three rows back. "Huh?"

"Yes sir, I did," said the journalist.

"For which paper," Smith demanded.

"*The Black Ink*," the young man replied, naming a campus student newspaper.

"I see," Smith acknowledged before trying to pick up where he left off.

Dean Smith is not a racist. In fact, the coach was a strong civil rights activist in Chapel Hill in the '60s. The coach demonstrated and "sat-in" at a local restaurant that refused to seat blacks during those volatile times. Smith also was the first North Carolina coach to recruit a black player. No, Smith was not intimidating the reporter because he was black. The coach was still upset with the young man for his questions in front of the student body two months earlier. The reporter, Charles Mills, had written a letter to *The Daily Tar Heel*, another student newspaper, which was published.

"I wrote the letter where I criticized Coach Smith and the program," Mills said later, remembering the chain of events. "And it caused a lot of heat, although I don't know whether or not he knew that I wrote it. Then back in late October of this year, Coach Smith had this little get-together in Lenoir Hall where students could come and ask him questions. Well, I went and sort of grilled him. I brought up a lot of stats, and we sort of argued back and forth for about five minutes.

"I pulled up stats like from 1978 to 1982 Carolina won 81 percent of its ACC regular season games and 81 percent of their ACC tournament games. But since that period, they've won 84 percent of their ACC regular season games, but only 54 percent of the ACC tournament games. So, I asked what was going on?

"He claimed injuries and the usual lame excuses. But then I said, 'Supposedly you're the best recruiter in the country — you have talent sitting on the bench,' but he responded by trying to give me examples of players in the past who really weren't as good as people claimed they were. We went back and forth for a while.

"Whenever I had him on the ropes a little bit, he'd crack a joke, and everybody in the room would laugh, and there was nothing I could do after that."

Dean Smith may never forget a face or a writer's copy, but he is also intelligent enough to listen even to those who voice displeasure. In response to critics such as Charles Mills, Smith and his team would later redouble their effort and place even greater emphasis on winning the ACC tournament in March.

The additional exertion would prove fruitless.

VANDERBILT 78, UNC 76

The game would have ranked as the second-greatest all-time North Carolina comeback.

A solid Vanderbilt team enjoyed a six-point lead over the top-ranked Tar Heels with just eight seconds showing on the Memorial Gymnasium clock in Nashville, Tennessee. Though the game had been close most of the early December afternoon, it finally looked like smooth sailing for the Commodores. However, Smith's team wasn't ready to strike its canvas. Jeff Lebo, smothered by two Vanderbilt players, hit his sixth three-pointer and the Tar Heels called for a timeout with three seconds remaining. Still down by three points, Dean Smith went to work.

During the timeout, the team assembled on the bench to hear the strategy. Smith always aims his comments at providing positive scenarios. He makes no contingency plans for missed shots. All strategies envision properly executed plays only. In this instance, the Tar Heels needed a steal, a turnover, or a failure by the Vandy team to make an inbounds pass in the allotted time. As soon as one of the three possibilities came true, another timeout would be called to set up a three-point shot to tie. The sequence went according to plan.

Vanderbilt's Charles Mayes inbounded a pass for teammate Barry Booker. It never got to him. Steve Bucknall, who came off the bench to play 27 minutes in the game, deflected and chased down the ball as his teammates called time. The fans and the television audience thought the game was over. The clock showed no time remaining. Then the officials stepped in, ruling there were two seconds on the clock. The brief stay was more than enough time for another scheme from the master.

Clearly relishing the challenge, Smith dismissed the elaborate and called for the obvious — a three-point play with Lebo as the designated shooter. Again the scenario was acted out according to direction. Kevin Madden threw the ball in to Lebo on the far side of the court. As the junior launched his shot, Booker slashed the point guard with a second still remaining, causing the ball to miss the basket. The game was in the hands of the officials. The closest referee saw a criminal act, but not an intentional one. He gave Lebo a two-shot opportunity.

"It was a good foul on their part if you're going after the ball," Lebo offered. "I thought he went for me and knocked me back, instead of going for the ball." Had the referee seen the play as Lebo and thousands of Carolina fans did, North Carolina might have won. Instead, Lebo connected on only one of the two free throws and the Tar Heels never regained possession of the ball.

"It was a fun comeback," Smith said of the almost miraculous turn-around. "Coming down the stretch like that will help us in the future." It would. The young team learned that they could stay in a game and fight back, even with only seconds remaining. The freshmen also got a chance to see Smith in last-minute action. They could now better appreciate their coach's remarkable skills. So could Vanderbilt head coach C.M. Newton. "Coach Smith milked the clock down the stretch like a real genius. Newton was right — but it wasn't enough. The Tar Heels suffered their first loss of the young season.

• • •

The most-remembered and often most-hyperbolized game in the Tar Heel history books is the clash between Duke and Carolina on March 2, 1974. UNC was fifth-ranked nationally and favored to beat a mediocre Blue Devil team that year. But Duke played an exceptional game and was on the verge of upsetting the home team. While many North Carolina fans headed for the door thinking tragedy, Smith's team staged its greatest comeback of all time.

Down by eight points with only 17 seconds showing on the clock, the Tar Heels went on an offensive and defensive run that still defies reason. Bobby Jones sank two free throws. Walter Davis stole an inbounds pass that John Kuester converted into two points. After another Duke turnover, Jones converted a teammate's missed shot. The Tar Heels had cut the lead to two points with six seconds remaining on the Carmichael Auditorium clock.

In the huddle during a timeout, Smith called for his players to intentionally foul. A Tar Heel complied. In turn, the offended Blue Devil stepped to the line and missed the front end of a one-and-one. UNC then called another timeout after capturing the rebound. Mitch Kupchak substituted into the game to make the pass that set up "the shot." Davis took the long inbounds pass, took three dribbles, and fired a bullet milliseconds before the horn sounded. His shot kissed the glass and exploded through the twine.

Overtime.

The ending is foggy to all but die-hard North Carolina fans. Duke jumped ahead briefly, only to lose down the stretch, 96–92. It was a great college basketball game. It demonstrated the kind of tradition that builds a great program.

• • •

The air was let out of Carolina's premature and highly inflated national rankings on December 8. The Associated Press gave the team what Coach

Smith insisted they deserved — a lower ranking. Smith's constant insisting, coupled with the loss to Vanderbilt, achieved the desired result. Carolina had fallen to the fifth spot.

The new ranking still wasn't where the coach or most knowledgeable basketball followers would have placed UNC, but it was a start at realistically wiping the bright red "S" off of the front of the North Carolina jerseys. The Heels had played like supermen in beating Syracuse in the season opener, but the team was not yet playing like the best in the country. They were definitely a power to be reckoned with, but most of the energy was potential. The refinement would take place faster without the added burden of maintaining a number-one status. The team could use the time to work toward deserving a high national ranking.

The new owners of the hot seat were Eddie Sutton and the Kentucky Wildcats. Kentucky, another blue chip college basketball program, was quick to use the same strategy Smith had. "Naturally, it's a great honor for our team and basketball program to be ranked number one," Sutton said following the announcement. "But I've said many times I'm not sure we're the best team in the country."

The official collegiate coaching line is to downplay any acknowledgment during the season, but then to overload the media guides and press releases with how many times, and where, the team was ranked the preceding year. False expectations are bad for the fans, but hype brings in the fans' dollars and, more importantly, the recruits.

High rankings are also vital to programs that haven't quite made it into the Fortune 500 of the collegiate basketball world. The rankings bring exposure and the exposure brings in talent, TV money, and a chance for the big prize at the end of the season — the NCAAs.

Vanderbilt, the team that knocked off the number one-ranked team and upped its record to 3-0, was not even voted into the AP Top 20 for its efforts. The polls are fickle. The night after the new poll was released, the Commodores took on the sixth-ranked and defending national champion Hoosiers of Indiana and came within a basket of beating them in Bloomington. Later in the season, the Commodores would perform well in the NCAA tournament, losing to eventual champion Kansas in the Midwest regional semifinal.

•   •   •

Meanwhile, former UNC basketball players in the professional ranks were dropping like flies.

Earlier in the NBA season, Kenny Smith, All-America guard and possible contender for NBA Rookie of the Year honors, had broken his wrist in a game. The Sacramento King was expected to be out for six to eight weeks. His former teammate, Joe Wolf, another first-round draft choice and member of the Los Angeles Clippers, underwent arthroscopic surgery on his right knee. Wolf had suffered an injury in a collision with Caldwell Jones of the Portland Trail Blazers on November 27. He would be out of action for three weeks.

A few hundred miles away, the Phoenix Suns placed Walter Davis on the injured list. Davis, suffering from disk problems in his lower back, was hospitalized after sitting out of the team's last four games. He would later announce that he would retire at the end of the season. He didn't.

Dudley Bradley's disappearance from the professional ranks may have been more permanent. The Milwaukee Bucks waived Bradley as the former Tar Heel had only appeared in two games during the season. Bradley, 30, had played for Indiana, Phoenix, Chicago, and Washington in his professional career. He had come off the Bucks' injured list on November 30 after recovering from a thigh bruise, but had failed to contribute consistently.

UNC 90, SMU 74

It was another healthy experience for the inexperienced.

North Carolina was called upon to show its mettle. The challenge was issued by Southern Methodist, a team that had upset then seventh-ranked Florida a week earlier. The game was played in the Smith Center exactly one week after the Tar Heels lost a game and their number-one ranking at Vanderbilt.

The visiting Mustangs galloped out to an early 23–8 lead after hitting their first nine attempts. It looked as if the Tar Heels would continue their descent in the national polls. The fifth-ranked Heels missed nearly everything in the first ten minutes of play, while the Mustangs scored from both the inside and outside.

Smith and company should have been nervous. They weren't.

"I wasn't real concerned," Smith said, "but their ninth shot was a layup and I was about to call a timeout then, and then we came back and started looking like we knew what we were doing."

In the next four and a half minutes, the team did turn it around by scoring 16 unanswered points. After Scott Williams threw up an airball from the free throw line with 9:18 left in the first half, the Heels corralled the hot Ponies on defense while balancing their offensive attack. J.R. Reid, Kevin Madden, and Pete Chilcutt drove to the hoop, while Jeff Lebo added a jumpshot and a couple of assists. North Carolina led 24–23 with 5:44 left in the half as the crowd sighed with relief. It was short-lived.

The Mustangs surged as Smith's substitutes made errors. Freshman

Rick Fox made a mistake and on the next dead ball he was pulled from the game. His punishment for poor play was the lack of acknowledgment from his coach and the loss of valuable playing time. Normally, in the course of a game, the coach greets a UNC player returning to the bench with a pat on the behind or a hand on the shoulder. When the coach is upset with the play of one of his protégés, he doesn't look at them or make any physical contact with them at the bench. The offending player knows he has been reprimanded without having to be embarrassed in front of the fans.

It is also a team policy that fellow players all rise and applaud any teammate leaving the floor. His teammates then move one spot down the bench to make room for the player next to the coaches. The farther one gets away from the coaches, the less opportunity for playing time. Fox, who would not have been scheduled for extensive play anyway, would only see three minutes of playing time against SMU. He eventually found his seat next to the walk-ons.

The visiting team wasn't concerned with who was on or off the UNC bench, though. The Mustangs wanted to knock off the home team. One way they thought they could do so was to employ a modified defense, a "diamond and one" with defensive standout Kato Armstrong soloing against Lebo. The defense worked — to an extent. Lebo was limited to three of five shooting while SMU stacked the middle, keeping the North Carolina inside game from developing.

"What made me happy about [using] the diamond and one was I didn't have to watch J.R. Reid spin on my post men and dunk," SMU coach Dave Bliss told reporters after the game. He couldn't have been too happy, though, with the way Madden and Ranzino Smith used the open space created in the key for short jumpers. Madden and Smith combined for 24 points in the second half. That and 16 more points from Reid broke the spirited Ponies and helped the Tar Heels rally to win handily, 90–74.

"Their strength inside is phenomenal," Bliss said. "It seemed to me to be the telling blow because we weren't able to get anything inside, and if you are primarily a perimeter-oriented team and you have to rely on that with all of the deep changes in defense they play, then pretty soon you're going to have a spell where tired legs aren't making the same shots."

● ● ●

Present at the game was senior walk-on Joe Jenkins' mother. Her health failing as she battled cancer, she nonetheless made the effort to see her son with his teammates in the battle against seventh-ranked SMU.

Dean Smith, aware of her journey to see the game, provided Mrs. Jenkins with a special treat. When starting power forward J.R. Reid raised his fist with the team "tired" signal early in the first half, the coach bypassed his normal rotation and called out Jenkins' number. Smith leaned over to assistant coach Roy Williams and said, "That will make her happy." His timing turned out to be critical, as Mrs. Jenkins would never see her son play again in person. She passed away on January 1, 1988.

•   •   •

The January issue of *Playboy* magazine hit the newsstands with a noticeable exception. The centerfold was intact, but another heavenly body was missing. In its annual in-house *Playboy* All-America basketball team layout, one player was absent. North Carolina's J.R. Reid, a consensus preseason All-American in everybody's book, was listed in a secondary group entitled "Rest of the Best." Leaving out a player who was the ACC's Rookie of the Year and named to the U.S. Basketball Writers' district All-America team belittled the players who made the team.

"It's ridiculous that they didn't honor J.R.," said teammate Jeff Lebo. "He should have been on the team like that [Lebo snapped his fingers]." Thousands of basketball aficionados would have agreed.

There was a reason for the slight, though it had nothing to do with basketball ability. The year before, Kenny Smith was chosen to receive the honor, which includes an all-expenses paid weekend trip together with the other honorees. He turned it down, citing a disagreement with the overall philosophy of the magazine and its stance on drugs. Many felt Linnea Smith, the psychiatrist wife of Dean Smith, had influenced the senior's decision due to her involvement with an anti-pornography movement. Interestingly enough, Kenny Smith wore a gold chain with a *Playboy* bunny logo attached in his underclass days in Chapel Hill. "Those were my younger days," he explained, saying that he didn't have any problems with the photographs contained in the magazine.

"I'm sure Kenny had his reason for turning it down," Lebo continued. "I'd probably accept [the honor] and go on the trip. It's another experience and an honor to make it."

Playboy changed strategy in late April 1988. "They've already called J.R. for this year [1988–89 preseason]," Dean Smith said. "I called J.R. and asked him if he would like to go on the trip and he said 'No, I don't believe in *Playboy* and my mother wouldn't like it' — so he turned it down this year. I didn't even turn my wife loose on J.R.

"I assume they won't discontinue asking. But I agree with my wife, totally. First of all, what's a preseason All-American? I was in it in 1976 and my wife was there too [on the all-expenses-paid trip]— we didn't even think about it. The NCAA ought to do away with it."

There *was* a centerfold of sorts, however, in the annual lampoon of *The Daily Tar Heel*, the Carolina student newspaper, entitled "The Smelly Tar Hole," put out by the N.C. State students a few months later. With a banner headline of "Non-Playboy All-America Kenny Smith" spread over two pages, there was a large photograph of a nude black male sprawled over a couch in typical cheesecake fashion. Kenny Smith's face was superimposed onto that of the model. A blue-and-white-striped basketball and other various UNC items also adorned the picture.

A "Ballboy Data Sheet" listed his dimensions and all of his favorite things.

• • •

Meanwhile, the trade of Ralph Sampson, a former two-time national player of the year while attending the University of Virginia, from the Houston Rockets to the Golden State Warriors on December 16 would be debated throughout the country's sports world for days.

The announcement caught Sampson, and basketball fans, by surprise. When the shock waves subsided, Dean Smith went on record to the *Durham Morning Herald*'s Kip Coons. "I've been a Sampson fan," Smith said, surprising Coons and many who read the column. Sampson had turned down the chance to attend North Carolina in order to attend UVa and be closer to his home and family in Harrisonburg, Virginia. The tight recruiting battle between Smith and the Cavaliers' Terry Holland refueled the ongoing feud that still exists between the two head coaches today. Apparently, Smith never let his feelings for Holland taint those he felt for Sampson.

"They don't know what I know from playing against him in college," Smith continued. "When he would come in and play in Chapel Hill, he was intense. In our games he would rise to the occasion."

There is little doubt Sampson rose to the occasion many times in his collegiate career, especially when the going wasn't so hard. Despite his personal laurels, however, Virginia teams he played on in Charlottesville never won an ACC tournament or made it to the NCAA finals. Sampson's critics frequently complain that he doesn't have the day-to-day intestinal fortitude when the game is on the line. But though he played in the shadow of Akeem Olajuwon the past three years, Sampson wasn't expecting to be traded.

The trade to the last-place Warriors team may have been just what Golden State needed, according to Smith. "They [the Warriors] won't be [in last place] for long, even this year." That remained to be seen.

While Sampson traveled west to join his new team, Tulane University's head coach and athletic director, Mack Brown, journeyed east to be named

Dick Crum's successor as head football coach at North Carolina.

Brown was already being favorably compared to Dean Smith, primarily due to his charismatic appeal to the regional media. It would take time before the UNC fans could see what kind of results the young coach could yield on the playing field, but there was little doubt his outgoing personality was in high contrast to his predecessor's.

UNC 98, THE CITADEL 74

North Carolina said goodbye to the Charlotte Coliseum and quite possibly to the Bulldogs of The Citadel on the night of December 17. It may have been a relief to the Carolina fans. After 85 games over 27 years, UNC would no longer be scheduling games in the 11,666-seat home-away-from-home. The next time UNC decided to play in Charlotte, it would do so in a new 23,000-seat coliseum scheduled to open in the fall of 1988.

In the recent past, games scheduled in Charlotte were done so as a gift to the many Tar Heel supporters who live in and around the largest North Carolina city. The games were little more than tune-ups for the Heels — generally against weak opponents — in order to give the school's local financial backers a chance to see the team. The team would showcase its skills and the faithful would roar their approval. But the constant one-sidedness of the games took its toll on the Charlotte audience. This last game was played before a less-than-capacity crowd on a night when the only competition for the game came from Bill Cosby's television show on NBC. No wonder. The last time the two teams met had been during the 1985-86 season when the Tar Heels more than doubled the Bulldog's score, 104-51. The 1987 game was closer, but in score only. And it wasn't as if the Bulldogs didn't give it the old college try, either. But then, The Citadel wasn't out to compete for national honors.

Though it seemed on paper that the Bulldogs didn't have a prayer of winning the game, the feisty scrappers twice managed to lead the Tar Heels by seven points. Considering the Bulldog front line averaged a fraction over 6–5 and North Carolina was about five inches taller, The Citadel must have wanted a victory a little more. Or at least for 15 minutes of the 40-minute contest.

With 5:53 left to play in the first half, Pete Chilcutt went to the line and made both of his shots to give the struggling Tar Heels a six-point lead, the team's largest lead up to that point. By the end of the half, the lead had climbed to 16.

The double-digit margin would remain for the rest of the game, with the lead reaching 28 at one time. Final score: Carolina 98, The Citadel 74.

The only surprise was how long the Bulldogs managed to stay in the game. UNC's Kevin Madden said the Tar Heels didn't expect the game they got from the weaker opponent. "We just wanted to come in and play our usual way," he said. "They played real well the first half, and of course we tried to get out to a good start, but we've been getting out to a slow start every game we've played this year."

The first half of the Citadel game may represent the differences between the North Carolina approach and that of most mainstream college basketball programs. Smith coaches his team to play against itself and contain emotion. A day on the floor for a UNC team is a study in concentration toward execution. Players are self-motivated, seeking only to please their teammates, themselves, and more importantly, their coach. *If I play well*, the player thinks, *and concentrate on unselfish play and strong defense, I'll play more and my worth goes up in the eyes of my peers and my coach.*

The UNC players know when they are playing a weaker opponent. And their motivation and concentration level is usually lower until challenged. Consequently, most opponents are not as confident going up against the likes of a North Carolina. But their motivation is usually sky high. *If I play well,* the underdog opponent thinks, *I'll be noticed and gain respect. If I don't, nothing is lost — no one expects me to play well against the established and proven winners, anyway.* Woody Durham, the "voice" of the Tar Heel Sports Network, remembers a game in which UNC's opponents were especially in awe of the Tar Heels. "One time, Rochester [the University of Rochester] lost to Carolina, 101–43, in 1977," Durham recalled. "After the game the Rochester players came down to the locker room to get some of the Tar Heel players' autographs. They especially wanted Phil Ford's." Few college players want to reveal that they are fans of their opponents.

Usually, the weaker team is looser and better focused at the start of its "day in the limelight." North Carolina, however, has the calm understanding that more than likely it will overcome any early adversity to put together a victory in the end.

The collective experience of the North Carolina program and its tried-and-true coach add up to quite an edge, especially when playing the not-so-established programs. The emotionally driven opponent can sometimes run out of steam over the long haul of a 40-minute game.

Still, UNC will not likely ever run out of Citadel-type opponents. Just having North Carolina on the schedule is priceless to the schools that aren't basketball powerhouses. "It's always impressive to play North Carolina," said The Citadel's head coach, Randy Nesbit, following the game. "It's important for us when we recruit players. They always ask us, 'How good is your schedule? Who do you play?' And when they find out they say,

'Yeah, I want to play North Carolina. I want to go to a school that plays a good schedule.'

"It also has a good financial reward, though it's not our biggest of the year. The Citadel has a good name and we're able to schedule virtually anybody we want by virtue of our academic reputation." It may, in truth, have been by virtue of its lack of basketball prowess. The Citadel, after this loss to the Tar Heels, was 28–101 against ACC teams. If the 23 wins against in-state foe Clemson, another school with a generally weak basketball program, were subtracted, the Bulldogs would have been 5–78 against the conference.

What is a "dream" game to The Citadel is an equally important "learning experience" scrimmage for North Carolina. Still, it's not always fun for the fans, who invariably prefer a closer, more exciting contest.

Dean Smith may have made an unintentional slip during his postgame press conference that evening. In speaking of the repetition of his comments concerning his team's play that evening and in previous games during the season, Smith said, "I thought we did some good things — this is getting to be monotonous — and we made some mistakes that we can't afford to make against a stronger team and expect to win."

What may have been monotonous was scheduling a team that was 0–16 against the Tar Heels.

•   •   •

A Tournament of Champions had been scheduled in Charlotte and set for the first week in December 1988. The tourney, the first of an annual event to be sponsored by Raycom Teleproductions, would feature North Carolina, Temple, Arizona, and Missouri — four of the best teams in the nation in 1987–88. According to Doug Verb, director of information and promotions for Raycom, and in keeping with its national stature, UNC would receive roughly 30 percent more to play in the tournament than any of the other schools participating — just one of the many advantages of having the best program in the country.

UNC 85, ILLINOIS 74

Sophomore J.R. Reid had missed his team's first appearance on national television when the Tar Heels surprised Syracuse in his absence. In Champaign, against Illinois almost a month later, he let the national viewing audience know he was still alive and kicking.

After a 30-point, 13-rebound performance, Reid acknowledged he had played well. "It was my best game, both offensively and defensively," Reid said. "A win away from home. Anytime you can do that, it's a blessing." According to Reid, it was only the Lord's intervention that made the difference. And considering the way the Tar Heels played in the opening minutes, maybe He did step in and lend a hand.

In the first nine minutes, the Tar Heels fell behind 5-16. During one span of seven minutes, UNC recorded only one foul shot's worth of offense. Credit the Illinois pressure defense. "We just didn't seem comfortable playing against it," Coach Smith said after the game. "I yelled at them at halftime and I thought we did better in the second half. I don't think anyone can press against us if we do what we're told." The team listened, and did what they were told.

In the second half, North Carolina outshot Illinois 71 percent to 40 percent, hitting 17 of 24 field goal attempts. But it was the overall UNC team defense that paved the way for the win. The Fighting Illini were held to 44 percent shooting, 40 percent in the second half. "We just could not contain them," Illinois head coach Lou Henson said of the second half. "They didn't have any trouble containing us."

Carolina's inside-outside game made the difference offensively. Jeff Lebo and Ranzino Smith converted five of six three-point attempts to keep the Illinois defense spread thin. The Fighting Illini could only muster a two-of-four afternoon from outside. "It was the key to the game, in my opinion," Henson said. "We tried to cover Reid with our best defensive post player, and even gave help, and he still got 30 points. They do a great job of getting him the ball where he can do something with it. And they have excellent outside shooters."

Still, Coach Smith didn't expect the win. "That was really a surprise to me," Smith said. "I didn't think we could compete with Illinois here." The accent was on "here." Smith, who relishes the role of underdog, though he seldom gets it, must find ways of handicapping his oft-favored team. One consistent way is to insist that the other team should be favored any time his team plays on the road. That way he can give his team proper motivation and protect them should they falter. There is no question a home crowd is an advantage. But it can also inspire the visiting team to play to its potential. When a North Carolina team plays to its potential, it is hard to beat. In 1987-88, Smith got extra mileage out of his youthful team by stressing its handicaps of youth and inexperience.

Coach Smith's job does not end with the satisfaction of the win on the road. Always the gentleman in public, and always preparing his team should it meet the same team during the NCAAs, Coach Smith graciously comments on the opponent's future success. After stating his surprise at winning the game at Illinois, Smith said, "I'd hate to have to play them again in

March." Should North Carolina and Illinois meet in the 1988 NCAAs, Smith could easily recall the remark and convince his team that not only were the Tar Heels lucky in December, but Illinois could easily reverse the outcome.

Call it smart gamesmanship.

Coach Henson didn't miss a beat, either. When he was informed that Coach Smith had said he would hate to play Illinois in March, Henson was ready with a reply. "We will turn down a bid to the NCAA tournament if we're assigned to North Carolina's region," he said, and smiled.

Call it returning in kind.

UNC 105, NANTES 79
UNC 87, GREAT BRITAIN 79

Why wait months for a crack at the NCAA championship when world honors were at stake? In a two-day holiday tournament at London's Crystal Palace Sports Center the week before Christmas, UNC conquered professional teams from France and Britain on successive nights to win the World Invitational Club Basketball Tournament.

On Monday night, the Tar Heels easily dismantled Nantes, the French team, 105–79. Getting the game started wasn't as easy. As late as two hours before tip-off, North Carolina didn't know who it was going to play. And when the Tar Heels took the floor for the scheduled 8:00 p.m. contest, their opponents were still en route to the sports center. The same bus that carried the North Carolina contingent to the game had been dispatched to bring the Nantes team. No problem. The smallish crowd of 2,000 on hand for the basketball game could walk next door for interim entertainment. Inside the Crystal Palace hundreds of young English boys and girls practiced aquatic moves in oversized pools. Just outside, another group of youngsters kicked soccer balls. The atmosphere was definitely amateur. Compared to the pressure play of the NCAA, competing in the United Kingdom was a quiet afternoon on the links of a Scottish golf course.

The championship game against the British Select team on Tuesday wasn't a gimme, but it was a game that wouldn't have been close if players hadn't been experiencing the rigors of international travel. "There's a five-hour time difference," Steve Bucknall said. "We stayed up at night and slept in the days." Combined with the fatigue factor was the unfamiliarity of the international rules that governed the games. UNC's starters began the game sluggishly, causing the season's first appearance of the famous Blue Team. The gang substitution, a staple over the years at North Carolina, was a shock to the British crowd. The announcer interrupted the quiet to proclaim "Coach Smith is committing to the uncommon occurrence of inserting five new players."

Smith's "uncommon" strategy worked. Trailing when they entered the game, the freshman and sophomore replacements captured a lead before the starters returned. The game seesawed until the last eight minutes of the game when the Tar Heels gained a seven-point advantage. Britain's Select team fought hard but couldn't catch North Carolina. With just over a minute left and a six-point lead, Smith called for the Four Corners delay, another longtime Tar Heel staple. (The Four Corners offense spreads the defense by utilizing the entire half court in a time-consuming display of passing and dribbling.) The game ended after UNC upped the scoring margin to 87–79.

Smith wasn't happy with his team's play. "I think we digressed," he said. "We played with intensity last night, but not tonight. Maybe jet lag hit us a day late." The players weren't concerned. The trip hadn't been made for the expressed reason of playing basketball. The flight to London was actually a sanctioned payment to one of the UNC players.

Steve Bucknall, the team's best defender, had persuaded his teammates to vote the trip into their schedule for selfish reasons. "It was a decision between Jeff Lebo, Ranzino and myself to go over there," said Bucknall, "but the whole team was behind me getting to see my family. It was good for them [his family] to see me play as they only get to see me in the summer." The junior had grown up in England, originally coming to the United States to play two years at the Governor Dummer Academy in Massachusetts, where he led his team to the New England Class C Championship. If possible, and the records support the notion, most out-of-state players find a game scheduled close to home sometime in the four years they are with the program. In 1988–89, Lebo, Williams, and Reid would all play a game close to their hometowns in Pennsylvania, California, and Virginia. And considering the international scope of UNC recruiting, the players need to keep passports and immunizations current.

The mini-vacation to England was another "learning experience" for the traveling party, a group used to jetting about in search of cultural and roundball knowledge. Dr. Gerald Unks, a professor at UNC, had organized the trip, which included sidetrips to various local sites, and gave the student athletes information about what to do once they got there. It wasn't the first time a North Carolina team had made the journey to London. In 1979, the Tar Heels had traveled to play in the London International Tournament. It was Carolina's play in that tournament, and later NCAA play, that made an impression on Bucknall. When asked a few years later to join the team, the young Englishman signed on the dotted line.

The Englishman's experience soured quickly, however. Bucknall isn't sure he made the right decision in accepting a scholarship to North Carolina.

"I regret it all the time, really," he said after the season. "I don't regret coming to school here, but I regretted the basketball [aspect] as I didn't get to play — and I really wanted to play. I'm happy socially and academically with the school, but if you'd asked me last year, I would have really regretted coming here." After sticking it out, Bucknall now feels that the years of limited play may turn out to be a positive experience if he makes it in the pros.

"If you're gonna be a good pro," he said, getting back to the company line, "UNC is the place to go. If you can make it here, you can make it anywhere."

• • •

Back in North Carolina, an article by *Durham Morning Herald* staff writer Tim Crothers revealed an insight into Dean Smith that doesn't often make the sports pages. When it comes to the delicate topic of recruiting, North Carolina's CEO is as tight-lipped as a Mafia boss subpoenaed before a grand jury. The master coach refuses to even address the subject, stating his standard line, "We don't discuss recruiting at Carolina." Period. End of discussion.

The inside information in this case came from a highly recruited former prospect who chose not to attend UNC. Billy Owens, who had announced his decision on November 19 to attend Syracuse, had been in Raleigh to participate in the *Raleigh Times* Holiday Tournament with his teammates from Carlisle High School in Pennsylvania. He recalled a question that Coach Smith put to him during his recruitment.

Smith had asked Owens to imagine himself as a member of the Tar Heel basketball team and then asked him if he thought the team could win the national championship. Owens remembered answering the coach with an emphatic "yes." While he may have thought that the team could bring home the title, he still felt that the Tar Heels would have to do so without his services.

"It was hard to turn down Dean Smith," Owens said. "I've always thought he was a great coach, and I've had great respect for him. It was a hard offer to refuse." Owens, a 6-9 blue chipper who was a prospect with most top college programs, seemed to be in line to follow in the footsteps of another current UNC player from Carlisle, Jeff Lebo.

Lebo, a junior on the North Carolina team, had guided his high school team to a state championship in his senior season. Owens had been a part of that same team that collected two more titles in his sophomore and junior seasons. It also didn't hurt Carolina's recruiting chances that the coach of the Carlisle High School team was none other than David Lebo, Jeff's father.

The town of Carlisle has embraced the Tar Heels for years, sending busloads of fans to Chapel Hill on occasion to cheer for its favorite son, Jeff.

But David Lebo hadn't pressed Owens to attend UNC. "I was caught in between because I am close to the Carolina coaching staff," Lebo said to reporters after his team, led by Owens' 32 points, destroyed Ocean View (California) High School, 86–49. "I tried to stay out of it [Owens' recruiting] as much as possible."

Jeff hadn't attempted to take advantage of his inside track, either. In an interview prior to Owens' decision, the coach's son had said that he would "love to see him come to North Carolina. I have just tried to be available to answer his questions and then let him make up his own mind."

But while the Lebos had tried to remain neutral, another voice may have been the deciding factor. Owens' brother Michael, a sophomore tailback on the 1987 Syracuse Orangemen's undefeated football team, had made it clear that he would like for him to attend his school. Still, Billy Owens stated that he'd made his decision on the difference between the two campuses and the style of play each basketball team favored. "I like a fast-paced running style of basketball and the Big East is a more fast-paced game than the ACC," Owens offered as his reason for opting for the team coached by Jim Boheim.

Crothers' article noted that Coach Lebo had pointed out that Syracuse's academic standards may have been less intimidating to Owens, who reportedly needed to raise his SAT scores or else sit out his freshman season as a Proposition 48 casualty (a set of national requirements for eligibility). In a local television interview the same weekend, Owens had said that academics and raising his SAT scores would be no problem. Regardless of what prompted his decision, Owens had decided not to study the game under Dean Smith in Chapel Hill.

In recent years, it has often been thought that "Dean Smith doesn't recruit — he selects." With the decision of Owens and other top national prospects like LaBradford Smith, Alonzo Mourning, Christian Laettner, LaPhonso Ellis, and Jerrod Mustaf to attend other schools, the times may be a-changing.

UNC 115, NEVADA-RENO 91

West Coast recruiting wasn't hurt by Billy Owens decision. The Tar Heels returned from the holiday jaunt to England only to continue their journey westward. And to celebrate its homecoming, North Carolina muzzled the Nevada-Reno Wolf Pack, 115-91, in front of the largest crowd ever to witness a game in the Lawlor Events Center in Reno. The game, which started out somewhat ragged, settled into a smooth Tar Heel domination of the inside. The height advantage that North Carolina possessed proved to be too much for the much smaller Nevada-Reno team.

Scott Williams hoped that his career-high 25-point performance was just a tune-up for the game against UCLA. Pete Chilcutt also hit his career best with 18 points and 10 rebounds in just 20 minutes of playing time. Ranzino Smith knocked in 19 and Kevin Madden scored 15 to help lead the way for the visiting team. J.R. Reid scored only nine points, half of his average, and Jeff Lebo attracted more than his share of Wolf Pack defenders, reflected in an eight-point effort. What made the game memorable for the assembled fans was a New Year's "gift" from the Wolf Pack bench via the officials. Nevada-Reno's Gabriel Parizzia fouled Williams in the act of shooting. Upset with the call, members of the home team growled until a technical foul was called on the Wolf Pack bench. Ranzino Smith went to the free-throw line to shoot the two technicals and missed both. But instead of Williams then shooting his free throws, the officials gave the ball back to Smith, who made a free throw. By this time the crowd and Wolf Pack head coach Len Stevens were protesting the mistake.

The officials conferred and decided to start the whole sequence over. Williams was sent to the line and made one of his two free throws. Smith was then allowed to shoot two technical shots and made them both. The bizarre turn of events was important only to Ranzino Smith. As the result of his disallowed free throws, the senior from Chapel Hill kept his perfect free-throw record intact.

Despite his differences with the officiating, Stevens was so impressed with the North Carolina program and Dean Smith that many of his remarks to the press contained glowing praise for the Tar Heels' play. "All of their players run the court very well," he said, responding to the way that UNC reacted to his team's full-court pressure. "I love the way that they play the inside-outside game. If those big guys don't have something inside, they pitch it back out. They have great patience on offense. Offensive patience is not easy to teach. You don't see them taking many shots that they don't want, which gets right down to coaching."

At age 45, Stevens is both a coaching veteran and a sharp diplomat. It was his first year coaching the Wolf Pack; he had previously been head coach at Washington State. Smart coaches know that playing a top-ranked team and then praising its head coach can do nothing but good, win or lose. Not only does their program get to see what its weaknesses are, but the added exposure and revenue doesn't hurt the program's chances to improve its position. Losing to UNC is much more beneficial than beating Small-town University any day.

"Everything he does is orchestrated," Stevens continued, speaking about the way Smith utilizes his bench. "Their substitution plan is excellent.

It looks like they always have fresh players on the court. It was great to play them on our home court. We got a good lesson."

UNC 80, UCLA 73

Two of college basketball's traditional heavyweights took the floor at the Pauley Pavilion in Los Angeles on January 2. And this time, only the fourth meeting between the two most prestigious programs in the country, the visiting Tar Heels emerged with the decision.

"We're happy to have won this game on the road," said Dean Smith after the game. "We didn't take them lightly. UCLA lost two starters and so did we. We're a capable team, but not a great team. We can beat anybody, but anybody can beat us on a given night. To come out with a win on the road — we're very pleased."

Smith has been known to downplay even his great teams and his stated view is that winning any game on the road is virtually an upset, but his assessment of his 1987-88 team was correct. The fourth-ranked Tar Heels should have had little trouble with the 4-6 Bruins. But then, the year before, the Bruins had knocked off then top-ranked UNC in what UCLA head coach Walt Hazzard called "one of the greatest [victories] in UCLA history."

The 1988 Bruins tried to recapture the magic of the year before, but the effort came up a few minutes short. "We need to execute at crunch time," Hazzard said of his team's poor play down the stretch. "Once again with this year's team, it was the same scenario. In the last three or four minutes we were right there. But from that point on, we don't do the things we need to do to win."

Ranzino Smith scored two critical baskets in the final 3:27, one his fourth three-pointer of the game and the other a goaltended breakaway layup. J.R. Reid led the Tar Heel scoring with 25 points while Smith followed with 18. Steve Bucknall was the only other North Carolina player in double figures, contributing 13. UCLA held Jeff Lebo to three points, his lowest tally in the season. Scott Williams, who wanted to play well in his homecoming to California, scored nine points and gathered six rebounds; his early foul trouble limited his playing time to 23 minutes before he fouled out of the game. Reserve center/forward Pete Chilcutt played well, including a key block in the final minutes.

Hazzard spoke highly of the way UNC plays at the end of a game. "I liked our effort, but it wasn't enough. That's a tribute to North Carolina. They seem to play that way at the end of games every season." UCLA's Trevor Wilson felt the same way as his coach. "Carolina just has that certain confidence about them. They know what they have to do, and they know when they have to do it."

Consider that a tribute paid directly to the program. One difference that sets UNC apart from a mainstream college program is the team's consistent reaction under fire. While thousands of Tar Heel fans are holding their breath and attempting to quell the pounding of their hearts, their team calmly addresses the task at hand.

• • •

Walt Hazzard would be fired after the season. Like his team, the Bruins' coach hadn't done the things necessary to win. Once a program reaches the heights of a UCLA or a North Carolina, the fans demand more than a winning season. UCLA finished the season 16–14 and failed to make the NCAA tournament, both unacceptable results for coaches at the top of the heap.

UNC 76, FORDHAM 67

Coach Smith had scheduled it as another tune-up game — another chance to flex some muscle and hone skills prior to conference play. It was an opportunity to play two back-to-back Metro-Atlantic Conference teams, the first in the friendly confines of the nearby Greensboro Coliseum against the lightweight Fordham Rams.

It would have been too easy. Though not by design, at least as far as the general public knows, the team found a way to handicap itself and make it interesting. North Carolina would eventually beat the Fordham Rams in overtime, 76-67, but not before the Tar Heels could pick up more valuable "learning experiences."

Gone from the lineup were starting guards Jeff Lebo and Ranzino Smith. Both were out due to nagging injuries. Lebo had injured the pinkie finger on his right hand in practice two days earlier. Smith had re-injured a thigh muscle. Steve Bucknall, another starter, was doubtful as late as the bus ride to the game. His "turf toe" (a severe stubbing of a toe) made it painful to walk. But head trainer Marc Davis did his best (ice, whirlpools, and ultrasound) to have him ready to go.

The point guard duties fell into the untried hands of freshman King Rice. The game would be a true initiation. Until the night of the Fordham clash, the 6–0 guard from Binghamton, New York, had seen only limited minutes in an understudy role. Rice had played in all of the previous 10 games, but his role was to spell Lebo for occasional breathers. This time out, Rice would be a headliner.

The word on Rice was that he would one day be another in the long line of UNC court-smart point guards. His major drawback, in addition to inexperience, was a reluctance to shoot.

Rice had been a solid scoring threat in high school. He knew his duty at North Carolina would be in assisting the strong inside game for which the program was known. Still, to keep the opposition's defense honest, he would have to make a good percentage of the shots that came his way. Coach Smith and Rice's teammates knew he wasn't a great shooter, but he would have to prove some accuracy from outside to wear the blue and white. Until the Fordham game, Rice was shooting a horrific 11 percent from the floor. The Fordham game could either boost or shatter what little confidence the freshman had left.

Rice chose the former.

Playing 44 minutes, more than any other player on either team, Rice delivered a first-class performance in the overtime victory. His 14 points and seven assists were helpful, but not as important as his increased stature on the team. "I was very pleased with King," noted Coach Smith after the game. "Of course he's not Jeff Lebo — but he played with poise and directed the team very well considering his lack of experience."

Smith, never one to overly praise a player's performance until the player is an upperclassman or has graduated from the program, knew how to give just the right amount of encouragement while emphasizing just how much work the player still needed.

It wasn't easy for the freshman. The Rams forced the issue.

Fordham coach Nick Macarchuk learned of UNC's backcourt loss during warm-ups. "We had already planned on packing [the defense] back in against North Carolina," Macarchuk said. "But then we saw Ranzino Smith in street clothes. We didn't know anything about Jeff [Lebo] until we got back from the locker room. Then we just pushed our defense even further back. We were going to make the freshman prove himself.

"He [Rice] shot once early and then became reluctant to shoot. But then he just had to shoot. He had no choice in the matter and he made a couple of shots. And now we had to play him a little bit instead of packing it in on Reid.

"I thought King Rice played a hell of a game. He was thrown into a position to do things that had to be done and he did them very well."

Rice's confident debut forced the Ram defense to cover the outside shot, thus enabling Reid and Scott Williams enough freedom to play inside. Reid's game high 23 points and 11 rebounds were also instrumental in the hard-fought win.

With the Tar Heel inside-outside game not working, Coach Smith, who dislikes using his timeouts, reluctantly called one with 6:39 remaining in regulation. "We called the timeout and said, 'OK, let's go inside,'" Smith noted. "J.R. delivered when we got the ball to him. Scott Williams did the same thing in the overtime." Reid complied with his coach's wishes after the timeout to the tune of nine of the next 11 Tar Heel points. Williams then accounted for the first five points of the overtime.

The three-point shot, a staple of the North Carolina offense since its insertion into the rules and the basis of the UNC outside attack, wasn't in evidence without Lebo or Ranzino Smith. Later, when asked if he had made a conscious decision not to use the shot prior to the game, Coach Smith answered with a half-smile. "Which one did you want to use it, J.R.?" Smith asked. "Scott, Kevin [Madden], and Jeff Denny are the only ones who have a green light on that. So I guess that was conscious."

Knowing every strategy and coaching decision is mathematically sound and well thought out by Smith, one could envision the entire guardless scenario as a *conscious* decision. Though highly unlikely, what better way was there to get a reluctant point guard's shooting touch wet than by throwing him into the stream of a regular season game in a must-perform situation? Without the safety outlet Lebo and Ranzino Smith provide, the freshman swam like a fish. The temporary setback of a non-conference loss early in the season would have been a minor cost if it would provide dividends later on.

The nagging injuries to Lebo and Smith that Coach Smith later referred to as so bad "they couldn't have played tonight if we were playing in the nationals" may have been actually just what the doctor ordered. At least for Rice, anyway.

In a notes column following the game, the *Durham Morning Herald*'s Steve Mann wrote that he felt Dean Smith "didn't think much of the officiating" in the win over Fordham. "I thought they [Fordham] got good officiating away from home," Smith said. When members of the media raised an eyebrow, Smith shot back defensively, "I'm serious. I'll show you on the film."

It was an interesting assessment from Coach Smith. UNC had been called for only 16 fouls playing a pressing man-to-man and Fordham, staying mostly in a tight zone, had been whistled for 23 fouls. (The Tar Heels made 22 of 36 free throws and Fordham hit 17 of 21.) The Tar Heels' last basket of regulation came on a Scott Williams foul-line jumper with 4:13 to play. From there, UNC hit eight of 10 free throws to end regulation tied at 65.

Fordham coach Nick Macarchuk, who had received a technical foul in the first half and had constantly badgered the officials, grinned when he was told of Smith's statement. "Yeah, I agree," Macarchuk said. "Coach Smith is a great coach. Anything Coach Smith says, I agree with."

UNC 96, LASALLE 82

There was no relief in sight.

Though LaSalle University coach Speedy Morris listed 12 players on his roster for the January 9 matchup in the Smith Center, he could have made the trip from Philadelphia with half as many. Two of his players, guard Rich Tarr and sophomore forward sensation Lionel Simmons, played the entire 40 minutes. Two others, guard Tim Legler and center Craig Conlin, played for all but three minutes. Starting forward Bob Johnson got limited playing time and reserve Ken Palczewski saw less than two minutes of action.

The six players, paced by an extraordinary offensive display by Simmons, beat the fourth-ranked home team for the first half of the scheduled contest. The second half, though, belonged to North Carolina and its sophomore giant, J. R. Reid. "They were a better team in the first half and we may have played one of our best halves of the year in the second half," Coach Smith said. "I thought defensively we tightened up and we put J.R. on Simmons and asked for lots of [defensive] help. I didn't want him [Simmons] to break all records."

Simmons did break the Smith Center scoring record set by the late Maryland star Len Bias in 1986. The LaSalle forward scored 37 points from all over the court, including two of three from three-point range. It wasn't enough to offset the entire Tar Heel team. Even though Coach Smith had called the injuries to Jeff Lebo and Ranzino Smith ones that would have kept them out of the nationals only two days before, both were able to start and play effectively against LaSalle. Both were able to hit long-range baskets, forcing the Explorers to cover the outside shot, and both hit 100 percent of their free throws, Smith keeping his season-long string intact.

Reid also produced another headline-grabbing performance. His point-a-minute 30 points, plus nine rebounds, led the way for the Tar Heels. His defense helped slow down a red-hot Simmons. "After talking with the coaches I realize that I should be able to play defense like that every night," Reid said. "After the first half, coach wanted me to play Lionel [Simmons] again because he was having such a good game. They have hard-nosed players. They're very competitive and they love to bang inside. They didn't have a defense, but they really gutted it out and I respect them for the way that they play basketball."

Reid gained back some of the respect he had lost with his early-season inconsistent play. The 6–9 forward exhibited the kind of performance Tar Heel fans expected from the sophomore. It was the kind of performance Reid expected from himself.

Reid's first 11 shots found the inside of the basket. (Of the 21 shots he took in the game, 19 added to his point totals.) Scott Williams added another 19 points, hitting six of nine field goal attempts. Kevin Madden enjoyed his most productive offensive game as he totaled 15 points.

North Carolina's 37–17 rebound margin and strong inside game made the difference. "Everybody in this field house knew that Carolina was going to go inside in the second half," Morris said. "Everybody except our guys out on the court. We didn't do what we needed to do. And we're disappointed."

The Tar Heels and their supporters weren't. Though not sure how the team would prosper during the fast-approaching ACC season, most were pleased to arrive with a relatively scar-free 11–1 record. "I never expected to be where we are as far as a win-loss record is concerned," Smith said. "We had one sure win on our schedule, which was The Citadel. We'll continue to improve — but so will everyone else. If we go 7–7 [in the conference] then we should make the NCAA tournament, which is one of our goals."

Carolina had been invited to the NCAAs in each of its past 13 seasons, equaling the longest all-time streak, set by UCLA from 1967–79 and, currently, the longest consecutive NCAA attendance record in the nation. Getting to the NCAAs has only become a spoken goal of North Carolina in the last few years. The Tar Heels stubbornly stressed winning the ACC regular season championship and the ACC tournament as their goals long after the NCAA started taking more than one team from a given conference in the tournament.

In keeping with its "one game at a time" philosophy, North Carolina has only recently acknowledged that a tournament berth is the ultimate goal.

•   •   •

On January 11, UNC Chancellor Christopher C. Fordham addressed the NCAA's 82nd annual convention in Nashville, Tennessee, concerning a number of topics on collegiate athletics. He complained of society's preoccupation with sports and the problems such a preoccupation entails. The editorial section of *The Chapel Hill Newspaper,* dated January 31, 1988, reprinted his complete speech.

Fordham's first "plea" concerned freshman ineligibility. He noted that prior to 1973, freshmen were ineligible to compete in varsity athletics, giving the student athletes time "to make the transition from home and school to college and university life." It was also Fordham's understanding that the ineligibility ruling was also done to cut budgets, thus establishing eligibility as an economic decision.

A concern of Fordham's was the possibility that increased costs, for a number of reasons, had created a smoke screen that thwarted efforts to reinstate freshman ineligibility. Fordham and Dean Smith share the same philosophy.

Fordham also raised a second topic: a decline in sportsmanship. He felt that there was a "tangible decline in sportsmanship and any sense of gentility between and among the contestants has eroded." He went on to theorize that "the commercialization of college athletics, which we all lament, is directly related to an excessive 'need to win' and that in turn translates into many other behavioral patterns."

The same chancellor had allowed UNC head football coach Dick Crum to be bought out of his contract (read: railroaded out of town) just a month earlier for not producing enough wins, and refused to take a tougher stance in defense of the beleaguered coach. Though Crum wasn't a favorite of the media or many UNC football fans, he stood strong on principle and in maintaining high academic standards at the university. He may have needed replacing, but his release could have been handled in a less hypocritical fashion.

"I am suggesting that these two issues, the academic value issue of freshman ineligibility and the human values issue of declining sportsmanship, together exemplify what I fear is the fundamental problem of sports in our society today, and that is a dispirited sense of values.

It was Fordham's next statement that provided the most puzzlement. "As important as economic considerations are, it may be that they are only symptomatic of the underlying confused and distorted values. We willingly pour countless millions of dollars into sports at all levels, while the poor do without medical care, people sleep in streets, and our schools and colleges are deprived of the support which they should have."

The chancellor spoke out on the evils of spending vast amounts of money on athletic programs, while the North Carolina basketball program is known far and wide for setting no ceiling on expense. He must not have been aware of the excessive expense incurred when the basketball team frequents the likes of The Park Lane Hotel in London, the Watergate Hotel in Washington, D.C., and The Mansion on Turtle Creek in Dallas. He must not have known that the team doesn't frequent many fast-food restaurants, either.

When the team travels by air, both charter and commercial, the players usually sit in first-class, which makes good sense in regard to the size of the athletes. Since everything about the program is also first-class, including the luxurious, fully upholstered high-backed seats the chancellor sits in at home games in the $33.8 million Smith Center, it's a wonder he didn't realize charity begins at home.

Fordham then went on to attack the media, claiming they distort and thus further increase the attention given to sports. "Even off-the-playing-field items become, of all things, front-page news — often suggesting that it is the colleges themselves which lack values."

One wonders where Fordham would suggest the newspapers place a story such as the arrest last year of former-UNC tailback Derrick Fenner, who was charged with an off-the-playing-field murder, possession of cocaine, and possession of a handgun.

Still, Fordham made some valid points — ones worthy of addressing. But they definitely didn't jibe with established UNC practices.

• • •

On January 12, the Tar Heels had climbed from the fourth to the second spot in the poll.

Arizona, which had fallen from the top spot on the second day of the new year after a loss to New Mexico, jumped over Kentucky and Pittsburgh to number one. Kentucky and Pitt had both lost at home, and dropped to the fifth and sixth spots, respectively.

• • •

What had started out as an innocent question two days earlier blossomed into a full-scale media event on January 13.

Paul Ensslin, a sportswriter for *The Chapel Hill Newspaper,* entered into a regularly scheduled ACC coaches' telephone conference call and asked a seemingly innocent question. (Members of the media had the option to call a telephone number hooked up to a line with all of the conference's basketball offices.) The answer proved to be the basis for widespread discussion both in the regional newspapers and on local airwaves.

"It was just a routine question," Ensslin remembers. "I just asked him [Smith] about J.R. Reid's future. I said 'in light of how well J.R. had been playing lately, how will you handle it if he doesn't return next year?' Reid played extremely well the past few games and some friends of mine and I had discussed the possibilities of him turning pro — so I asked Dean about it.

"Dean gave his regular response with something like 'there's a time every spring that I call around the NBA to be assured when a player might be chosen so that I can advise him on his options.'"

Dean has given similar advice to many of his NBA-caliber players over the years. Four Tar Heels were advised to leave school prior to graduation to pursue professional basketball. Bob McAdoo, a junior college transfer, was the first, leaving in 1972 after only one year with the program. Joining him in the pro ranks were Phil Ford in 1977, James Worthy in 1982, and Michael Jordan in 1984. All except Ford took his advice and signed lucrative contracts. All have since obtained degrees at UNC.

Basically, Smith's advice to his players is, "If they're one, two, or three in the NBA draft, they should go." The prospective pro pick must declare hardship prior to being drafted, so any advice Smith could provide is likely based on knowledgeable speculation. Inside information or direct consultation with NBA representatives is illegal.

In speaking of Reid so early in his career, Smith realized he might be sorry for even addressing the question with the press. "Both of J.R.'s parents are schoolteachers and they want him to get his college degree," Smith said. "It hasn't even been discussed. [It was discussed the next day with Reid in Smith's office.] The first they'll [Reid's parents] hear of it will be in the papers, so I probably opened a can of worms."

And the regional media was quick to take the bait. The following morning the *Durham Morning Herald* ran a piece by Steve Mann entitled "Smith Tells Reid To Take NBA Offer If Time's Right," with a teaser on the front page.

John Feinstein, then head basketball writer for *The Washington Post,* heaped coals onto the fire a day later in a story about UNC. In a column entitled "Tar Heels Develop Aura of Vulnerability When All Is Not Well in Chapel Hill," Feinstein wrote, "One wonders exactly what is Reid's role at North Carolina. Great player that he is, there has been talk — made public recently by Smith — about his leaving after this season. How happy is Reid at North Carolina? How happy is North Carolina with Reid?"

Feinstein said he based his information on conversation with two potential North Carolina recruits, Christian Laettner, who had committed to Duke University, and Jerrod Mustaf, who had committed to Maryland. According to Feinstein, both said they had been told by Dean Smith that Reid would be leaving early. If true, the obvious reason for Smith relating such inside information to the two recruits would be as an added incentive for them to attend Carolina and to assure them of more playing time.

Smith, who is quick to point out that he never promises playing time or a starting role to a high school recruit, would have been just as quick in pointing out to the two potential Tar Heels what the possibilities might be if Reid left early.

Ensslin, the writer who had started the ball rolling, chose not to use Smith's reply to his question in print. He did refer to Reid as "the top professional pick several newspapers rumored him to be this week" in a game story following the upcoming Maryland game. Still, the innocent question he posed would be a topic for continued discussion all year.

After the Maryland game, the first one after the teleconference, Smith tried to quell the questions about Reid. "All of you listen carefully," Smith interrupted as soon as a writer began to ask if Smith was encouraging Reid to turn pro. "I was asked a question 'Will J.R. Reid stay four years?' and I simply gave the same comment that I would have given three weeks ago, or a month ago, or ten years ago. The next thing I know I'm saying I'm recommending — if the factors are there [for Smith to check on whether or not Reid would be drafted high], but then I might check for Lebo, Chilcutt, Williams — the whole works.

"I'm just amazed that I answered the question, 'Do I think J.R. Reid will stay the whole four years?' I don't think [Duke's] Danny Ferry will stay the whole four years. His father [Washington Bullets General Manager Bob Ferry] may try to get him for the Bullets."

Even with Smith downplaying the possibility, many fans and members of the media weren't sure Reid would be one of the top three selected in the 1988 NBA draft. In a *Durham Morning Herald* story, Mann quoted an NBA scout who said he thought Reid should stay in college. "My advice is that he's not ready," NBA scouting guru Marty Blake said to the *Baltimore Sun*. "Michael Jordan was the only player in the last few years to come out early and make an immediate impact."

The article went on to say Blake felt that Danny Manning, a 6-10 forward at Kansas, would be the first college player selected. After that, said Blake, "There are a lot of guys, and a lot of guys the average fan hasn't heard of."

The average fan has heard of J.R. Reid. In the five games prior to the Tar Heels ACC opener, Reid was shooting 77 percent from the field, and averaging over 23 points. It would be hard to believe most NBA teams wouldn't list him first or second on their wish list. NBA great Julius Erving had remarked during a national telecast a year earlier that Reid would be his first choice in starting a new NBA franchise.

"Sad" Sam Jones, a former NBA standout and currently a scout for the Detroit Pistons, agreed. Jones, who was in College Park to see the UNC–Maryland game, said during a lull in second-half action, "He'd [Reid] go number one right now if he decided to go hardship. Manning would go number two. But, he'd have to announce first."

Reid responded to questions concerning his future with the standard patter, saying he had no intention of leaving the program early. "If he [Smith] thinks I should, he'll let me know," Reid said, repeating his coach's sentiment. "His philosophy has been the same for 15 years. But he hasn't said anything, yet."

The subject of Reid's future at Carolina was reopened 11 days later following UNC's game at N.C. State. Smith related that he had spoken with Reid's parents and that they wanted him to stay in school four years. "They are very vehement about it, in a nice way," Smith said. "They want him to stay and get his degree on time. I want [him to get] his degree, too.

"And J.R.'s extremely happy — I don't know where that ever started," Smith added in reference to Feinstein's piece in *The Washington Post*, "And we're happy with him. Somebody who says we're not happy with him has to be silly. Come to practice one day, he works very hard every day."

The probable departure of Reid looked much more likely in 1989, the end of his junior year. It would be a minor miracle if the sensational J.R. postponed the life of a millionaire until the beginning of the next decade.

IV.
SECOND HALF

UNC 71, MARYLAND 65

What contrast.

It was the old against the new. The collegiate game's most respected program taking on the league's youngest.

The 11–1 Tar Heels traveled to College Park, Maryland, on January 14 to play in their league opener. The Terrapins, 9–3 overall and 2–0 in the conference, had already doubled Coach Bob Wade's preseason goal of winning an ACC game. A game against second-ranked North Carolina and a follow-up game on Saturday with seventh-ranked Duke would give the young Maryland squad a true indication of how they compared with the league's elite.

It did and it didn't. And not in that order.

The Terps never got into the game with the Tar Heels. Though UNC won the game by only six points at 71–65, the Heels led throughout the game by greater margins. The difference in the game was Maryland's lack of mental preparation and their mediocre shooting. "I thought we played very poorly," Maryland coach Bob Wade said after the loss. "Our execution and defensive rotation was poor, and we didn't do a very good job of getting the ball inside."

The Terps didn't do a good job of getting the ball inside the hoop, either. From the free-throw line, Maryland hit only four of 13. From the floor, the Terps didn't make half of their shots. They accounted for almost a third of their total point production from three-point land, but at a poor 31 percent rate of return. Interestingly, the reason for the Terps' poor play was not from intimidation. Young teams often suffer at first when faced with the North Carolina tradition. Many of the Maryland players, largely as a result of their fast start with consecutive wins over Wake Forest and Clemson, were overconfident.

"Our attitude tonight going into the ball game was that we were going to win," sophomore guard Teyon McCoy said in the locker room after the game. "Intimidation wasn't a factor."

"The guys on the team thought we had the personnel to win," added

107

junior college transfer Rudy Archer, the Terrapin starting point guard. "But we came out tonight a little too overconfident. We were thinking about winning the game instead of concentrating on doing the things we had to do. We were overconfident after the two ACC wins and we overlooked Carolina."

A team would have to be exceedingly overconfident to overlook North Carolina, one of the country's traditionally talented teams. "We felt that Carolina was not as good as they were last year," Archer continued. "They proved us wrong tonight."

Coach Wade claimed his team just couldn't hit the shots, either from the floor or the free-throw line. Coach Smith felt it was his team's defensive effort that was the difference. "I was impressed with our poise on the road and our defense, particularly in the first half. It was a fun victory for us, they're hard to come by up here, particularly against a fine Maryland team."

Either way, the "fine Maryland team" wasn't in evidence until the following Saturday night when the Terps traveled to Duke's infamous Cameron Indoor Stadium and beat the Blue Devils, 72–69. With a 3–1 conference record, Maryland was regaining its stature among the league, and thus, the nation. The aftermath of the Len Bias tragedy was fading with the emergence of Wade's team.

While the quality gap between Coach Wade's rookie program and the former Terp basketball powerhouse led by Charles "Lefty" Driesell narrowed, the gap between the North Carolina and Maryland approaches to basketball widened. Though the athletes and the skill levels of both teams are comparable, the programs are quite different.

The Maryland basketball program's approach to college athletics at the time was low-key and truly representative of "amateur" sports in the strictest sense of the word. Though the team members took basketball seriously, they looked and acted like a well-coached high school team. The players were inexperienced at handling the attention from their fans and the media — true student athletes in terms of basketball.

UNC's demeanor is always professional. The players are skilled at providing clear, yet often vague, responses to questions. The highly visible Tar Heels are used to crowd adoration and give off an aura of bored acceptance underneath their practiced smiles. They are also student athletes, but they are graduate-level student athletes in terms of basketball — far removed from any "amateur" level.

The ready access to both academic and basketball figures at College Park would be unheard of in Chapel Hill. At the game that evening, Maryland's former chancellor John Slaughter sat underneath one of the goals near press row on a folding metal chair. Fans, students, and "bigwigs" have easy access to the distinguished scientist and dedicated humanitarian. When Chancellor Christopher Fordham, a distinguished leader in medicine and academics, attends a game in the Smith Center, he sits at center court in a chair that would rival a first-class seat on a Concorde. Ushers divert those who don't hold tickets in that section.

Cole Field House, the Maryland indoor sports facility, seats 12,004 in a Quonset hut-like building. Financed with funds from a self-liquidating bond issue and a special student activity fund, the building was completed in 1955 and cost $3.3 million. Students holding tickets are seated first come, first serve in the best seats courtside. The Maryland media guide contains five paragraphs about the facility. The Dean E. Smith Center seats 21,444 in an ultra-modern naturally lit arena. Though located on a state-owned campus, private contributions paid the $33.8 million tab for the Smith Center. Most students lucky enough to get tickets sit in the end-zone and upper-deck seats. The UNC media guide devotes two full pages to a descriptive article written by Deana Nail, a Smith Center marketing and public relations assistant.

On the day of the Carolina game, Maryland senior Kirk Bell and one of his fraternity brothers casually dropped by Coach Wade's office without an appointment to talk hoops. "We stopped by this afternoon to talk to him about recruiting — to talk about some high school kids we saw in a high school game," Bell said prior to the game. "We sat and talked for a while and we also gave him a sweatshirt [emblazoned in bright red with SWAT TEAM] for his kid [Darion, age 11] to wear to tonight's game. Bob's very personable."

Dean Smith is personable, too. But it is highly unlikely that a couple of fraternity members could drop in for a chat during the season unannounced, much less on a game day. And should anyone get past Smith's receptionist-secretary Angela Lee and executive secretary Linda Woods in the first place, no one, other than staff and perhaps a few "chosen" confidants, would ever be allowed to discuss recruiting.

UNC 87, VIRGINIA 62

On January 16, six nights prior to the Mike Tyson–Larry Holmes bout in Atlantic City, the second-ranked Tar Heels knocked out the Virginia Cavaliers in a regularly scheduled 40-minute brawl in Chapel Hill. The tally of takedowns, holds, shoves, and pushes numbered only slightly less than the combined scores.

The two schools have played each other tough since Terry Holland took over the coaching duties in Charlottesville 14 years ago. Although the Tar Heels consistently win three out of every four games they play against

Virginia, the Cavaliers have just as consistently kept UNC on the ropes throughout the last dozen years.

This game began with both teams playing solid basketball. North Carolina worked the inside, with Scott Williams scoring five of six baskets from the paint, and the outside, with Jeff Lebo connecting on five of nine. Virginia's scoring was achieved mainly through the efforts of veteran forward Mel Kennedy. The score seesawed until midway through the first half when referee Dick Paparo called a technical foul on Coach Smith for displaying displeasure at an earlier call.

"It must have been something that I did," Smith acknowledged later. "Don [Vaden, one of the officials] said that I kicked my leg in the air. I didn't know that was a technical nowadays."

Regardless, Smith's not-so-innocent body language set off a wave of personal foul calls that eventually changed the course of the game. The technical foul worked in favor of the Tar Heels. The Cavaliers' resulting bonus shots gave them a one-point lead, but it proved to be their last lead of the game. UNC went on to build a 38–30 lead by halftime and the visiting Virginians never recovered.

In the second half, Reid awoke from his first-half slumber and the Tar Heels resumed their strong inside game. Reid's 19 points were largely the result of 11 free throws, as the Virginia defense was determined to keep him occupied in the paint. "It's hard to shoot when you have two or three men hanging on you," Reid said after the game. The height advantage of Reid, Williams, and Pete Chilcutt proved to be the difference inside. Within minutes, North Carolina literally put the game out of reach.

Virginia released its frustration as the physical nature of the game evolved into an NBA-style shoving and holding match. Virginia's John Johnson and Lebo refused to give each other an inch, and the intensity between the two guards increased until Johnson retaliated against a Lebo hold with an intentional foul. Minutes later he was called for another, this time on substitute point guard King Rice. "The first time it was definitely retaliation, which was dumb on my part," Johnson admitted. "I got caught and that was that. The second one wasn't intentional."

In all, three intentional fouls and two technical fouls figured into the game's 38 called infractions. Still, only one player, Jeff Daniel, a Cavalier reserve center who didn't score a point, fouled out of the game. The disruptive calls may have kept the contest from getting out of hand, but they didn't affect the outcome. The game had long been over. With six and a half minutes left to play, the Tar Heels enjoyed a 26-point advantage. Yet the starters for both squads were still on the floor. A weak argument can be made for keeping the losing team out on the hardwood. There is a lesson to be learned in defeat — when there is a remote possibility the game can be turned around. There was *no* reason for keeping the starting Tar Heels in the game.

Players from both teams looked like they wished they could be elsewhere. Anywhere. The game had long been decided and players, fans, and the media were ready to call it an evening. Substitutes for both teams did eventually get into the game, but the changes should have been made much earlier. Perhaps it was the continuing feud between the two head coaches.

It's no secret the two coaches don't care for each other — to put it mildly. The beginnings of the rift developed in 1966 when Smith "stole" Charlie Scott, Carolina's first black player, away from Lefty Driesell at Davidson, where it was thought the talented Scott would enroll. Holland played and later coached under Driesell before taking the head coaching job at the school. In 1974, Holland landed his current job at Virginia. With just three years under his belt there, Terry Holland made a remark that forever set the tone between the two coaches.

"There's such a gap between the man and the image the man tries to project," Holland said, speaking of Smith. It was the same year that a Virginia player, Marc Iavaroni, accused Smith of shoving him in the hallway at halftime. Smith later denied pushing Iavaroni. Holland spoke about the incident five years later to Gary Smith, who was writing an article for *Inside Sports* magazine. "In this particular case, Dean Smith was very wrong," Holland said. "There seemed to be no apology forthcoming, like he was right and our player was wrong. If Dean thinks he's at the point where he's right all the time, and the people of North Carolina don't even question him, then that's wrong. The point I was trying to make was, I don't think he needs to be afraid of being a human being. The man's achievements are incredible. That should not preclude making errors. Sure, I'd feel more comfortable if he'd admit his competitiveness to me. But he has no reason to."

Smith would admit his competitiveness three years later in a recruiting battle. The two coaches competed for the services of Ralph Sampson, an eventual three-time National Player of the Year. It was a battle Smith lost. Sampson elected to stay close to his home in Harrisonburg and play in Charlottesville. For four years the Virginia–UNC games took on greater significance. In the end, however, Smith won the war. During the Sampson era, Virginia never won an ACC or an NCAA championship. North Carolina, in the same time span, won two conference titles and the national crown.

In an interview, Smith will be the first person to say that the two men and their wives get along handsomely. "In fact, Terry and Ann and Linnea and I have been out to dinner," Smith said. "I think he's a very good coach and he and I usually agree in coaches' meetings." Smith may be content to let bygones be bygones — at least superficially. Holland isn't. On three different occasions prior to and during the 1987–88 season, the Virginia coach refused to speak about Smith and the North Carolina program.

In the past, Holland had been quoted as saying he renamed his dog Dean because he whined all night. Dean must still keep the Virginia coach awake.

DUKE 70, UNC 69

Dean Smith wasn't pleased with the timing of the scheduled showdown with conference co-leader Duke. "It isn't best to play a good team which is coming off an unexpected loss," Smith stated in a North Carolina news release dated two days prior to the January 21 contest. "But, we can't do anything about that. We'll just have to play as if we've lost, too."

Smith didn't want his opponents to have any psychological edge coming into the Smith Center, but the Blue Devils' recent loss to Maryland at home gave them one. A lot was at stake besides staying on top of the conference standings and maintaining a lofty national ranking. North Carolina was enjoying a streak of 16 consecutive conference wins and a Smith Center record of only one loss since beginning play in the domed facility. Additionally, Duke hadn't won a game in Chapel Hill since 1985, and the Tar Heels hoped to continue their winning ways over the Blue Devils.

The Tar Heels came within one shot of sustaining those records, losing to Duke, 70–69. Duke sophomore forward Robert Brickey deflected that shot, a 20-foot jumper, to ensure victory. "We didn't get the shot I diagrammed," Smith said after the game. "I wanted to get the ball to J.R. at the end." Instead, the ball ended up in the sure-shooting Jeff Lebo's hands. Normally, Smith would have been happy to let Lebo take the last shot. But after hitting only two of thirteen attempts for the evening, Lebo found himself with the ball and not enough time to get it inside.

"I knew I had to shoot, and he knew I had to shoot," Lebo said. "I tried to get off a shot before he got there [to block it]." It was fitting that a defensive play preserved the game. Both teams played defense as if the game depended on it. It did.

"The sign of a good basketball team is that they never relax on defense," Duke coach Mike Krzyzewski said. "Both teams showed that tonight." Neither team had the time to relax. Duke tied the game 44 seconds after the opening tipoff and never trailed in the remaining 39 minutes. North Carolina was able to tie the game with 2:42 to play, but could never get ahead. "We had our chances," Coach Smith said. "Maybe it's that we're a young team, or maybe it's that we weren't really sharp. I might not have had 'em ready to play."

Duke was certainly ready. In fact, almost to a man the Blue Devils spoke of knowing they were going to win. "This is a difficult place to play, and North Carolina is a very, very good basketball team. But we came in here to win — expecting to win," said senior guard Kevin Strickland, speaking for his team.

UNC didn't lose without a struggle. After trailing most of the game and down by 11 points with just under 12 minutes to play, the Tar Heels went on a 14–6 run. Reid scored 12 of the points, tying the game with 1:23 to play with a layup. But they missed two chances to go ahead when Lebo missed a three-pointer and Pete Chilcutt missed a tap-in opportunity.

Duke didn't help its chances offensively, either. The Blue Devils didn't score a field goal in the last seven minutes. It turned out they didn't need one.

"It was a great basketball game," Krzyzewski said as he sat exhausted behind a battery of microphones, "and I think I would have said that even if Lebo hit that last shot. We feel very fortunate to win here, and beat an excellent team. But, it's still only one game."

It was more than a game in the current rivalry between the two coaches. Krzyzewski had won only one game in Chapel Hill in his career. If Duke was to break the hold that the Heels held on home victories, it needed to find a way to win at the Smith Center. Coach "K" had succeeded in building and maintaining a Top 10 program. He had also come a long way in personal growth. At one point in his career at Duke, Krzyzewski had taken on the full wrath of Smith when he let loose with a verbal barrage suggesting that there was a double standard when it came to playing against North Carolina and its famous coach.

In a close game in Durham during Michael Jordan's junior year, Dean Smith ran to the scorer's table. A referee was about to put the ball into play and Smith wanted to insert a player. When the official failed to notice the player and no horn was sounded, Smith reached over the table and slapped at the electronic clock in an attempt to hit the buzzer. The timekeeper shoved Smith back; Smith slapped the timekeeper's arm down in retaliation. While one official ran over to unravel the mess and readjust the scoreboard, Krzyzewski was swearing up and down to another official that Smith should receive a technical foul for touching the clock. In the end no technical foul was awarded and Smith was able to substitute a player. The Duke coach had let loose after the game, precipitating a cold war between the two men.

Time has matured both coaches. The long-standing rivalry is extraordinary between the two schools, but only recently has the coaches' respect for each other grown to match that rivalry.

An ongoing rivalry exists between the two schools' student newspapers as well. Each year in this decade, the two papers have spoofed each other on the eve of their respective home basketball game. North Carolina lampoons *The Chronicle* with "The Comical" and Duke counters later in the season with "The Daily Tar Hole" to replace *The Daily Tar Heel.* Both schools always know which sensitive spots to probe. The Duke students pick at Dean Smith's amply proportioned nose knowing Carolina will retaliate against Mike Krzyzewski's similarly styled beak. UNC writes about the craziness of the Duke fans. Duke retaliates with a story saying the UNC athletic director plans to place electric prods in the seats in the Smith Center to get its normally complacent crowd to "react violently to a 10,000-volt surge of electricity through their bodies."

One story in a past "Daily Tar Hole" quoted fictitious Velma Stiller, who claimed Dean Smith was none other than the paternal father of both Kenny Smith and Ranzino Smith. The article was penned by Langston "Lenny" Wertz, after the official Coach Smith dislikes. In the piece, Dean Smith's only comment is a repeated, "I think we should be the underdog against Duke."

The annual spoofs are always taken and given with tongue placed firmly in cheek. "Each school uses its college newspaper as a learning lab," said Anne Fulcher, director of publication for *The Daily Tar Heel* at North Carolina. "There's even communication between the technical staffs of each school to properly match the correct typestyles." Neither school was concerned about any legal ramifications. Fulcher did mention, however, that *The Daily Tar Heel* carries a $1 million libel insurance policy.

• • •

Early deadlines are a curse for weekly news and sports periodicals.

Most of the nation had received copies of the latest *Sports Illustrated* (January 25), and though the lead stories on the two National Football League conference championships were timely, the national college basketball rankings found farther back in the issue were a shambles. In a season when upsets abound, it's almost impossible to print a Top 20 poll that isn't dated before it hits the newsstand.

Sports Illustrated's Top 20 ranking placed North Carolina ahead of Duke for the first time in the year. All season, the nation's best sports magazine had picked the Blue Devils higher than the Tar Heels. The Associated Press, United Press International, *USA Today*, and every bettor's tout sheet had sung the praises of North Carolina over its cross-town rival.

It took Duke's unfortunate loss to Maryland almost a week before to cause the *SI* staff to change its tune. UNC jumped ahead of Duke to third (up from fifth) and Duke fell to eighth (down from second). With Carolina's one-point *upset* loss to the Blue Devils in the Smith Center, *Sports Illustrated* and all of the nation's pollsters would be whistling still another melody. It would be anybody's guess as to where the Tar Heels and Blue Devils would land when the new rankings appeared the following week.

UNC 77, N.C. STATE 73

On January 24, the first football-free Sunday since the early fall of 1987, college basketball filled the void on the airwaves for national sports fans.

One of the day's best matchups featured two schools with North Carolina in their monikers. The game between UNC and N.C. State University meant the difference between sharing a tie for first place or falling to fifth place in the ACC. It was a game between two nationally ranked teams. More importantly, it was simply a game between the Wolfpack and the Tar Heels, two intrastate roundball rivals since 1918.

Prior to the matchup, broadcast nationally by NBC, the Tar Heels held a 105–63 advantage in the series between the schools and, in recent years, still held the advantage in regular and postseason play. In 1983, however, the Wolfpack had knocked off the Tar Heels in the ACC tournament and gone on to win both the ACC and the NCAA tournament in a Cinderella season. N.C. State had accomplished the feat just one year after the Tar Heels had brought home Smith's first NCAA title. Though publicly pleased for the Wolfpack's laurels, most North Carolina fans felt that the over-achieving "Cardiac 'Pack" had diluted UNC's 1982 accomplishment.

The popular North Carolina slogan for years was "Duke is puke, Wake is fake, but the team I hate is N.C. State." State's dynamic new head basketball coach, Jim Valvano, changed those feelings. Largely on the strength of his startling success, both he and the public couldn't seem to get enough of each other. The effervescent young Italian soaked up the media exposure and catapulted the Wolfpack and himself into the national lime-light.

The gap that existed between the two programs and the two coaches began to close. In 1987, the Wolfpack rose again to dampen North Carolina's spirits by beating the Tar Heels in the finals of the ACC tournament. It was the only loss to a conference team that year as UNC had delivered a perfect 16–0 record against league opponents before that game. Now, in 1988, when the number two Tar Heels traveled to Raleigh's Reynolds Coliseum to take on the number 20 Wolfpack, hoop fans felt there was a chance the gap might close further.

It did, and it didn't.

The game, won by North Carolina, 77–73, showcased a little of everything. Coach Valvano, normally an energetic cheerleader, donned his athletic director's hat and attempted to quell any abnormal exuberance prior to the contest. He took the public address microphone and requested the State fans to treat the visitors as they would like their team to be treated on the road.

"I had read in our student newspaper that our students would be shouting 'guilty, guilty, guilty' [aimed at two of the North Carolina players] and I didn't think that it was appropriate," Valvano said in his postgame remarks. Valvano could have taken a page out of the Dean Smith book on acceptable fan behavior. Smith is a firm believer in polite crowd response. While 99 percent of the schools allow the student body free rein in cheering the home team on to victory, Smith prefers a more sportsmanlike approach.

The most obvious difference is behind-the-basket distraction tactics. Most schools seat students in the end-zone sections directly behind the glass backboards. When a visiting player is at the free-throw line, thousands of arms are waved in conjunction with bloodcurdling screams and cheers to distract the hapless shooter. Sometimes the distractions are more ingenious. At a game at Jacksonville University in December 1985, point guard Kenny Smith received a distraction of a different nature. Just before shooting a free throw, Smith caught a glimpse of a pretty coed stationed prominently underneath the basket in the front row. As he got the ball and set his feet for the shot, the coed opened her raincoat and flashed an itsy bitsy red bikini. Smith concentrated and made both shots. He noted to reporters after the game that she was quite attractive. Though a clever interruption and one that is not against the rules, it was a distraction.

No such shenanigans take place at a North Carolina-hosted contest.

The ever-gracious Smith not only disapproves of any arm waving or crowd noise during an opponent's free-throw attempt, but he will send ushers to reprimand any fans who haven't been properly schooled in his strict etiquette. There has been some discussion in the media that Smith's actual strategy is that the sudden quiet might be even more unnerving to free-throw shooters. In any case, in the tradition of Frank Sinatra, Dean Smith does it his way.

Valvano's etiquette appeal was met with mixed reactions. His pregame requests for good behavior elicited cheers, but later the same fans' rowdiness (represented by thrown objects) caused two delays in the game. The game announcer warned that technical fouls would be called if another outburst occurred.

"At least I tried," Valvano said.

J.R. Reid and Steve Bucknall, due to their well-publicized skirmish in

A beleaguered Dean Smith meets the press. (Photo by Hugh Morton)

(Above) Dean Smith served as an assistant coach to Frank McGuire before taking over the head coaching reins at UNC. (Photo by Bill Pronty)

(Below) Vesta and Alfred Smith watch their son coach the Tar Heels in the arena that bears his name. (Photo by Hugh Morton)

(Above) Smith chats with North Carolina State coach Jim Valvano. *(Photo by Alex Webb)*
(Below) Smith visits with Virginia coach Terry Holland. *(Photo by Hugh Morton)*

(Above) Smith and a star-studded UNC alumni team in Los Angeles for a classic rematch with a UCLA alumni team. From left, Mike Pepper, Lennie Rosenbluth, Michael Jordan, John Kuester, Kenny Smith, and Phil Ford. That's Doug Moe on the right with his back to the camera. (Photo by Steve Holstrom)

(Left) Senior Ranzino Smith gets a hug from the coach before his final home game. (Photo by Shea Tisdale)

(Above) A dapper Dean Smith enjoys the dedication of the Smith Center. (Photo by Bob Donnan)

(Below) The misty enshrouded Smith Center rises out of the Carolina pines. (Photo by Bill Richards)

A typically determined J.R. Reid clears a rebound against Clemson. (Photo by Shea Tisdale)

All Tar Heel players rise and applaud a teammate's good play. (Photo by Shea Tisdale)

Jeff Lebo displays his three-point shooting form during the Blue-White scrimmage. (Photo by Matt Plyler)

Scott Williams jams one home. (Photo by Shea Tisdale)

(Left) Ranzino Smith scores on a breakaway against N.C. State, as Vinny Del Negro watches. (Below) Smith and fellow senior Joe Jenkins clasp hands before the Senior Day game. (Photos by Shea Tisdale)

Kevin Madden rises to block a shot by Duke's Kevin Strickland. (Photo by Nell Rittenburg)

(Left) Rick Fox drives past Wake Forest's Cal Boyd. (Photo by Nell Rittenburg)
(Right) Pete Chilcutt looks to pass around Duke's Danny Ferry. (Photo by Shea Tisdale)
(Below) King Rice, guarded by SMU's Kato Armstrong, looks for an open Tar Heel. (Photo by Nell Rittenburg)

Steve Bucknall converts a wraparound layup against N.C. State's Avie Lester, Jr. (Photo by Nell Rittenburg)

(Above) J.R. Reid scrambles for a loose ball against the Soviet
National team.
(Below) Jeff Lebo takes a charge from Virginia's John
Johnson as Kevin Madden blocks the way. (Photos by Matt
Plyler)

J.R. Reid rattles the rim against Duke in the Smith Center. (Photo by Nell Rittenburg)

(Top) Exhausted and disappointed, Tar Heels Jeff Denny, Jeff Lebo, J.R. Reid, Rodney Hyatt, Pete Chilcutt, and David May watch as the Duke Blue Devils cut down the nets after winning the 1988 ACC Tournament. (Above) A dejected Steve Bucknall tries to block out the same scene. (Photos by Nell Rittenburg)

Raleigh before the season began, expected to be the brunt of many catcalls and jeers. The two UNC starters weren't disappointed. Handheld signs alluded to the spitting and assault charges with phrases like, "Who gives a spit about J.R." and, "Don't hit me, J.R." There were students dressed in prison garb with Reid's name on their backs and coliseum-wide chants of "guilty, guilty, guilty" whenever Reid committed a personal foul. One enterprising State fan collaborated with the Wolfpack pep band. He wore a large bone (through-the-head-type) apparatus that spelled out "Herman," Reid's first name, while the band played the theme song from *The* (Herman) *Munsters*, a popular '60s television show featuring a Frankenstein monster look-alike.

The real show took place on the floor.

Both teams had done their homework. Valvano's plan, one that many teams utilized throughout the season, was to slow down Reid's inside attack and deny Jeff Lebo any uncontested jump shots. UNC did likewise, taking the Wolfpack's leading scorer, guard Vinny Del Negro, out of the game, and keeping pressure on State's big men, Chucky Brown and Charles Shackleford, in the paint. "They did exactly what we did," State senior guard Quentin Jackson said. "We took Lebo out of the game, and they took Vinny out."

Both teams were then forced to counterattack with increased efforts from secondary starters and substitutes. The on-again, off-again Shackleford was on, especially when Reid was forced to the sidelines with foul trouble. North Carolina got strong all-around play from its bench and meritorious support from sixth-man Kevin Madden. The substitute's seven-of-eight shooting performance and UNC's 23-of-26-made free throws were the difference in the game. That North Carolina shot 66 percent to State's 46 percent for the game didn't hurt matters, either.

Though no excuses were offered, the Tar Heels went into the game wounded and emerged with still more battle scars. Lebo was diagnosed as having an inflamed plica, an injury (to the tissue around the knee) he had sustained in the previous game against Duke. "I didn't think Jeff Lebo should play," Smith said. "He begged to play. He's got a real bad knee. I think he showed tremendous courage to play that long. He probably won't be able to walk tomorrow."

Few fans knew of his injury prior to the game and it wasn't obvious from the stands, although a slight limp did develop from time to time during the 36 minutes the junior played.

Ranzino Smith's problems were more noticeable. Coming into the game, Smith had seen very limited action since rebruising his thigh in practice January 4, playing in only two of the four scheduled games. The senior started against State, but his rustiness and a three-point airball caused an early return to the bench. When he managed to return to the action, an errant elbow from State backup center Avie Lester sent him back to the pine by way of the locker room. The officials missed the blow, and when Smith returned to his bench, Coach Smith sent the bleeding senior back out onto the floor to display his fresh wounds. It was Coach Valvano, not the North Carolina bench, who offered a towel and some momentary comfort to the dazed guard.

Smith returned to the game in the second half, but not before receiving 12 stitches in his head. A three-inch white bandage accompanied the football thigh pad already adorning Smith's body. His courage and gutty contribution was important for team morale, floor leadership, and for two critical baskets that halted a State rally midway through the second period.

With a slight lead, North Carolina was poised and ready to run a delay with its best ball-handlers and foul shooters controlling the ball. "My great plan was to throw the ball to Ranzino for the foul shots," Coach Smith said. "He's our best foul shooter. But, [after Ranzino missed one, his first miss of the season] at least that 100 percent jinx is over now. But then it could have been the 12 stitches he took in his head."

Smith felt the blow to his senior was intentional and that Valvano did the correct thing in benching the culprit. "I understand that's why he [Lester] didn't play much [after the incident]. Jim may have noticed it [the swung elbow], and I admire that."

Valvano disagreed, saying Lester's blow was unintentional and that the reason he wasn't in the game was just a matter of rotation. He also noted that a later call on UNC's Kevin Madden for a similar infraction was not an intentional foul, either. Ranzino agreed with Valvano's assessment after the game. Though the unfortunate injury to Smith was a cause for concern, its only effect on the game was to provide additional color for the fans.

The Wolfpack lost the game due to poor shooting caused largely by excellent defense from UNC. Still, it was clear that the degree of dominance UNC enjoyed over State was not as strong. Valvano's success as a basketball program builder, though overnight in many respects, was not just a momentary flash in the pan. The Wolfpack program under entrepreneur Valvano might never achieve the longstanding success Carolina enjoys under Smith. But it proved it belonged in the league's upper echelon just the same.

Despite a one-point loss to Duke in the Smith Center and the close victory over N.C. State at Raleigh, the Tar Heels fell only one spot in the Associated Press rankings.

Arizona held on to its number one ranking, missing a unanimous selection by only four points. It marked the third week in a row that the

Wildcats prowled on top of the standings, their fifth week overall.

Purdue rose from fifth to second place by virtue of a hot winning streak after losing only its first game of the season. The Boilermakers had won 16 straight games and were undefeated in Big Ten Conference play.

Duke took a giant stride after wins over UNC and Wake Forest, moving into the vacant fifth spot past Temple. The Blue Devils nearly tripped in their next game, however, against the Stetson Hatters in Daytona Beach, Florida. Duke overcame some late-game mistakes to hold off Stetson, 81–78.

N.C. State was not so fortunate. After conference losses to Wake Forest and UNC, the Wolfpack dropped from the Top 20 after only one week in the bottom spot.

Indiana, curiously absent from the Top 20 after winning the NCAA championship a year earlier, was not listed in the polls, but it did make the sports pages. Bobby Knight, the ever-colorful coach of the Hoosier team, denied rumors he was resigning after his team's subpar performance up to this point. Knight attempted to thwart the rumors on his radio talk show, calling the news stories "bull."

The defending national champions were currently 9–6 after a 72–60 loss to Michigan. The Hoosiers' conference record was 1–4.

WAKE FOREST 83, UNC 80

Thousands of members of the UNC student body were torn in making social plans on the evening of January 28. The two main choices were between rocking and rolling on campus or driving to Greensboro, just 45 miles away, to watch the Tar Heels take on Wake Forest.

The students who decided to attend the Smith Center saw Sting and ensemble replace Smith and company for the evening. The popular rock star filled the Dean Dome with a mixture of jazz and rock while the Tar Heels and the Demon Deacons took turns making string music in the Greensboro Coliseum.

Marginal basketball fans felt they could miss the game because, in all likelihood, the Tar Heels would make mincemeat out of the Deacons. Those who did make the decision to hear the concert on the basis of the past six years of Wake Forest-North Carolina matchups made a critical error in judgment. The Deacons, who hadn't beaten the Tar Heels in regular season action since January 21, 1982, stunned the basketball world. In a foul-plagued but well-shot game, overlooked Wake Forest knocked off the third-ranked UNC team to claim the season's biggest upset, 83-80.

It wasn't done with mirrors.

The Tar Heels took an 11-point lead in the first half, forcing Wake's floor leader, forward Sam Ivy, to watch from the bench due to foul trouble.

He did leave the floor with 14 first-half points, however. Ivy picked up a fourth foul in the second period, but never fouled out of the contest. UNC's two big men weren't so lucky.

J.R. Reid and Scott Williams fouled out of the contest, leaving Pete Chilcutt to mount the inside attack for the Tar Heels. Kevin Madden, normally a strong sixth or seventh man off the Carolina bench, was sidelined with an ankle injury. In addition, both Jeff Lebo and Steve Bucknall were playing with four fouls. If the Tar Heels were to catch the hot-shooting Deacons, they would have to do so from the outside.

They couldn't. Jeff Lebo and Ranzino Smith did manage 30 points between them, but it came up short compared to the two Wake Forest guards' tally. Junior Cal Boyd hit 18 points, including a four-for-six effort from three-point distance, and his backcourt partner, sophomore David Carlyle, scored his career-high and the game-high 21 points in a variety of ways.

"We just couldn't stop Carlyle," Dean Smith said. "And it's unbelievable what Boyd did to us. We had our chances to put them [the Deacons] away, but they [Boyd and Carlyle] just kept hitting." The Tar Heels had their chances all right, but uncharacteristically lost their composure during crunch time.

"Wake Forest played a tremendous game," Smith continued, "and made a lot of people happy. I can still hear it going on." In a spontaneous celebration, many of the 14,500 roaring fans took to the floor and screamed for the Deacons and their coach to come out for a curtain call. The Deacon mascot climbed atop the basket to lead the cheers as other jubilant fans cut the nets.

Wake coach Bob Staak returned to the floor with a few of his players and the Greensboro imitation of Mardi Gras continued. Staak took the win in stride, stating humbly, "Every win is a big win, but tomorrow we have to get ready for Virginia."

Carlyle, arguably the MVP for the night, went on record contrary to Staak's reserved comments. "It's the biggest win I've been associated with. I've always wanted to beat Carolina, growing up, all my life." His memories of the game would last a lifetime. And the win was more important for Staak than he let on publicly. Beating North Carolina, combined with an earlier win over North Carolina State, would definitely strengthen Staak's future at Wake Forest, a school that emphasizes academics more than sports.

Deacon alumni wouldn't expect their basketball coach to win every time the home team took on the Tar Heels, but they, like any collegiate supporters, do demand the occasional upset. Ex-Tar Heel football coach and new Wake Forest football coach Bill Dooley had delivered the goods last fall when his Deacon squad knocked off the Tar Heels in Chapel Hill, and now Staak gave the Wake Forest fans another dose of victory over the intrastate rivals.

As far as many North Carolina fans were concerned, it was a better night to have listened to a concert.

UNC 73, GEORGIA TECH 71

The night before, Jeff Lebo and Brooke Ferguson, a UNC varsity cheerleader, had watched a rented videotape entitled *From the Hip*. The title aptly described the game-winning offensive display the junior guard delivered the following evening. In breathtaking fashion, the good-looking marksman led his team to a 73–71 win over Georgia Tech.

The game belonged to the Yellow Jackets until Lebo pulled out his six-shooter and blasted five consecutive three-pointers to pull out a victory for the otherwise misfiring Tar Heels. Had the Yellow Jackets not dribbled themselves out of the last 40 seconds of the game, Lebo might have needed to fire his last round. "I hit five [three-pointers] in a row," Lebo acknowledged, "but we still only won by two. They were coming down and scoring, so I think our defense needs to get a little bit·better."

The UNC defense wasn't that shabby. The Tar Heels played hard, challenging the Rambling Wreck to stay with the strong inside game North Carolina is known for. With the game on the line, and Tech in possession, UNC's defense did muster an airtight case. After Lebo's fifth extra-pointer gave the men in blue a two-point lead, Tech seemed content to run off the clock and return to Atlanta with a close loss.

"I was kind of disappointed in myself that we didn't get off a shot there at the end," Georgia Tech coach Bobby Cremins said. "We were a little confused when [Craig] Neal called timeout."

Cremins took the blame, but his floor general was the one who lost the battle. Earlier, during a Carolina timeout with one minute remaining, Cremins had told his team what to do if UNC scored. "We wanted to get it inside to [Tom] Hammonds. We were a little tentative and then I was afraid we were going to let the clock run out. I didn't want the game to end with us dribbling the ball, so I called timeout."

Tech still had five seconds to inbound and score — and North Carolina still had five seconds to prevent a score. Tar Heel freshman Rick Fox deflected the inbounds pass to Scott Williams, who kept the ball in play by bouncing the ball between his legs to Lebo. Lebo held on to the game ball that was rightly his, and Carolina emerged victorious.

The game plan Tech utilized was becoming more and more familiar to the Tar Heels. North Carolina had to win the game from the outside. With an ever-tightening Tech zone forcing J.R. Reid and Williams farther away from the basket, UNC still tried to force the ball inside. Against the zone and without room to work, Reid and Williams contributed only 29 points, less than half of the UNC total. Luckily, the outside duo of Lebo and Ranzino Smith were up to the task. Before this game, both were off the mark. Lebo had been nine of 34 in the previous three games and Ranzino was gradually getting his shooting touch back after being sidelined by a thigh injury.

With the consistently strong inside game the Heels possess, most teams would be content to pack it back against them and force the outside shot. Though Lebo and Smith can be deadly from three-point range, opposing teams, as well as the two guards, know their coach prefers the higher-percentage inside shot. "Our first priority is to get the ball inside," Ranzino Smith reluctantly admitted, "but if the defense is stacked back, then we have the green light to put the ball up."

Lebo agreed. "It always helps. If you can get a couple of three-pointers it loosens things up inside. We want to get the ball inside to J.R. The guy's shooting 66 percent from the field and every time he touches it he usually scores or gets fouled. You want to get him the ball as much as possible, but we could be forcing it in too much."

It's hard to argue with the success of the North Carolina offensive philosophy over the years. Times do change, and those who refuse to adapt will eventually be left behind. Smith and company may drag their heels in respect to some tried-and-true team strategies, but the integration of the three-point shot and a 45-second clock into college basketball has effectively brought about some fundamental changes.

The difference in the game, after Tech chose to employ a zone defense, was the three-point shot. Both teams shot 47 percent from the floor, with UNC making one more field goal in two more attempts. But they shot 10 of 23 from outside the bonus stripe, while Georgia Tech could only muster three of 11 from the same distance.

"They [Tech] gave Ranzino and Jeff the three-point shots," Coach Smith said after the game. "We have to take those shots. I told Jeff at one of the timeouts that he needed to take those — we even had a play called for him and he didn't shoot it. He didn't feel real comfortable."

Smith quickly offered assurance for Lebo's benefit. "He's a great competitor. If it didn't come tonight, then it would've the next game." Lebo had come around with the game on the line. The resulting two-point win kept Carolina tied for second place in the conference standings. Had UNC lost, the team would have dropped three spots to a tie for fifth.

"We were very fortunate to win that game," Smith said. He was right.

•   •   •

As expected, the loss to unsung Wake Forest the previous week took its toll on the Tar Heels' national standing. Falling five spots to eighth place, North Carolina was slowly but surely working its way down from its inflated early season rankings.

Arizona was but one vote shy of being the unanimous top pick in the Wildcats' fourth week at the top spot.

Duke, narrowly beaten for third, still improved to fourth.

Temple, the only non-conference game still scheduled on the Carolina slate, also improved by moving up to fifth.

•   •   •

On February 2, 1988, there was more excitement for the UNC Athletic Department. On Derrick Fenner's behalf, his attorney accepted a guilty plea to one count of cocaine possession. It was just one month after the former North Carolina football star had escaped a murder charge.

It had been hoped by Fenner and university officials that all charges would be dropped completely, as had been the case with the murder charge. Clearing the athlete's name would go a long way toward restoring some of the shine to UNC's tarnished image of late. No such luck.

Fenner was accused of illegally transporting a handgun and possessing cocaine after he was pulled over by police while driving a friend's truck in May 1987. Apparently the prosecutors had too strong a case. The case wasn't dropped. Instead, the prosecutors and Fenner's attorney reached an agreement acceptable to Prince George County Circuit Judge Jacob Levine. Sentencing would be on March 23, with the maximum penalty being four years in prison and a $25,000 fine.

It might be a while before the young tailback would carry another football.

Fenner had tried to re-enroll at UNC in the hopes of continuing his education and eventually returning to the gridiron to showcase his football talents. As a sophomore tailback, Fenner had been the leading rusher in the ACC. He wouldn't carry the ball for North Carolina again. The university refused to re-admit him.

UNC athletic officials were wondering if the fallout from the Fenner "situation" would ever subside and thus keep the sports pages clear for news about the basketball program.

The next day in Durham, coaches Dean Smith, Jim Valvano, and Mike Krzyzewski met as members of the same team to help a drug-prevention campaign promote anti-drug basketball trading cards. They were joining various local police departments, area businesses, and an adolescent care unit in an effort to educate area youth about misuse of drugs and alcohol.

The program had begun a year earlier when the Tar Heels alone had adorned the trading cards. In an effort to expand the program, both the State and Duke basketball teams joined the consciousness-raising effort. Over 500,000 of the trading cards would be distributed to the fourth through sixth grades of area public schools. The cards were not for sale.

"I think we all realize that our players are role models, whether they like to be or not," Smith said. "I think they handle it well, and certainly this type of use of their name goes with their blessing."

In addition to a full-color photo of a player or coach on the front of the card, the back contained biographical information about the individual and an anti-drug message. J.R. Reid's read: *In basketball, if you score the most points you will win the game. If you score with drugs, you will be the big loser.*

The coaches pointed out that the program allowed the athletes and the athletic departments a chance to show the positive side of collegiate athletics. Krzyzewski wanted the public to know how much of a community asset collegiate sports are. "I hope it's an indication to the media, especially, what a positive influence intercollegiate athletics can be," he said.

Coach Valvano took the anti-drug issue personally, as he has children in the age bracket receiving the trading cards. "I see the problems they have with drugs and we have to get the message across — don't do drugs." Valvano, always one to make the most of any chance to display his great sense of humor, got in a mild dig at Smith. The N.C. State coach and athletic director asked the program sponsors a show-stopping question. "How many Jim Valvano cards does it take to get a Dean Smith card?"

The question was rhetorical, for no Smith cards had been printed for the 1988 distribution, making them priceless. A more important question might have been, how do the individual athletic programs deal with drug and alcohol usage among their players? North Carolina point guard Jeff Lebo later said that the drug issue is addressed annually in Chapel Hill. "We have drug seminars two or three times a year. The FBI came to talk to us. And Mike Helms talked to us. He played at Wake Forest and got into drugs — he told us how it ruined his life. Coach had us visit Central Prison this year. Everybody should visit a prison. It's like a slap in the face."

The policies and speeches must be working. Though North Carolina cannot claim that its basketball players have never abused drugs or alcohol, news of substance abuse within the program has never reached the public in anything other than rumor form. Smith, his coaches, and his players prefer to leave such choices up to the individual, and hope that no one will disgrace themselves or the university. To date, only a few former players have stumbled, and then only after leaving Chapel Hill.

UNC 88, CLEMSON 64

Points of view differ depending on which hometown newspaper "reports" the news. Utilizing the same amount of two-column space, two newspapers, within 150 miles of each other, delivered headlines that expressed different opinions of the Tar Heel's win at Clemson on Thursday, February 4.

The day following the game, the *Herald-Journal* in Spartanburg, South Carolina, titled its UNC-Clemson game story "Tar Heels take Tigers, 88–64." *The Chapel Hill Newspaper* saw fit to proclaim "UNC whips Tigers, 88–64." Action verbs notwithstanding, neither newspaper's headline gave justice to the closeness of the game.

Clemson coach Cliff Ellis set the record straight. "The score was not indicative of the way the game was played. We took some gambles at the end and had to foul."

"At the end" was immediately following Jeff Lebo's three-point play with 4:42 remaining in the game. His acrobatic drive and an Elden Campbell foul resulted in a three-point play. That slowed what had been a Clemson onslaught, and when Campbell fouled out on the next UNC possession, it became the starting point for a 22–2 North Carolina closing spurt. Until that point, the Tigers smelled an upset.

The "deaf valley" crowd roared behind the struggling home team, hoping to upset the eighth-ranked Tar Heels. Clemson, beset by guard problems, including the loss of Donnell Bruce two nights earlier to a broken hand, needed strong 40-minute performances from its guards and stellar support from the remaining starters. It managed the first, but with Campbell and sixth-man Dale Davis on the bench with five fouls, the Tigers and their fans lost their growl.

"Lady luck has not shined on the guard position at Clemson this season," Ellis noted. "When you go back to last April, this is the fourth player we have lost at the shooting guard position. First, [upperclassman] Michael Tait was not granted a hardship year. Then [would-be senior] Michael Brown was dismissed from the team in September. [Sophomore transfer] Chris Duncan left school at mid-semester and now this injury to [Donnell] Bruce."

Lady luck didn't shine on the Clemson shooters, either. The Tigers only managed 42 percent from the floor, including a two-of-17 effort from three-point range and four of 17 from the free-throw line. Dean Smith felt his team's defense was the reason. "I thought we played our best defense of the season in the first half," Smith said. "On the stat sheet, it only showed 10 turnovers for Clemson, but we were tipping a lot of balls, deflecting a lot of passes."

Smith has long discredited the stat sheet (actually the official NCAA basketball box score prepared by the sports information departments of the hosting school) as not providing the complete picture. His coaching staff feels that there are many important factors superseding those that show up in the final box score. Though there are many statistics the UNC coaching staff notes, points per possession is the most critical.

Smith provided the gist of his philosophy in the introduction of his textbook entitled *Basketball: Multiple Offense and Defense*, published in 1982. In the book, Smith credits the statistical evaluation system's origination to a joint effort while he was an assistant to Bob Spear at the Air Force Academy in 1955. First written for Coach Frank McGuire's book *Defensive Basketball*, Smith called the system "possession evaluation." "Possession evaluation is determined by the average number of points scored for each possession of the ball by a team during the game. A perfect game from an offensive viewpoint would be an average of 2.00 points for each possession. The perfect defensive game would result in holding the opponent to 0.00 (scoreless). Our goals are to exceed .85 points per possession on offense and keep our opponents below .75 points per possession through our defensive efforts."

Obviously, with the incorporation of the three-point shot, the points per possession average slightly increases. In a North Carolina perfect-game situation, however, the offense wouldn't need to utilize the three-point shot. Smith's offensive objective is to look for and to score the highest percentage shot. Though various shooters (Jeff Lebo, Ranzino Smith, Kevin Madden, and ultimately Steve Bucknall and Scott Williams in 1987–88) have the green light to attempt the outside shot, the long-range jumper is still a secondary objective in the overall offensive strategy at UNC. Exceptions occur only when North Carolina faces a tight zone that isn't penetrable or when the Tar Heels are behind late in a game.

•   •   •

With most of the ACC in action, the Tar Heels began the weekend with anything but basketball on their minds. It was their first weekend off since the second weekend in November and the players were looking forward to it. Vacations are rare with the North Carolina Tar Heels.

The weekend had actually begun for the team following class the day before. After the 9 p.m. game against Clemson Thursday night, the team made a quick exit for the bus to the Spartanburg Airport to catch a chartered plane back to Raleigh-Durham Airport. From the airport, the team boarded another bus for the 40-minute ride back to Chapel Hill. Nobody got into bed before 2:30 a.m. The company rescheduled the travel plans at the last minute to ensure that Ranzino Smith and another teammate would not miss a test in a 9 a.m. class. There was to be no practice until the following Monday.

The players could catch up on whatever sleep they had missed over the long weekend, but most of the players weren't looking forward to sleeping the extra time away. "We don't play a game for another week and we've got a couple of days off," Ranzino Smith said, speaking for many of his teammates. "We're going to catch up on our studies, relax, and catch up on our social lives. The only thing I may do that has to do with basketball is do a little bit of running to stay in shape."

"Yeah, the only basketball I'll see this weekend is what I see on television," Steve Bucknall added. The team's eyes would be glued to the tube Saturday afternoon to watch the game between N.C. State and Duke. Considering a Wolfpack win would throw the conference into a three-way tie for first place between Duke, State, and UNC, it wasn't hard to figure out whom Tar Heel fans were rooting for.

The Wolfpack delivered a 77–74 victory and the conference race began afresh. If the season were to end the next day, it would mark the 24th straight season the Tar Heels finished first, second, or third in the ACC. Another UNC tradition would continue.

• • •

While Duke, State, and Carolina were equal as far as the conference standings and all three had been to the Final Four in the '80s, there was at least one stark contrast in the three basketball programs. The programs chose three different travel plans after playing the Tigers of Clemson. The Tar Heels chose to fly home via a chartered jet. The Wolfpack would fly commercial. And Duke, currently ranked fourth in the nation, made the trip back home in a bus.

• • •

With nine active North Carolina alumni playing in the NBA, it could be argued that the leading professional roundball training ground is in Chapel Hill. Four of the nine players led their respective NBA teams in terms of salary. UNC also contributes to the international scene by sending many of its former starters and role players overseas to play in the European leagues. A degree in basketball from North Carolina is a virtual guarantee into a gymnasium anywhere in the world.

The reigning Ph.D. of hoops, and easily one of the finest players ever to grace the space above the floor, demonstrated much of what he learned in his brief stay at UNC. The Chicago Bulls' Michael Jordan went airborne Saturday, February 6th, to win his second straight NBA Slam Dunk contest, and didn't land until after he secured the NBA All-Star Most Valuable Player award Sunday afternoon. He did it all in front of his new hometown crowd in the windy city of Chicago. Scoring 40 points on a 17-of-23 shooting performance, grabbing eight rebounds, stealing the ball four times, and adding four assists, the 24-year-old made an indelible mark in the record books.

"The whole weekend was fun," Jordan told reporters. "I felt I was home. It felt really good and it's something to remember. It was my first opportunity to win the MVP."

One million fans provided the opportunity, voting Jordan the top (most popular) All-Star. His teammates on the Eastern squad ensured the weekend was one to remember. Isiah Thomas, Larry Bird, and former UNC teammate Brad Daugherty helped clear the runway for many of Air Jordan's takeoffs. "The players were paying me a homecourt tribute," Jordan said. "It was a great display of great gratitude from my peers." One of those peers, Dominique Wilkins, Jordan's slam-dunk rival on Saturday, could have won the MVP honors had he not played so unselfishly. His 29 points and high-soaring efforts were just slightly less dramatic than Jordan's.

"We wanted to put on a good show," Wilkins said, "and he did it. It's his town and he did very well."

Carolina was well represented in the All-Star ranks. On one memorable series in the second period, Jordan stole a pass and led a fast break with Daugherty filling the middle. Jordan passed to the swooping Cleveland Cavalier center, who leapt to lay in the ball — but out of nowhere came a third former Tar Heel to block the shot. James Worthy, playing despite tendonitis in his knees, managed to thwart the Jordan–Daugherty effort. The three Tar Heels kept the game in hand for a few more minutes, as Daugherty found Jordan with a blind pass on the next possession for an easy two points and Jordan then fouled Worthy for a three-point play at the other end of the floor. For a few brief moments, Tar Heel fans were in heaven.

• • •

The next day, the Temple Owls made their first appearance at the top of the Associated Press rankings, tallying 23 first-place votes. Temple jumped over four other teams after a week of several Top 20 losses to become the fifth team to hold the nation's top ranking. Since the last poll, 13 ranked teams had lost at least one game to tumble downward in the sportswriters, and broadcasters, poll.

North Carolina, with only a win against a decimated Clemson team to show for the week's effort, still climbed up two notches to the sixth spot. Duke, previously the fourth-ranked team, dropped into a tie for eighth after losing at home to N.C. State. The Wolfpack, by virtue of the Duke upset, rejoined the Top 20 at number 16.

With fortunes changing at the drop of a hat, Coach Smith was convinced North Carolina's rankings were still inflated and his team didn't stack up to other UNC teams in the past. "We're not a Final Four team," Smith said after the Clemson win. "We're not a good team. I think last year was a Final Four team; we just didn't make it. That's why they play the tournament.

"I don't think we have a Final Four team this year, but maybe we'll get lucky."

UNC 75, N.C. STATE 73

After managing a three-way tie for first place in the ACC with a 5–2 record, UNC began the second round of conference action with a no-holds-barred thriller in the Smith Center on February 11. The sixth-ranked Tar Heels and the 16th-ranked Wolfpack, also tied for first, fought for 45 minutes in an overtime contest that showcased the strengths of both teams, and more noticeably, both coaches. Dean Smith and Jim Valvano, two of the nation's better coaches, used every trick up their sleeves to grab a victory and stay atop the conference standings with Duke.   "Obviously, it was a heck of a ball game," Valvano said after the game. "It was a great one to win, and an extra difficult one to lose."

The win could eventually decide where each team began the NCAA tournament a month later. With the Smith Center designated as the first round tournament site, both teams wanted a crack at playing before a "home" crowd. Both teams had a shot at playing in Chapel Hill, but the conference champion had the best chance.

"I've said this before," Valvano continued, "and I won't change my mind about this. Teams shouldn't be allowed to play on their home courts in the tournament, but as long as it's the way it is I would like to play here again in front of our fans."

But whoever got the chance wouldn't know until later. In the meantime, the fans, 21,444 boisterous individuals, created the most vocal and demonstrative crowd ever to witness a game in the Smith Center. Charles "Lefty" Driesell, one of only two coaches to win a game against Smith in the Dean Dome, remarked that the crowd sounded like the ones that used to cheer against his old Maryland team in Carmichael. (ESPN had assigned Driesell broadcast duties for the national telecast of the game.) And while the crowd's aspirations rose and fell with their respective ballclubs throughout the momentous game, only Driesell calmly went about his business of predicting what each coach would do as each new situation arose. His experience of coaching and winning against both coaches qualified his insights. Though he didn't know the outcome, he knew the moves and countermoves of the two master tacticians even before they were made.

The game wasn't predictable from the fan's point of view, however.

North Carolina's Jeff Lebo stole the opening tip and J.R. Reid scored on a jump hook just 11 seconds in the game. The two points may have been the difference in the 75–73 win by the Tar Heels, but the game wasn't over until the final second ticked off the clock. Reid's total offensive output didn't affect the game as much as his defensive work on State's Charles Shackleford. After only five minutes of play, both Reid and Shackleford had scored the majority of the points they would tally in the game. The name of the game turned into stopping the opponent in the paint. Carolina's Reid and Scott Williams won the battle against Shackleford and Chucky Brown on the inside, outscoring their counterparts 26–16. Rebounding was about even. What little edge the Tar Heels gained in the middle, the Wolfpack made up for outside.

State's starting guards, Vinny Del Negro and freshman Chris Corchiani, scored only two points from the field in the first half, but along with help from another freshman, Rodney Monroe, the trio delivered a series of outside jumpers in the second half to force an overtime. The Tar Heels led throughout the second half and were seemingly in command with a six-to eight-point advantage down the stretch. With a seven-point lead and only 1:06 showing on the clock, a few fans were poised and ready to bolt for their cars. But knowledgeable observers were too familiar with the State-UNC rivalry to move prematurely.

True to form, both coaches knew the game was far from over. Valvano and his 1987-88 version of the infamous Cardiac 'Pack could employ numerous strategies to narrow the margin, although the Tar Heels were ready with the latest edition of the famous Four Corners delay game. The game was just beginning.

Monroe, who was instrumental in the Wolfpack charge with four of six three-pointers, came off the bench to give State a three-guard attack. It worked. Carolina's Kevin Madden had substituted into the game for defense in place of Ranzino Smith. That was a mistake. Madden was not 100 percent recovered from an ankle injury and suffered in quickness. The quick-shooting Monroe whisked down the floor and scored a 20-footer from the right wing to cut the margin to four points at 76–63. Chucky Brown fouled Reid on the Tar Heels' next possession, but the future pro missed the front end of a one-and-one. State scored again, this time on a 10-footer from

Brown. Carolina held a two-point lead, but looked tentative in trying to run off some time and Madden threw the ball away.

"It's my fault Kevin threw that last pass away," Smith offered in defense of his sixth man. "I had made up my mind that I wouldn't play him, but I looked down there [on the bench] and he wanted to play — it wasn't fair to put him in there with that ankle. It was my fault."

Brown, who tipped away Madden's pass, almost converted on a layup to tie the score. It didn't matter. Del Negro was right behind Brown to tip in a follow shot that tied the game. It was anybody's ball game with 23 seconds remaining in regulation. Scott Williams signaled for a Tar Heel timeout.

North Carolina set up to get the ball into Lebo's hands. The Wolfpack was ready to foul anyone except Lebo or Smith, who rejoined his team as a one-man offensive platoon. Valvano's decision was to foul early, force a Tar Heel to shoot a pressure-packed one-and-one, and then have a chance to tie or win the game. Smith's plan was to keep the ball in the hands of either Lebo or Smith, both excellent free-throw shooters, and try to work the ball inside to Reid. Both teams flunked their assignments. The Wolfpack had a chance to foul Reid at :14, but didn't.

"The new [intentional foul] ruling is tricky," Valvano said later, reflecting on the play. "The 25,000 fans know that we're going to foul, Lefty [Driesell] is telling everyone watching the game on television that we're going to foul, and the referees know that we need to foul — hey, we're going to foul. But if we do it too aggressively, then we'll get an intentional foul and that's the ball game. If we're too cute about it, then it might not get called."

Meanwhile, Lebo evaded a series of Wolfpack defenders, but couldn't elude the sure hands of Shackleford. The point guard penetrated the paint and looked to dish off to Reid or Williams. Both were covered, and Lebo had no choice but to put up a weak layup. His attempt was slapped into the third row of seats by "the Shack." With five seconds still showing on the clock, UNC primed for one more attempt. Lebo again took the shot, missing wildly from three-point range.

Overtime.

Neither team had demonstrated enough prowess to win the game outright, but neither team was willing to concede anything. After an official timeout, both teams came out on the floor with their starting lineups still intact. With five full minutes to play, each team was determined to carefully work the ball inside and see what happened.

State won the tip, but couldn't convert. UNC did, with a Reid layup off of a Smith alley-oop pass. State answered with a Brian Howard tip-in to tie the game at 69. UNC's Steve Bucknall, who performed yeoman duty on defense all evening, committed his fifth turnover. State missed a shot. Bucknall seized the opportunity to make up for his previous error by zipping a pass to a streaking Williams for a slammer. State missed again. Coach Smith felt it was a good time to insert King Rice as a defensive platoon for Ranzino Smith. It worked, but on the offensive side of the floor. Rice fed Reid in the lane for an easy two points. The Tar Heels led by four, at 73–69. Bucknall fouled Del Negro, who made both shots. Smith inserted his offensive platoon, Ranzino Smith, with the Tar Heels up by two. Rice took the quarterback spot in the Four Corners, spotted Williams underneath the basket, and delivered a semi-lob pass for another slammer. State called timeout and Coach Smith inserted Rick Fox for Ranzino Smith.

Down by four points with only seven seconds on the clock, the Wolfpack needed a three-point shot with a foul, or two two-pointers, to tie and force another overtime. They got neither. Corchiani danced to the three-point line with Rice draped all over him and still managed a shot. From the stands it looked as if another Valvano prayer was answered — the shot was good, and it looked like Rice had fouled him in the process. No whistle sounded, however, and Corchiani quickly called for a timeout. His shot had been made with two seconds remaining, but the buzzer sounded before he could call time. The officials ruled his shot good for two points only. Final score: Carolina 75, State 73. The Tar Heels remained in a tie for first place.

Dean Smith was brief in his remarks to the press, and UNC sports information director Rick Brewer announced to the assembled media that the Tar Heel locker room would only be open for 15 minutes. One would have thought the Tar Heels had lost. Writers could choose between hearing Smith or questioning his players.

"I'm very pleased to have won," Smith understated. "I was very proud of our team to come back and win in overtime after losing the lead and not playing smart at the end of regulation. We congratulate N.C. State on a great comeback. We didn't do the things we should. We're not a young team any more and that's why it is disappointing to make the mistakes we did at the end."

North Carolina had indeed made too many mistakes, but they were made throughout the game. The Tar Heels turned the ball over 23 times, twice in overtime. In addition, the team shot poorly from the free-throw line, an area where UNC players usually shine. The mistakes should have been more costly, according to State's Chris Corchiani. "We had three opportunities to win in overtime," Corchiani told reporters in a quiet locker room, "and that still wasn't good enough. Anytime a team gives you three chances to go up two points in overtime — there's no excuse — you should do it."

• • •

It was obvious Valvano wasn't pleased with the end result, either. A chance to beat his nemesis in the Smith Center doesn't come too often. The Italian coach had never won a game in Chapel Hill, and he reminded his players of that fact after the game. Reporters waiting outside the State locker room to interview the players overheard a tongue-lashing that would have made a sailor's wife blush.

But Valvano regained his composure before addressing the press. "We played about as well as we could in the first 13 minutes, but then our offense struggled in the second half. That was mainly due to Carolina's defense, not because we weren't putting out the effort. In overtime, we really had every opportunity to win. I think we had two chances to take the lead and we didn't."

Valvano's mood lightened as he realized his team had still played an exceptional ball game. The quick-witted coach from Seaford, Long Island, always has time for the media, win or lose. His easygoing manner is in direct contrast to Smith's. Few writers are ever relaxed enough to ask Smith a tough question, fearing a rebuke. Valvano takes on all questions, rarely ridiculing the occasional student reporter's uninformed query. His remarks are candid and refreshing compared to the controlled and repetitious answers given by Smith.

"You know what I'm going to do?" Valvano offered after noting he has never won a game in Chapel Hill. "I'm going to schedule a game over here next year and win. It won't be Carolina, though. We've won five times in eight games at Duke, and everybody says that's supposed to be the toughest place in the league to play. We've won at every place in the league at least once, except here. I may never win here."

UNC 64, VIRGINIA 58

Just when it looked like North Carolina was going to be sweet and present arch rival Virginia with a gracious Valentine sentiment, the fickle visiting team from Chapel Hill decided to be a tease instead. Though the Cavaliers led throughout the Valentine's Day game, the 18–3 Tar Heels snatched a win in the final minute to further depress the 12–12 Virginia basketball program and its coach.

In lieu of flowers or candy, sixth-ranked North Carolina rolled into Virginia's University Hall and presented the Cavaliers with a different kind of gift. It was a gift the Tar Heels seemed reluctant to give. In just a little over six minutes of very intense basketball, UNC gave the Cavaliers an 18–2 lead. Virginia came out smoking, hitting 10 of its first 11 shots, including five three-pointers and two other jumpers from just inside the bonus area. The Tar Heel's aggressive man-to-man defense kept the Cavaliers outside the paint, but not outside the basket. UNC answered by playing its worst offensive basketball of the season. The Heels were able to get the ball into J.R. Reid, but not into the hoop. Reid managed only two of nine attempts from the floor in the first half. "Sometimes we can be very stubborn about getting the ball to J.R. inside," Jeff Lebo said after the game. "He was having a tough time, though. He couldn't get the shots to go down."

Smith's team didn't appear rattled by the opening minutes. The Tar Heels requested no timeouts, though they suffered until the 11:36 mark. Luckily, ESPN needed a chance to air a couple of commercials. Smith's distaste for calling timeouts to halt momentum makes sense in a second half. It is critical to have an adequate number of timeouts at the end of the game. But not using a timeout during a first-half 18–2 run smacks slightly of arrogant stubbornness, although it can be argued that a televised game supplies more than enough breaks. Another possible defense for Smith's decision may have been the desire to continue the up-tempo game and tire out Virginia's starters.

Still, the discipline Smith demands of his team pays off in clutch situations. The loyalty that develops between a coach and his team is crucial. Smith takes his team to the edge and back so often that the players would follow him over a cliff if asked. In the Virginia game, Smith wanted to get the ball inside to Reid, and inside to Reid it went. The fact that Reid wasn't able to score didn't alter the strategy. The indifference to anything outside of the planned strategy is both laudable and inflexible.

On one hand, North Carolina's unwavering sense of purpose works toward what has been described as a will to win no matter what the odds. Smith makes no secret of the fact that the games he relishes are those whose outcomes are determined in the final seconds. Since many of their games appear to go down to the wire regardless of the opposition, it's smart to instill a sense of "we can win in any situation." Each time the team escapes with a win there is one more "learning experience" committed to memory. In win-or-lose sudden-death situations, North Carolina, more often than not, wins.

On the other hand, Smith's dogged determination to use what is "percentage-wise" the best strategy in a given situation sometimes works against the team's best interests. If the other team is playing them straight up, with no special defensive strategy, the Tar Heels' odds of winning increase. Their teams are always stocked with an abundance of talent that can compete with anybody on the collegiate scene. If the other team is prepared for their predictable "work-it-inside" game plan, the odds of a

UNC upset are greater. In 1987-88, North Carolina's basic game plan was to work the ball inside to Reid, and then to kick the ball back outside to Lebo or Ranzino Smith if there was no shot for him — a well-tested "inside-outside" strategy. If the opponents can shut down either or both, then their odds of winning multiply.

This said, wins over North Carolina are few and far between, especially for Virginia's head coach, Terry Holland. UNC has beaten the Cavaliers 13 of the last 14 times the teams have played each other. Overall, Smith has a 24–7 winning record over Holland-coached teams. With the ongoing personal feud still subtly in place, the game will continue to carry greater significance for the two programs. After the Virginia game, John Feinstein, a *Washington Post* writer always on the lookout for controversy, asked Dean Smith a loaded question. "Do you dislike playing Virginia more than any other team in the league?"

"Any other questions?" Smith responded, after a pause for nervous laughter. "I'll answer your question. Terry and I differ a lot on how men can move without the ball. The defense cannot jump out by rule. He interprets the rule that if I have possession, I can play with you the whole day."

Feinstein interrupted, asking the coach if he was saying yes.

"Naw," Smith said, refusing to succumb to Feinstein's loaded question. "They have a class program at Virginia . . . I like playing them . . . when we win, put it that way."

Since their earlier, more turbulent times, both coaches go out of their way to tone down in public their personal feelings for each other in private. Still, the bad blood has a way of trickling into the system of each new player for both programs. Real blood has a way of flowing when the two teams take to the floor.

"Whenever we play Carolina, it's the same thing," Virginia guard John Johnson told Kevin Record of *The Daily Progress* in Charlottesville the day before the game. "You always get into a fight with them or a shoving match. Things just get totally out of hand." Teammate Mel Kennedy likened it to a battle. "I'm not going out there thinking it's going to get ugly, but I'll tell you right now, I know it's going to be a war. Almost like a fight. I'm just going out there to play hard and destroy my opponent. The team has got to get it through their heads that it's not going to be any kind of a soft game. There's going to be elbows flying, there's going to be pushing, shoving, talking, spitting — whatever."

Reid, one of the objects of the Wahoos' affections, stressed that he liked a physical game. He knew he would get one against Virginia. What he didn't know was how much Virginia's physical attention would affect his shooting touch. "Virginia likes to make up for a lack of talent on defense," Reid told reporters in an unintentional slur. "They body-up hard down low, getting underneath you and riding you out, trying to make you change your normal shots." Reid's shots were so altered that his highest percentage shots, normally jump-hooks from close range, were those from the free-throw line. He made 10 of his total 16 points from the charity stripe. In the second half, Reid only scored from the floor once.

Coach Holland's game plan was to stop Reid with a barrage of fresh Cavaliers. It worked. "I thought we did a great job of staying between Reid and the basket," he said. "Let's face it, he's a fantastic player. But somewhere along the way they [the officials] have to call them the other way, too."

Holland's "sixth man," the vocal crowd of 8,200 on hand, also did an effective job of letting the sophomore from Virginia Beach know his annual "homecoming" wasn't appreciated. From pregame warm-ups until the final buzzer, Reid, who at one point considered attending Virginia, was the center of attention from the stands. Every time Reid touched the ball, the crowd booed. Every miscue was roundly applauded. Cheers of "way to go, J.R., way to go" echoed off the ceiling of the domed arena when he missed a shot. Reid managed to overcome his offensive woes with a strong defensive effort.

"There're going to be games when you don't shoot well and things don't seem to go your way," Reid acknowledged to reporters when asked about his performance, "But you can always go out and play defense. That's what the coaches always tell us. Nobody really shot well today, so we had to make it up on defense. That's how we got the victory. It was all on defense."

The North Carolina defense was the only constant in the game. After Virginia cooled off midway through the first half, the Tar Heels slowly mounted an offense. Smith wanted to trim the 16-point lead to 10 by the half. He got his wish as the Tar Heels went into the locker room down by a 33–25 margin.

In the second half both teams started out slowly. The Cavaliers maintained an eight-point cushion, but in less than five minutes the intensity picked up, as did the number of Virginia personal fouls. In one 30-second spurt, officials whistled the Cavaliers for five fouls, including a technical on Holland for "running down to the other end of the bench" away from the action after Virginia reserve Bill Batts picked up his fourth foul. The sequence did little to cut the scoring margin, but eventually the Virginia foul situation softened up the middle. Two minutes later, UNC scored 10 unanswered points to cut the lead to three. Virginia ran its lead to four points one last time before the Tar Heels kicked in an eight-point scoring run to take the lead for good. Virginia, within two points with 12 seconds remaining, had to foul Lebo and then Smith, who were running the Four Corners delay. They both made the clutch foul shots. Final score: UNC 64, Virginia 58.

Senior Ranzino Smith, one of only a few Tar Heels who knew that close games are common UNC occurrences, summarized the game simply. "Down the stretch, we did what we had to do." Nothing more, nothing less.

• • •

In the polls that week, the top four teams held fast, but North Carolina edged upward to the fifth spot of the Associated Press poll. Their narrow win at home against N.C. State and road victory over Virginia were not instrumental in the move; Pittsburgh dropped from fifth to eighth after losing to Syracuse and beating Villanova. Duke moved up two rungs to the sixth spot.

Temple, scheduled to meet the Tar Heels in the Dean Dome the following Sunday, retained its top ranking by beating both Villanova and George Washington handily. George Washington Coach John Kuester, a former Tar Heel role player under Smith, said that he felt Temple was good but didn't think it was the nation's best team.

"There are probably 20 number one teams," Kuester told the Associated Press. "Right now they deserve it. They have good inside people and can shoot from the outside." Ditto North Carolina. The game against Temple loomed as a big one, but two games still remained for the Tar Heels before they could think about playing another top-ranked team.

UNC 80, WAKE FOREST 62

"We felt all along that the key was to keep them from getting hot with the three-pointers," Steve Bucknall said after the second meeting between Wake Forest and North Carolina. "But we had some lapses."

Wake Forest was hot all right, shooting 75 percent from three-point distance, but not hot enough to burn fifth-ranked UNC. This time, the contest was won by Carolina. It was a game of quantity, not quality. The Tar Heels converted more baskets, made more steals, blocked more shots, and delivered more assists. The visiting Demon Deacons had more turnovers.

"We played very hard for 40 minutes," said Wake Forest head coach Bob Staak, "and I think if we had protected the ball better, we could have been right there at the end. They did an excellent job in forcing tempo and creating some turnovers with their traps."

The fast tempo greatly affected the outcome. Wake Forest came into the contest with only seven scholarship players. Two injured Deacons, Tony Black and Daric Keys, who had played against the Tar Heels when the Deacons upset then third-ranked UNC in January, watched from the bench.

"Although they didn't play any real significant roles in that [previous] game," Staak said, "I think Tony Black's decision-making at the latter part of the game when we had the lead was very helpful to our win. Keys was able to come off of the bench and give us some time to rest some people." The first breather for starting guards Cal Boyd and David Carlyle didn't arrive until UNC had safely salted away the victory late in the game's final moments.

In the first half, the Deacons controlled the contest, keeping the sold-out Dean Dome audience out of the game. All five Deacon starters scored within the first three minutes. Wake's "junk" defense held the primary North Carolina scoring weapons, Jeff Lebo and J.R. Reid, tightly in check. The Deacons played a 1–3 zone, with the remaining defender assigned to Lebo. Lebo would only shake the defense twice from the floor in the game, both times for three-pointers. Reid was also held well below his season scoring average, with just three baskets in 32 minutes. Instead of the usual firepower provided by the inside/outside attack of Reid/Lebo, UNC's current sixth man, Kevin Madden, ignited the offensive sparks.

Madden, still hampered by a nagging ankle injury, came off the bench to add outside scoring power to the lineup. He turned in an almost flawless offensive performance, hitting six of six from the floor, including three three-pointers, for 15 points. His only miss was from the free-throw line. Bucknall added 15 more to share the team-high scoring honors, but his 10 assists and strong defensive play were just as important. Bucknall shrugged off any personal credit, saying that he felt the team demonstrated a new cohesiveness.

"That's what we've been striving for this season — to be a team. Everybody says we're a young team. Then they started saying that we should be experienced by now. But we're growing together. We've got a lot of good players on this team. We don't have to have good games from J.R. and Lebo to win. They can't be perfect every time out."

If the Tar Heels had a major flaw, that was it, thinking they had to get the ball into the hands of either Reid or Lebo to win. The rigid philosophy of working it into the inside, embraced by most college coaches and especially Dean Smith, was gradually evolving into something more flexible. The new line of thinking went hand in hand with the three-point shot. If the inside was cut off, then the outside shot would be open. Though the Tar Heels paid lip service to "the shot goes to the open man," in truth the shot went to those brave enough to take the shot. Missed shots translated into missed playing time. Consequently, younger players like Pete Chilcutt and Rick Fox would pass up an open six-foot shot attempting to get the ball to a covered Scott Williams or Reid for a two-footer.

Coach Smith found he needed to encourage his players to *take* the shot, while still stressing the importance of patience and looking for the *best* shot. It is a fine line between the two, but if the team wereto develop into a great team, it would have to incorporate the best of both worlds.

•   •   •

At the game, *USA Today* had provided thousands of ballots for fans to vote for an All-Time Final Four team in honor of the 50th anniversary of the NCAA Division I Men's Basketball Championship. The ballot, broken down into five decades, listed ten players from each ten-year period. A panel of championship coaches and tournament directors had chosen the nominees. Only North Carolina could claim players listed from three decades: Len Rosenbluth from the 1957 team, Charlie Scott from 1968–69, James Worthy from 1981–82, and Michael Jordan from 1982.

UNC 74, MARYLAND 73

With two home games on tap for the February 20–21 weekend, the company line was, of course, that the only important game was the conference game against Maryland. The following day's game against top-ranked Temple University was, in Dean Smith's words, "for fun." The game against Maryland was a chance at the regular-season championship. To a man, the Tar Heels had only the Terps on their minds. The immediate goal was an ACC win to stay on top of the conference standings. If the fans wanted to think ahead to Sunday's game, so be it. But the UNC squad would concentrate on the task at hand. At least for the first twelve and a half minutes of the game.

North Carolina began the game with its best start of the season. Ranzino Smith and Jeff Lebo nailed a couple of early baskets around the perimeter and Scott Williams and J.R. Reid slammed in a few in the paint. The Terrapins weren't held scoreless, but with 7:38 left in the first period they were down, 28–11. The fans sat back further into the plush seats and began to dream of a Tar Heel domination of the Owls 24 hours later.

Losing the fans at a North Carolina basketball game is nothing new. Since the program's move to the Smith Center, the majority of the fans close to the action have attended only to be passively entertained and not to actively support the team. There was no real need to actually cheer on the home team — the home team always won. Better to just attend in lieu of watching prime-time fare on television at home. The Smith Center was comfortable and never deafening. In the name of sportsmanship, Dean Smith encourages the ushers to keep a watchful eye on the sections behind the baskets lest a rowdy fan let loose and wave his arms during an opponent's free-throw attempt. Though Smith's sense of fair play is commendable, his overly cautious attitude further stifles fan involvement.

The students, like students anywhere, are not pleased with cheering restrictions. Despite the pleas of highly charged cheerleaders, the sedate Educational Foundation fans are not interested in becoming hoarse for the sake of the team. The attendees from the student body are too few and far removed from the court to create a serious din. For this game, a new mascot was introduced in the Smith Center — a man in a ram costume. The ram, normally associated with the school's football program, has been the UNC mascot for over 60 years, but his appearance here didn't cause much of a reaction. In fact, the majority of the fans didn't know he was there, and the ones that did weren't enamored of the sheepish mascot. "Almost none of the students are in favor of it," said Andrew Podolsky, a sportswriter for *The Daily Tar Heel*. "There was a rumor going around that a student passed a note to a television broadcaster saying, 'The students at UNC claim no responsibility for the mascot on the floor.'"

One reporter was overheard commenting on the lack of effectiveness of the new mascot in stirring up fan support. "Another typical crowd in the Dean Dome," quipped Kip Coons of the *Durham Morning Herald*. "One ram and 21,000 sheep." Actually, the mascot acted quite sheepishly himself. The UNC student newspaper later ran a plea asking for the ram to be slaughtered or given some pep pills.

At the Dean Dome, an army of ushers in North Carolina blue jackets watch over the fans quite carefully. Hand-lettered "pep" signs are not permitted in the arena, either. "We don't allow any signs in the Smith Center," Willie Scroggs, assistant athletic director for operations, said after instructing an usher to confiscate a smuggled-in sign reading "Kinston Loves Carolina." "A professor told us that if we allowed any signs, we would have to allow all signs no matter what they said. Rather than have a sign that uses profanity or says something off-color, we choose to not allow any signs."

The brief unveiling of the small cardboard sign must have distracted the Tar Heels on the floor as well. Maryland began a run of its own, cutting the 17-point North Carolina lead to three, before an official timeout stopped the Terp momentum. UNC added five more points before going into the locker room with a comfortable eight-point lead. The fans stood, stretching and yawning, thinking the game was well in hand.

"The way we played defense in the first half," Smith said, "I felt we should have been ahead by 20 at the half. But our ball-handling wasn't very good in one stretch late in the half. We even threw it away with the numbers advantage on fastbreaks. We threw it away when we had three on twos, three on ones, and two on ones."

Maryland coach Bob Wade agreed. "We did a poor job of handling their pressure. We weren't coming to the ball strong. I told our guards not to pick up their dribbles. Carolina thrives on having people pick up their dribble so they can force a turnover with their trapping defense. But then we forced a few turnovers, too."

There were 42 recorded turnovers in the game.

Over the years, North Carolina's pressure defense has been good at forcing an opponent to turn the ball over. But in the past, the Tar Heels made the most of the additional scoring opportunities. In 1987–88, the team had not been able to capitalize on its opponent's mistakes. In a game that relied so heavily on momentum to determine the outcome, North Carolina had never developed a consistent killer instinct. Even with commanding leads, the Tar Heels weren't putting away teams. One additional reason for the many close games was their lack of ball-handling skills. The great point guards North Carolina has been famous for were missing. The Phil Fords, Jimmy Blacks, and Kenny Smiths had departed. UNC had recruited a potential point guard in LaBradford Smith, but he had elected, at the last minute, to attend Louisville, much to the surprised displeasure of Dean Smith. King Rice, a second choice, hadn't developed as fast as the need dictated. Though Rice could fill in and was picking up defensive skills quickly, his turnovers and lack of offensive firepower kept him out of the lineup.

To fill the vacant spot, Dean Smith was forced to convert an excellent number two shooting guard, Jeff Lebo, to the position. The added responsibilities hampered the sharpshooter's scoring abilities, and his lack of speed slowed down the North Carolina fast break. The Tar Heels were forced to rely on a secondary fast break to pick up easy baskets. Two number-two guards had emerged to play where Lebo could have excelled alone. Senior Ranzino Smith possessed a variety of offensive skills, but hadn't played up to his coach's defensive expectations and still made too many mistakes. Kevin Madden, a big guard/small forward, lost a lot of the momentum he had gained as a freshman. After sitting out a year to work on raising his grades, the redshirted sophomore didn't have the necessary quickness to play guard or the height to oust Reid or Williams from the front line. Steve Bucknall had earned the small forward spot by virtue of strong defense and was slowly developing his offensive talent.

On a basic skill level, the Tar Heels were excellent. Only quickness and a true point guard kept the team from being another great North Carolina team. This 1987–88 team was vulnerable — particularly in their ability to maintain big leads.

Maryland's senior leader, power forward Derrick Lewis, knew as well as anyone else that the current UNC squad was as beatable as any to come along in a long time. "We knew we could come back when we got down in the second half," he said later. "We're not going to give up until the final horn, and that was evident today."

It certainly was. The Terps fought hard for the first 15 minutes of the second half, trying to keep the North Carolina margin from climbing. UNC constantly got the ball to J.R. Reid, and he delivered on 10 of 13 from the floor for 21 points. But the Tar Heels couldn't pull away from the determined Terrapins, and Maryland's perseverance paid off. At the 4:34 mark, Wade's troops had whittled a 15-point lead down to just three. Dean Smith began his familiar platoon tactic to utilize Ranzino Smith's scoring ability and King Rice's defensive skill. With five seconds to play, Lebo blundered, committing his third foul, sending Maryland guard Steve Hood to the line. After Hood drilled both shots to cut the margin to two points, North Carolina called its first timeout.

Coach Smith made sure the ball would be inbounded to Ranzino Smith. Coach Wade made sure his team fouled immediately. After Smith hit both free throws, Maryland was down by four points with one second showing on the clock. The Terps inbounded the ball to Teyon McCoy, who turned and launched a 35-footer that found the target. Too little, too late. Final score: North Carolina 74, Maryland 73.

"We definitely did some positive things out there today," Lewis said. "We played hard even though we were out-manned. They had the size advantage and the home court advantage, but we kept fighting and we almost came away with the victory."

The game was close, and yet the crowd had never felt the outcome was in doubt. Smith and his team knew better. A concentrated 40-minute effort had once again evaded the immature team. They were no longer the young and inexperienced team that started the season —they were good enough to give Coach Smith his eighteenth consecutive 20-win season, however. His streak is the longest by any coach in the history of collegiate basketball.

The Temple Owls had been in town since Friday to prepare for the Sunday meeting with the Tar Heels. Head coach John Chaney had requested tickets for his players to attend the Maryland/UNC game, but was told there were no tickets available. The back-to-back games were sold out. Regardless, it is highly unlikely Dean Smith would have wanted a Top 10 team, much less the nation's top-ranked team, to scout the Tar Heels in person. The Owls settled in for the afternoon to watch North Carolina narrowly avoid an upset loss to Maryland.

TEMPLE 83, UNC 66

Less than 20 hours after beating unranked Maryland by a point, the fifth-ranked Tar Heels donned their Converse high-tops to take on the top-ranked Owls of Temple. The sneakers were still warm from the previous day's action, but the North Carolina squad was not. In its worst home loss in 13 seasons, UNC was pummelled, 83–66. The televised game showed the nation that Temple's 1987–88 team was for real, a true basketball strength. Just as important to future North Carolina opponents, the contest revealed UNC's weaknesses.

If the Tar Heels' offensive attack had a middle name, it would have been "Achilles." No longer hidden from view was the fact that the inside-outside offense mounted by J.R. Reid and Jeff Lebo was too predictable and too one-dimensional. Prior to the Temple contest, UNC was able to stick to its stated philosophy, and eventually it overcame most opponents in the final minutes of a game. Not against the Owls. Temple made sure the outcome was determined well before the Tar Heels could mount a late-minute challenge. Temple head coach John Chaney's plan was to pressure the ball out of the Tar Heels' hands and into the Temple basket. His team executed to perfection.

"We knew they had the capability to turn the ball over 20 or 25 times," starting Temple forward Mike Vreeswyk said. "But they won't do that unless they're under pressure. We force the tempo on defense more than we do on offense." The fierce zone pressure Temple exerted caused a record 29 North Carolina turnovers.

Still, it was Temple's fireworks on offense that added to UNC's demise. Temple converted better than 68 percent of its shots in the second half, including five of eight from three-point distance and 14 of 17 from the free-throw line. The Owls outplayed the Tar Heels in every aspect of the game except rebounds. In this instance, the Owls didn't need rebounds at either end of the court.

"Their offense was the key to the second half even though we weren't scoring," Dean Smith said after the game. "I didn't have our team prepared and that's my fault. We aren't a great ball-handling team and we tried to force too many passes." It was an interesting assessment from a coach who lives by the pass. Over-passing and unselfish play is so drummed into the team mindset that it's no wonder they can't adapt to another style of play at will. Couple those fundamentals with the fear of being jerked from the game for missing a shot and the whole team can look tentative at times.

On at least two occasions, Ranzino Smith was removed from the game promptly after missing a three-point attempt. His total playing time of 16 minutes was far below his average, and his absence hurt the team's outside chances. Substitute point guard King Rice, previously 0–4 from three-point distance and shooting 32 percent for the year from the floor, and swingman Kevin Madden, still not 100 percent after an injury, logged more time in the game than Smith. Against a zone defense, it was puzzling that the senior sharpshooter didn't play more. The North Carolina coach may have been making a statement to Ranzino about his defensive effort, but in sacrificing his shooting ability, the overall Tar Heel offensive production suffered.

Temple's Chaney has a different way of treating a cold shooter. Forward Mike Vreeswyk badly missed three of four three-point attempts in the first half. But his coach stuck with him and in the half the Owl's designated shooter hit four three-pointers en route to a 26-point game-high performance. "Coach [Chaney] never takes you out for missing shots," Vreeswyk said later. Chaney agreed, and said he never has to tell the high-scoring player to keep shooting. "Most of the time I just tell him he's the worst shooter in the world. But he doesn't believe it — he just keeps shooting." UNC players don't get the chance to miss many outside shots without risking a return to the bench.

One weakness North Carolina hadn't displayed before rose to the surface in the frustration of the onslaught. Unable to penetrate the Temple defense, the Tar Heels uncharacteristically waved a white flag. After a strong Temple run in the beginning of the second half, the Tar Heels made a brief effort to come back, only to give up prematurely. Even Smith, known for last-second tactics, pulled his starters off the floor.

Coach Smith maintained that the 1987–88 edition was not a great team. But in defense of its close wins and losses, he also noted that the team was very competitive. In its previous three losses, and four of its wins, the final outcome had been determined in the final seconds. If any single word described the current squad, it was "competitive." At least until midway through the second half of the Temple game.

Starting the second period down by five points, the Owls hooted for 19 unanswered points. Freshman guard Mark Macon and Vreeswyk lit up the scoreboard with a combination of dunks, layups, short jumpers, and three-pointers. While they were busy scoring, two teammates, forward Tim Perry and guard Howard Evans, were busy shutting down the Tar Heel offense. Perry led the charge inside, combining with his teammates in a matchup zone that thoroughly tied the hands of J.R. Reid in the paint. On the perimeter, Evans was busy creating havoc in the passing lanes, forcing altered passes, double dribbles, and walking violations. The frustration showed clearly on Reid's face. Even Evans, whose back was to the UNC basket, knew the sophomore All-American was losing control. "I could see

J.R. getting frustrated," he said later. "I've seen Carolina play a couple of times, and I knew the key to them was J.R. and Lebo. We weren't concerned about Scott Williams or Ranzino Smith. The key is J.R. and Lebo. We wanted to deny J.R. and frustrate him. He started talking to the refs."

The refs weren't listening.

UNC's floor general, Jeff Lebo, was trying to communicate to his teammates. Evans' heads-up play thwarted his efforts as well as his physical communiqués. "Every pass we made and every shot we took was contested," Lebo said after the game. Since he took most of UNC's passes and shots he would know. "We couldn't seem to get easy passes, anywhere. All the passing lanes seemed to have arms and legs in them."

Most of the arms and legs belonged to Evans. The 6–1 senior guard was a one-man wrecking crew. Starting at the point position in the Temple zone, Evans tallied seven steals, and he had more than ten deflections. "Our game plan was to make them rush their passes and shots. I was trying to read the guards and after a while I could read their passes." Evans kept his reading glasses on for the entire 40-minute game.

Dean Smith, recognizing a need for change, substituted guards continuously. Seven Tar Heels saw action in a guard role, including one who was virtually nameless to the crowd and the national television audience. Doug Elstun, a walk-on clad in a jersey without a name on the back, managed two minutes against the Owl first-stringers. At one point the Tar Heels, normally the picture of composure, didn't know who was supposed to bring the ball up the court, forcing one inbounder to attempt a full-court bullet pass. In another instance, Coach Smith had to yell to his substitutes while they awaited a Temple free throw, telling them who was to take the ball out of bounds. No UNC starters were in the game. Reid, Williams, Smith, and Lebo were on the bench.

"Kevin [Madden] and I were in the game at the four and five position," freshman Rick Fox said of the inbounds mix-ups. "I didn't know the four or five spot, so we were just trying to improvise with the guys who didn't know what they were doing." The mass confusion was atypical of a Tar Heel team.

Temple took no chances, playing three starters for the entire 40 minutes.

Chaney referred to the demonstrative win as "a morale builder." Dean Smith saw the rout as merely a disappointment and "a good learning experience." When questioned about what the team could learn from the blowout, Smith was curt, saying he wasn't sure. "That's something we'll have to talk about this week."

Smith could have used the game as a learning experience himself. Even a crafty veteran needs to be flexible in his philosophy at times. During the second-half 19-point run, Smith never called a timeout to try to halt the Owl's momentum. His longstanding belief that timeouts must be saved for the end of the game may have directly contributed to the eventual outcome. The Owls took control of the game immediately after halftime, running off 12 unanswered points before a TV timeout came to the Tar Heels' rescue nearly five minutes later. It proved to be too late, and UNC never recovered.

If the players felt they needed a brief respite, they didn't dare voice such mutinous thoughts in public. Even the freshmen knew how to handle the touchy subject of calling a timeout. "This is my first year," Fox said diplomatically. "I'm not sure when we should call them, but we need to learn more from experience. Instead of calling a timeout, we need to regroup even without a timeout. We just need to look to Lebo and Ranzino for leadership on the floor."

Ranzino couldn't have been any help, since he was on the bench doing penance for an earlier sin. Lebo said that the team was in its offense, but couldn't hold on to the ball. "We made some careless passes and it led to some easy baskets for them. It seemed like the harder we tried, the worse we got. I don't know why. I guess we'll just have to look at the films." Perhaps Coach Smith could have provided some answers. There seems to be little sense in protecting timeouts until the end if the end has already been determined.

"We did learn a few things about our weaknesses," Lebo continued. "We know the things that we need to work on. There's a fine line between being an average team and a good team and a good team and a great team. I think we're a good team, but we've got a lot of work to do to cross the line a be a great team."

Temple, by virtue of the 19-point run early in the second half, seemed to cross such a line. The Tar Heels had just three regular-season games left to make the transition.

There was *one* happier bit of news that evening.

A UNC News Bureau press release passed out in the press room in the Smith Center announced that Kimberly Ann Stewart had been named the first recipient of the Dean E. Smith Academic Scholarship at the School of Education. The $4,000 scholarship was awarded by the Dean E. Smith Foundation Inc. with monies given through a grant from the UNC Educational Foundation Inc. The Dean E. Smith Foundation had been created in 1987 by friends and admirers of the coach.

• • •

The fallout from the bomb that top-ranked Temple dropped in Chapel Hill began to settle. North Carolina, by virtue of their 83–66 loss to the

Owls, dropped from fifth to ninth in the AP basketball poll.

Duke moved into the Tar Heels' spot, up from sixth. The Blue Devils needed an overtime win on the road against unranked Kansas to keep from falling. N.C. State fell four spots to 18th after losing to Georgia Tech. The win by Tech allowed the Yellow Jackets to join the three other ACC teams in the rankings.

Georgia Tech had been 18th in the preseason standings, but had dropped out in the first regular-season ranking. The latest voting returned them to the fold and marked the first time that four ACC teams had appeared in the same poll in the same season.

•   •   •

On February 23, Coach Smith, sounding slightly depressed over his team's loss on Sunday, hooked up with the weekly ACC coaches' teleconference call with the media. The coach made no opening remarks, preferring to open the lines for questions. After responding to a question about North Carolina's next game at home against Clemson, Smith was asked if the loss to Temple would have any beneficial impact on the team.

"You never know," Smith answered. "Maybe a month from now we'll look back and say it was beneficial. It isn't beneficial right now the way the team, the staff, and I feel." Smith went on to graciously give credit to Temple, but couldn't hide his disappointment. "I feel like we were blown out, and we haven't had that happen around here for a long time. It could have a positive impact — at least it gets the players' attention. It won't be an easy week of practice."

When a program like North Carolina loses, thousands of fans are also depressed. A loss is not only unexpected, but personal. In North Carolina every office gathering place and every bar will overflow with fans debating possible solutions. Sportswriters working within the five-state ACC region quickly offered their opinions. Eddy Landreth, sports editor for *The Chapel Hill Newspaper*, tried to give the Tar Heel fans some inspiration during their despondency. In a column entitled "Early Spring," Landreth noted that March may have come a month early for the North Carolina program.

It was no secret that many fans and detractors felt UNC was the best basketball program in the country, but was notorious for losing the big games down the stretch in the NCAAs. Since 1981, North Carolina had lost to the eventual national champion during the tournament three times; they had lost one final and won another by a point. Getting into the NCAAs was no longer a serious challenge to the program. As far as the program's fans were concerned, the only truly successful season was one where North Carolina won it all.

Landreth felt the early "big-game" loss might take the place of a tournament loss later. In a few paragraphs that sounded evangelical in style and inspiration, the recent UNC grad wrote:

"If the Tar Heels keep the Temple disaster in the back of their minds as fuel to drive them, then they could become this year's team of destiny.

"Others will continue to use UNC as a measuring stick for success, and the only way for the Tar Heels to overcome that is to become driven, to mentally settle for nothing less than victory when they enter the upcoming tournament season.

"UNC has to be the team that, from beginning to end, refuses to yield, absolutely refuses to accept defeat. Carolina must be a team that doesn't play to not lose, but instead, claws, scratches and plays to win."

While national sports pages seemed to be offering more and more stories and columns concerned with curbing violence in collegiate basketball games, Landreth was proposing that the Tar Heels needed to ignite competitive fires.

Dean Smith wasn't concerned with his team's competitiveness. Though obviously not pleased with the lopsided loss to Temple, the coach finally had an example for his team that he might be able to use to its betterment. The team spent the entire week getting back to fundamentals in an effort to do what Smith called "realizing our limitations." The coach systematically called each player into his office for a personal interview to review the player's strengths and weaknesses.

Since the beginning of the season, Smith had voiced concerns about the team. While the country's media and coaches had voted UNC into the Top 10 continuously, Smith had contended the team was really not that good. In years past, Smith had cried wolf, saying similar pessimistic things about even his great teams. This season was different. The year before, North Carolina had possessed a stable of thoroughbreds, but the racehorse (point guard Kenny Smith) and the sturdy workhorses (forwards Joe Wolf and Dave Popson) had since left for the greener pastures of the pros.

On the strength of tradition — the program and the coach — UNC was still a national power. On a game-by-game basis, however, the team was just one of many strong college basketball teams. The media chose to illuminate tradition; Smith hoped to improve upon his current team.

The week featured intensive practice sessions and team meetings. No game would disrupt the journey back to fundamentals until the following Sunday. The week was free for a review before the big "test." If there was one skill stressed in practice, it was holding on to the ball. Throughout most of the season, the Tar Heels had handled the ball like it was greased. Against Temple, they had turned the ball over 29 times. "That wasn't going to happen again," said J.R. Reid, who had committed five turnovers against Temple. "We worked on protecting the ball all week. We had an added incentive in practice. If we lost the ball we had to run."

The weeklong practice session provided a rejuvenation of sorts. It was also a chance for the team to recover from the embarrassing blowout of a week ago. UNC hadn't been blown out by a team in years, and the taste of such a bitter memory needed to be washed out. With no game on the schedule, the Tar Heels took out their frustrations on each other, in hard-fought practice sessions.

"We had some very intensive practices," said Jeff Lebo. "There was a lot of pushing and shoving going on. There was much more diving for loose balls and stronger protection of the ball. Everyone seemed to have an extra spark in their eyes — even Coach Smith seemed to have an extra spark. Everyone was embarrassed by what happened against Temple."

If effort was going to be incorporated into the team's final grade, the Tar Heels were working for an "A."

UNC 88, CLEMSON 52

On Saturday, Clemson school officials released the news that two basketball players had been suspended from the team for involvement in selling complimentary passes. The school had suspended sophomore forward Sean Tyson for the season, and sophomore center Elden Campbell would miss the next day's North Carolina game.

"This situation was first brought to my attention this past Wednesday," Clemson head basketball coach Cliff Ellis said. "We did not have all the facts until Thursday and we reported the situation to the NCAA and the ACC office when we had all the facts."

Campbell, the top scorer on the team and the ACC's leader in blocked shots, would be sorely missed in the game the next day. Clemson was 2–9 in the conference and was not expected to win with or without Campbell. Still, with the Tar Heels reeling from the Temple loss, anything was possible.

The next day was Dean Smith's 57th birthday. The coach wanted any extra media attention to concentrate on his departing seniors. The game with Clemson would be the last home game for starting guard Ranzino Smith and practice player Joe Jenkins, but it was also the last time two senior managers would get the chance to toss towels to the team they worked for.

"I was happy for Joe Jenkins and Ranzino Smith," Dean Smith said in his postgame remarks to the media. "Ranzino's given us four years of doing exactly what we like. He's been a model citizen and he'll get his degree in May. Joe had two great years of JV — and made me think I should have played him last Sunday [against Temple] the way he knocked those [shots] in. We'll miss our student managers Mike Ellis and Kendria Parsons. If you have space, please list their names, it'll mean a lot to them." Smith has long favored UNC senior day festivities for two reasons. First, both senior starters and role players alike get a chance to start for the team in their final home game. His reasoning is that they should be rewarded, no matter how briefly, for the years of effort they have contributed to the team. Standing ovations were the order of the day.

"I'll never forget today," Jenkins said in a gush following the game. Experiencing the questions of the media was also a new adventure for the seldom-used forward. "I worked hard on the JV team and was very fortunate to get a chance to help the team this year on the varsity."

Secondly, Smith knew he would get a solid effort from the rest of his team. Senior Day usually occurs at a time when a conference win is important to the team's ACC standings and Smith is always looking for a psychological edge to help motivate them. The team is anxious to send off its upper-class heroes with a bang, and the seniors want to oblige their coach one last time in front of the home crowd. Ranzino's farewell was even more special in that light. The senior had grown up in the small town, playing and starring in front of its citizens since junior high, and eventually became the first local hoopster to receive a scholarship from Dean Smith. Ranzino Smith entered into his last home game as the third-leading scorer on the team, behind J.R. Reid and Jeff Lebo.

"It was very emotional for me," Ranzino said of the game and the experience. "It felt so good to know that I've worked all these years and lived to reach my goal. This was a great way to go out." Especially when you consider that Dean Smith tried to discourage the young man from ever attending the school. The 6–1 guard had dominated play on Chapel Hill High School's team — a program that won the state championship in 1980–81 and lost in the finals the following year — on the way to becoming the school's most prolific scorer ever. Ranzino was equally impressive at the North Carolina basketball camp and was singled out to demonstrate the correct way to shoot free throws by Coach Smith. Still, Dean Smith had been reluctant to offer the local hero a free ticket to UNC.

Dean Smith had been quoted as saying he hadn't intended on recruiting that year, as the present team was young, and set for the immediate future. The year before North Carolina had recruited Kenny Smith, Joe Wolf, and Dave Popson to add to a well-stocked team. But Smith had relented, and had added Ranzino and fellow prospect Matt Brust to the team, and still had room for two upper-class walk-ons, James Daye and Gary Roper. Smith had felt that Ranzino was too much of a defensive liability, and he told the young man he would not see much playing time. Much to the chagrin of the fans, who had always liked the guard's offensive firepower, Ranzino never shook his coach's initial impression. But all that was in the past. On Senior Day, Ranzino was only an asset to the team.

Clemson head coach Cliff Ellis grabbed at the special occasion to sidetrack attention from his depleted team. "We always seem to catch them at the wrong time," he said of UNC. "I think this is the fourth time we've played them on Senior Day. It always fires them up."

It was good that the coaches had a topic such as Senior Day to discuss. The game itself was a disaster. Down to ex-football players, freshmen, and walk-ons, the Tigers were extremely weak inside. The Tar Heels walked away with an 88–52 win. Only the UNC third-stringers enjoyed the game, with every member of the 14-man squad getting to play at least three minutes.

To sum up the game, writers and broadcasters needed only a paragraph or two.

Clemson kept the game close for the game's first 10 minutes by spreading out the North Carolina defense in a game-long Four Corners offense. UNC contributed to the early stalemate by squandering fast break opportunities. Neither team could put the ball into the basket. The Tars Heels shot horribly, connecting for only 32 percent of their shots, but the Tigers were worse: only 29 percent of their attempts found the inside of the hoop. Clemson freshman Colby Brown even tossed up an airball on a layup.

"We missed so many easy shots in the first half," Ellis said after the game. "We missed four- and five-footers, and just couldn't finalize the shots. It could have been a lot closer at the half." Had it been closer than the 35–18 halftime score, the television network covering the game would have been a lot happier. Droves of viewers switched channels by halftime. Thousands of the fans attending the game walked past the concession stands and headed for their cars.

To watch the second half took effort. Dean Smith took the opportunity to substitute for his starters, utilizing everybody suited up to play. Cliff Ellis took the opportunity to retire, choosing to coach the entire half without leaving his chair.

"We took better care of the ball today," Smith said in his obligatory remarks following the mismatch. "And I was pleased with our defense. It's obvious that Clemson was not up to strength. But I thought they had a tremendous idea." The idea turned out to be one he had shared with Ellis in his brief remarks to the coach at midcourt following the game. Lou Bello, a former referee and current radio broadcaster, asked Ellis what Smith had talked to him about immediately following the game. "Ellis said Smith told him that the spread offense that Clemson played was a good idea," Bello said. "He [Smith] said he should try it against Duke this week."

The elder head coach either complimented Ellis or merely was trying to encourage his counterpart at Clemson to beat Duke. At the time of their conversation, Duke was trailing UNC by only a game in the conference rankings. Smith didn't want the Tar Heels to need two more wins to gain the ACC regular-season crown; their difficult final game was to be in Duke's Cameron Indoor Stadium. With Duke's loss to Georgia Tech two hours later in Atlanta, the Tar Heels were assured of at least a tie for the regular-season laurels. North Carolina had two tough road games left to close out the season. A win at either Georgia Tech or Duke would give the Tar Heels their second consecutive outright regular-season championship. With the exception of 1986 when UNC finished third, the Tar Heels had finished first or second 21 times in 22 consecutive years.

Smith didn't get his birthday wishes answered completely. He knew his team had responded well to a week of work on fundamentals. The starting team had only turned the ball over five times, with only three more from the reserves. But he still didn't know if the team was improving and capable of beating a Top 10 team. "After this week of practice we would have been tough for anybody, but now we don't know, because Clemson is so far down without Campbell and other people and missing those easy shots — we don't know if we've improved. We still have the two toughest games on our schedule — at Tech and at Duke."

Both games would help provide the answers Smith sought.

•   •   •

Leap year meant leapfrogging for ACC teams.

For the fourth consecutive week, the nation's top four teams held fast in the AP college basketball poll. Temple had survived a scare, after disposing of UNC, to dig in at the top of the hill. Purdue, Arizona, and Oklahoma maintained their positions. The jockeying for top rankings, and ultimately good seedings for the NCAA tournament, was still heated throughout the other 16 positions, however.

Duke, after losing to N.C. State and Georgia Tech, dropped to ninth from the fifth spot. North Carolina jumped up three spots on the strength of losses by Duke, Michigan, and Pittsburgh. The team's lopsided win over Clemson didn't affect the polls. Valvano's Wolfpack was in the hunt, moving up to the 16th position. Georgia Tech rambled upward as well, jumping seven spots to 13th.

Odds were that the ACC teams' national rankings would again change before the season was over. With the possibility looming of a four-way tie in the ACC title race, it was anybody's guess who would walk away with the conference crown.

•   •   •

On Tuesday, March 1, the team held an afternoon practice in the Smith Center as a final tune-up for Georgia Tech. As usual, the main area of concern was defense, with the concentration on sprinting back to stop any Yellow Jacket fast breaks. The practice was smooth and efficient, and the team looked ready, willing, and more than able to slow down a rambling wreck on a seven-game winning streak — except for one thing.

On the sidelines for the entire practice was the team's main man. J.R. Reid, his thigh bandaged with a thick wrapping, hugged a ball and contented himself with providing verbal encouragement for his teammates. Wearing the blue jersey of the second team, Reid looked like a man without a country for the two-hour stretch of hoops. In addition, Scott Williams, the other half of the inside one-two punch, threw in the towel after only 45 minutes, limping to the trainer's room for rehabilitation. Williams returned minutes later with an ice pack wrapped around his right knee to sit and watch the remainder of the practice. It looked as though North Carolina would need a super effort from the rest of the team to offset the probable loss of their two big men. Without starters Reid and Williams, Tech would have a field day with the Tar Heels.

UNC 97, GEORGIA TECH 80

With the possibility of the ACC regular season ending in a four-way tie, the pressure was squarely on the shoulders of the Tar Heels Wednesday to determine their own fate. With ACC eyes focused on Atlanta, Georgia Tech relinquished its home court advantage at the on-campus "Thriller dome" for the much larger Omni Center a few miles away. It might just as well have been a thousand miles away. The Yellow Jackets' fans were buzzing for the home team, but their sting was removed midway through the second half. UNC quieted the crowd of 16,400 and its vocal detractors by crushing Tech, 97–80.

"All week long all we heard was 'four-way tie for first,'" Rick Fox said after the game, speaking for the team. They wouldn't hear that phrase again. By virtue of the team's best performance of the year, North Carolina had won the regular-season crown outright prior to its last game with Duke. It was sufficient cause for a Tar Heel celebration at midcourt after the game. UNC, usually a contender for the conference title, had not been overlooked in 1987–88, but was not the unanimous choice of all sportswriters. Midcourt celebrations were few and far between since they had attained superpower status. With the Tar Heels expected year in and year out to dominate most teams, the "underdog" celebrations became less frequent. During the Tar Heels' last few seasons, Smith had actually encouraged his team to visibly rejoice on occasion. On those rare occasions when the team is challenged beyond the norm, it is important to savor the moment.

"We proved everyone wrong," Jeff Lebo said with a smile. "We've been up and down — we're a young team, but we all stuck together. We had a goal and we accomplished it and it's really special this year because nobody thought we could do it. We don't get a chance at the underdog role very often."

They don't. But it should be pointed out that North Carolina had been narrowly chosen by the ACC sportswriters as the preseason favorite to win the conference championship in spite of losing two starters to graduation. Betting odds narrowed as the season progressed, however. And had the public known J.R. Reid hadn't practiced the night before, and that Scott Williams was able to run for only half of the workout, the odds against beating Georgia Tech and winning the championship outright would have been even greater. As it was, the team's best-kept secret stayed that way. There was no evidence in the game that either player was physically disabled. Both Reid and Williams each played 29 minutes of the contest and both could have played more if needed. Whether Marc Davis, UNC's trainer, had worked miracles overnight, or the duo had employed some form of mind over matter, wasn't important. The way in which they led their team was.

Williams, a streak player at times, was in full stride all evening. From the opening tip until Coach Smith inserted his blue team with two minutes to play, he provided much-needed leadership. He took charge of both boards, grabbing nine rebounds. From the free-throw line to the 17-foot jumpshot to the rim-rattling slam dunk, Williams seemed to score his 21 points from everywhere. He had two assists, one steal, and limitless emotion. Reid, another dominating force inside for the Tar Heels, outscored Williams with 24, shooting six of eight from the foul line. With Pete Chilcutt and Rick Fox adding points and rebounds, UNC was able to score inside at will. During one eleven-and-a-half-minute spurt, the Tar Heels hit 16 straight baskets. The offensive boards belonged to them as well, with the Tar Heels enjoying a 46–27 margin over the cold-shooting Yellow Jackets.

"That's the worst shooting performance that we've had in a long time," Georgia Tech coach Bobby Cremins said after the game. "We have to shoot well because we are a perimeter team — a team without a center. When we don't shoot well, it puts a lot of pressure on us defensively." And the Tar Heels jumped at the chance. The Tech fast break, so prevalent lately, never materialized.

Smith started his big lineup, with Kevin Madden in lieu of Ranzino Smith, intent on boxing out and out-rebounding the centerless Georgia Tech squad. King Rice filled in as the primary guard substitute and Ranzino was left riding the pine. It affected the Tar Heel attack, but not the eventual outcome.

With Ranzino out and Lebo cold from outside, the Tar Heels finished the game two of 11 from three-point distance. It didn't matter. Their inside attack caused Georgia Tech lots of foul trouble. The Heels also scored more than enough points to offset their weakened outside game and hurt the Yellow Jackets in other areas as well.

"To put it bluntly, they just killed us on the boards, and we couldn't hit anything from the outside," Georgia Tech center Tom Hammonds said, nursing his right ankle with an ice bag. Two other Yellow Jacket starters didn't help matters when they picked up their fourth personal fouls early in the second half. Forward Duane Ferrell picked up his fourth at 16:55 and headed immediately for the bench, and Craig Neal, Tech's floor leader, joined his teammate there a few minutes later. Within minutes UNC doubled its lead and turned on the cruise control for the rest of the contest.

In his postgame comments, Smith attempted to soothe the Georgia Tech ego and downplay his team's exuberant victory. North Carolina could very well face the Georgia Tech team in the ACC and/or NCAA tournaments, so it wouldn't be advantageous to do much celebrating or boasting. "I'm sure Georgia Tech had a letdown following the Duke game [win]," Smith said. "It was an emotional game and they were sky-high. We were lucky to be playing them right now. They are certainly an outstanding team and that's what makes this win seem so much better for us."

What really made the win so much sweeter for the team was attaining one of its goals — a goal set before to the season but considered unlikely by the ever-pessimistic head coach.

"I never thought we would win the regular season this year. The team really wanted to put on the ring as ACC regular-season champions," Smith continued, allowing a pinch of pride to show through. "There's room for other things if they can win any other things." The other things he alluded to were, of course, an ACC and an NCAA championship. From the looks of the second half against Georgia Tech, the two additional laurels looked possible. Smith's 1986–87 team had been even better during the regular season, winning all 14 games. But this year's team was another story, according to Cremins.

"This is a different North Carolina team," he said. "I have the feeling that Dean is trying to get this team to peak at a different time. In the past years

North Carolina has been the best team in January and February, but had some trouble in March. I wouldn't be surprised if Dean isn't peaking them different this year." Though Coach Smith had probably considered such a strategy, he was quick to say it wasn't the case. "We're doing the same as we've always done," Smith said. "We hope to be peaking at the tournament and again, I think we have been playing our best basketball. If you go by points per possession we played great in the [1987] ACC tournament. In the second half against N.C. State, we played about as well as we can offensively. In the NCAAs we continued to have our best points per possession, even against Syracuse. I would have to disagree with Bobby. We haven't changed. Our main goal was to get into the NCAA tournament — I wasn't sure we had that goal until February."

One of the reasons they met their goal was the sporadic but prolific scoring outbursts by Ranzino Smith. Opponents could not be content guarding Lebo on the outside and Reid in the paint. Smith could score from anywhere. From the season's opening game —when Ranzino was named the MVP after scoring 21 points — to the last, the senior guard ignited quite a few offensive fires. When the ball was in his hands in scoring position, Ranzino saw nothing but the front of the rim. Everyone on the floor knew Ranzino could fill the bucket, and filling the bucket was, after all, the object of the game. Not at North Carolina. There they rewarded defense and unselfish team play before any scoring exhibitions.

Apparently, Ranzino's skills were no longer considered important. In the Georgia Tech game the sharpshooting guard managed only eight minutes of playing time, far below his average. Lefty Driesell, providing color for the regional broadcast, remarked in the press room and later on the air that he thought Coach Smith must be mad at his guard. Ranzino, for his part, was quite upset. Following the game, the maligned senior was so distraught that he prepared to quit the team. But instead of clearing his locker, he cleared his mind with a phone call to former player Buzz Peterson, another shooting guard whose playing time had been curbed at North Carolina.

"Ranzino called me after the Tech game and told me he was quitting," Peterson said. "I told him not to do it. He only had a few games left in his senior year and it would have hurt him more than the program. I told him to stay with it and said, 'You'll need Coach Smith to help get a job after school.'" (Smith did just that for Peterson. The former guard is an assistant coach at Appalachian State University in Boone, North Carolina.) Ranzino gave it some thought, took Peterson's advice, and stayed with the team.

On his coach's program the following Sunday, Dean Smith said that Ranzino needed to contribute more scoring down the line. But in the regular-season finale later that day, Ranzino's playing time again was limited, with just 13 minutes. The former starter contributed three points on one of two three-point attempts as a reserve. During the Duke contest, NBC's Al McGuire noted Ranzino's absence, saying that the Tar Heels needed his outside scoring ability.

•   •   •

Before the completion of the North Carolina–Georgia Tech game, news of another ACC contest rocked the Omni and the television audience. Cellar dweller Clemson had risen out of the depths to stun second-place Duke at home, 79–77. Smith's earlier advice to the Tiger coach must have paid off. "I did spread my offense a bit," Coach Cliff Ellis said later, remembering Smith's comments after his team lost in Chapel Hill. "But I'd planned on doing that anyway."

So much for a four-way tie for first place in the ACC. Both Duke and Georgia Tech were currently three games out with only one game remaining.

•   •   •

While the team enjoyed the fruits of its labor, conference rival N.C. State was busy securing second place in the ACC with a win over Maryland in Raleigh. And while the Tar Heels and Coach Smith felt like champions, Coach Jim Valvano insisted that UNC's accomplishment was meaningless. Following the Wolfpack's 74–68 win over the Terrapins, Barry Jacobs, sports correspondent for *The New York Times*, told Valvano a headline had appeared in *USA Today* saying that North Carolina had clinched the ACC title.

"I guess I just don't understand that," he said, shaking his head. "I've been in this league eight years, and I still don't understand it. I hear they're going to get a banner, and a ring, too." Valvano has always contended that the true ACC champion is the team that wins the ACC tournament following the regular season. The regular-season winner receives only additional consideration in the seedings for the postseason NCAA tournament. "That's my approach and will always be my approach," Valvano argued. "When we have a conference meeting, and they decide there will be a crowned, regular-season champion, and they present awards to them, then I will say okay. But, we don't do that."

Jacobs told Valvano that at one time there was a vote, 7–1, in favor of crowning a regular-season champion. "Obviously, I wasn't here then," Valvano replied. "No one's ever voted on it while I was here and no one's ever brought that up at any meetings that I've attended."

Valvano heaped coals on a competitive fire still burning from the previous season. In 1986–87, North Carolina had amassed a 14-0 regular-season record followed by two ACC tourney wins, only to lose to the Wolfpack in the conference tournament final. While UNC had lost only one of 17 ACC bouts, the Wolfpack had claimed the conference championship. It was a sore point for North Carolina, to say the least. Should the two teams manage a rematch to determine the new champion, motivation would not be a problem for Smith's charges.

While other conference coaches are seemingly content to leave Dean Smith as the reigning coach of record, Valvano seems obsessed with Smith. "That's an impression I have," Rick Bonnell, sports correspondent for *The Charlotte Observer*, relates. "I don't really have anything to back that up with except that Dean always crops up in his conversations a whole lot more than vice versa. It may be fairer to say that Jim is preoccupied with Dean Smith. I don't think Dean Smith is in his nightmares, but Jim is more worried about being in Smith's shadow than say Mike Krzyzewski is. And Jim represents the way everyone at State feels about Smith and North Carolina.

"Valvano is always fighting a battle in this state for recognition for his program," says Bonnell. "Here they won the national championship, play great in the ACC tournaments, and yet they are fighting a losing battle for exposure and recognition in this state." His program may not get as much attention as North Carolina, but Valvano's personality has already focused national attention on the glib young coach.

Valvano is easily the choice of the media and the fans as far as personality is concerned, but Smith is still the godfather of basketball. The Italian-American coach from Raleigh always pays his respect in carefully chosen and rehearsed remarks, but it isn't hard to sense that Smith's vast power is envied by the relative newcomer. It's inevitable, with the two coaches' contrasting philosophies of basketball and life, that they would clash in some respect. Valvano is a gambler when it comes to a season of basketball. Tournaments are the only prizes that matter. In practice, Valvano has his team prepare for future glory by actually cutting down the nets. His teams reflect his simple and direct philosophy. Win enough national games during the season to be noticed, get national exposure for future recruiting, and ensure a bid to the NCAAs is Valvano's three-fold strategy. Win at least half of the regularly scheduled conference games and most of the "should wins," go all-out for the ACC tournament, and then do the same in the NCAAs.

Smith, on the other hand, strives for consistency. Every game is "a learning experience" for the team, with the lessons best learned through hard-fought victory. Any loss, especially to a weaker team, could be considered an embarrassment, so winning is always essential. There are built-in excuses for road losses — Smith feels the home team is almost always to be favored. But Smith's program embraces a philosophy that every game is important to overall success.

Valvano's personal philosophies coincide with his program's: grab the spotlight whenever possible and make the most of any opportunities that present themselves. Winning the national championship in 1983 provided the colorful coach with instant credibility. His national prominence catapulted him onto the airwaves and into the hearts of the country's basketball fans. His candid, humorous remarks caught the attention of the media like a breath of fresh air — tinged with garlic. Contracts with television and radio networks, endorsements with regional and local businessmen, and even a line of clothing resulted. He entertained — and commanded — thousands at speaking engagements. Huge corporations like IBM and Ford hired him to motivate their employees. He wrote and published a cookbook. The coach parlayed his winning ways into the N.C. State athletic director's job, the only combination basketball coach/AD position in the conference. There is no stopping Mama Valvano's boy. And he knows it. If Valvano has a fault, it's his tight grasp of the 'me first' generation.

His personality and dramatic results also attract blue-chip recruits, though not in the droves that the UNC program does. His teams are usually overstocked with quality athletes — so much so, that defections and transfers became a regular occurrence. His teams often record roller-coaster seasons and his player graduation rate is less than great. Yet, the shortcomings haven't dampened his enthusiasm or his personal success or satisfied his detractors. Even Smith, the opposite of Valvano in personality and philosophy, would be hard-pressed to dislike the energetic fast-talker from Long Island. With the strong competition for conference and national attention from Duke's Mike Krzyzewski and Georgia Tech's Bobby Cremins, Coach Smith, like his program, is constantly under attack for king-of-the-hill honors. Adding Valvano and the Wolfpack to the list is merely taken in stride by the reigning ruler.

Two weeks after Valvano's comments Smith was asked about the significance of winning the ACC regular-season championship, obviously in response to the claim that winning the most games in the conference regular season was worthless. "I don't think it makes much difference whether there's a line in the ACC bylaws that says you're the champions," Smith countered. "I know in 1960, North Carolina proposed that it be changed and I just think no one has gotten around to it. The ACC tournament winner is playing to be the NCAA tournament representative and sure, we'd like to win it very much.

"What it is [not having the regular season champions recognized] is that some of the old guard don't want to change. It was right to say that [the ACC tournament determines] the championship and the tournament is played to determine the NCAA representative."

Neither Valvano nor Smith would claim the championship in 1988, but it was announced later by Rick Brewer, the UNC sports information director, that the Tar Heels would receive rings after the season for winning the ACC regular-season unofficial title.

DUKE 96, UNC 81

As a regular-season finale, the annual North Carolina–Duke matchup has become a national classic. Basketball fans didn't expect the 1988 version of the rivalry to be any different.

Though UNC's conference standing wouldn't be affected, a Duke loss could send the Blue Devils reeling into the ACC tourney as the fourth-seeded team. Just as importantly, the ninth-ranked Blue Devils needed to regain their winning ways after losing three straight conference games. The sixth-ranked Tar Heels wanted to win because Duke had beat them in Chapel Hill in January. UNC pride was also at stake, though, as Duke had been the runner-up preseason favorite to win the conference, and North Carolina hoped to prove that it was the better team. Even without ulterior motives, the Duke–North Carolina game at Duke is most often *the* game of the regular season. And not just because of the great basketball played on the court. The Duke fans themselves are also a very important part of the festivities.

The Blue Devil "sixth man" is always ready and waiting to ambush its opponents. Known for their quick, often off-color, wit, the Duke fans look forward with relish to the verbal onslaught they can inflict in the close confines of Cameron Indoor Stadium. Whatever minute flaw they can find in an opponent is magnified a thousandfold during the course of the contest. No game means as much to the team as the annual Duke–North Carolina clash at Cameron.

"No question about it. Nothing can be finer than to beat ole Caroliner," said Duke senior Greg Slover in an affected accent. "Hey, I've been ready for this game since last Tuesday — wait, make that I've been ready for this game all year." Slover spoke for thousands of "Dookies" spread around him in various costumes and painted faces.

At Cameron, in direct contrast to the Smith Center, the students surround the court. The seats are not upholstered chairs, but uncomfortable bleachers. It hardly matters, for the students are too busy standing and cheering the team on to sit and watch. And those seats are not reserved by the purchase of a ticket or a lottery chance. At Duke, it's first come, first served. And at Duke, at least for the North Carolina game, it means camping outside of Cameron for up to a week for a prime location in the free student seating areas.

Like all tent cities that crop up for a cause, the new community takes on a flavor and a personality of its own. For the week prior to the game, sportswriters covered the student ticket-line campers like they would Super Bowl fans. Krzyzewskiville, as the new township came to be named, became the focal point of the quiet campus. While thousands of students flocked to the Florida beaches for spring break, a few hundred "Dookies" staked claims in line by punching a tent peg into turf outside Cameron. (If you think the hardy souls who brave the brisk February-March weather are rugged outdoorsmen, think again. The same brainpower that got the students admitted to Duke unleashes clever new ways to offset the drudgery of lawn sitting. Over the years, campers have found ways to fight boredom and the cold without having to resort to studying. Power cords are run from Cameron to juice up color televisions, VCRs, toaster ovens, electric blankets, and blenders. Satellite dishes and hot tubs have frequented the mini-city and local beer distributors have made many a secret on-campus delivery.)

Even the unofficial mayor of Krzyzewskiville, the Duke head coach whom it's named for, dropped by with pizza and soft drinks to show his appreciation. In 1987, the Duke basketball players chipped in and bought the campers a keg of beer. "We wanted them to know we don't take them for granted," said senior defensive star Billy King. "And we couldn't shake every hand in the place." The relationship between the players and their fans is unique at Duke. "You don't feel you're doing it for the fans here," Krzyzewski has said. "You feel you're doing it with them." As part of their close relationship, the Friday preceding the 1988 game Coach "K" and the campers assembled inside Cameron while a downpour drenched Durham and the newly constructed township. Krzyzewski prepared the student fans for the upcoming contest by showing a videotape of the last meeting between the Blue Devils and the Tar Heels. With a running commentary, Coach "K" humorously pointed out various points of strategy and some officials' miscues in the game. The coach even prompted the fans to join in the game and let the officials know by name when they failed to call a foul. "When they don't call that, say 'Hey Dick! Call those things!'" he said. "But be nice to him when you say it."

But they are not always nice. The fans have occasionally overstepped the boundaries of good taste through the years. Duke students are sharp and quick to jump on opponents' off-court shortcomings, and though most of the pranks have involved players from N.C. State, Maryland, and North Carolina, it is open season on players and coaches from all schools. Notable Tar Heel slurs have been directed in the past at Mike O'Koren, Sam Perkins, and Steve Hale. O'Koren was singled out as the "Oxy-1000 poster child" because of a severe case of acne, Perkins' long arms were made fun of when a Duke student paraded courtside with broomstick-handle arms topped with gloves, and Hale, still on the bench with a punctured lung from earlier in the season, received a verbal cheer of "In-Hale!" from one side of the gym while the other responded with "Ex-Hale!"

There are always cheers and jeers for Dean Smith. One year after the Duke students were X-rated in dealing with a player from Maryland charged with sexual misconduct, Duke President Terry Sanford, later elected senator, challenged the students to be "clever, but clean," and G-rated for television. When Smith and company arrived at Cameron for the next home game, they were greeted with roses and signs saying "Welcome Honored Guests." Referees, usually bombarded with "Bullshit! Bullshit! Bullshit!" after questionable calls, instead heard a polite chant of "We beg to differ."

As expected, the 1988 reception planned in Cameron was primarily directed toward J.R. Reid and Steve Bucknall. The media attention given the pair since their altercation in Raleigh and subsequent punishment was cause for celebration in Durham. The Blue Devil mascot sported a Jim McMahon-style white headband adorned with "Shooters II," in reference to the nightclub where the two scuffled with an N. C. State student. When the two players came out on the floor for warm-ups, the stands erupted with "Assault and Battery!" The cheers warmed the bodies that had camped out in early March for the privilege of watching the game, but it was the game itself that warmed their hearts. For the second time in the season, the Blue Devils controlled the outcome, winning handily, 96–81.

"If Duke plays in the [NCAA] tournament like they did today, they are national champions," said Dean Smith, both in praise of Duke's performance and in defense of his team's strong effort. Through the first half, both teams played evenly with each team scoring 36 points. Kevin Madden, a regular starter now, led the Tar Heel scoring with 10 points, all from the paint. Reid was held to two baskets by Duke forward Robert Brickey, and Scott Williams also managed only two field goals. Though UNC was successful in quality from the outside (two of three three-pointers), the quantity was inadequate. Duke stayed even by taking more shots. While the Blue Devils' outside game was non-existent (zero for nine three-point attempts), Brickey hit six of six overall and forward Danny Ferry added 10 points and six rebounds. The real difference in the half, and ultimately in the game, was the Tar Heels' inability to take care of the ball. Sixteen UNC turnovers allowed the Blue Devils to stay in the game and restored their confidence. The Blue Devils were trying to regain their winning formula after a three-game losing streak that threatened to ruin their season. North Carolina couldn't capitalize on its mental edge; its players seemed to lack concentration.

Duke emerged from the locker room refreshed and eager to win the game. Each team scored a basket and then the game broke wide open. In less than a minute, guards Quinn Snyder and Kevin Strickland put up three successful three-pointers. Duke was hot and the crowd turned the heat up even higher with a chant of "go to hell, Carolina." Continuing the frantic pace, the Blue Devils streaked to a 60–45 lead in the first five minutes of the second period. Dean Smith called a rare timeout when the lead reached 51–40, but it didn't curb Duke's scoring appetite. They stretched the lead twice to 17 points, but to UNC's credit, the Tar Heels didn't fold.

With Reid in foul trouble and Jeff Lebo hounded by Duke's best defenseman, Billy King, they looked to Madden and Steve Bucknall to put points on the board. Both responded with career highs, Bucknall contributing 22 points, with three of four three-point shots, and Madden added 19. With 5:46 to play, Reid made the first of two free throws and Rick Fox gathered the rebound on Reid's miss and scored. At 76–71, Duke's formidable lead had been whittled down to five.

Snyder, who had been on the bench with foul trouble, sprinted back into the game and immediately ensured a solid victory. The point guard lofted a fast break pass to King for a layup, nailed a three-pointer, fed Strickland for another, and then hit six of Duke's next 10 free throws to lead the way. North Carolina redesigned its offensive attack with new designated shooters, but the turnover plague that had confounded the team throughout the season descended again. Duke's pressure defense enabled its transition game to flourish while stunting any UNC resurgence. While North Carolina's 60 percent shooting in the second half should have been enough, Duke shot better than 73 percent.

"We congratulate Duke on what I thought was a marvelous second half," Smith said after the game. "That's the most points per possession ever scored on us in a half. They could have beaten any team in the country today." But he also credited his team for fighting back and for clinching the regular-season championship. "I thought Bucknall and Madden played great games today. Of course we won the ACC regular-season championship on Wednesday, but we still tried very hard to beat a good Duke team today. It wasn't so much our doing — we shot the ball very well — Duke was just great today."

So were the Duke fans. "They really make a difference," said the mayor of Krzyzewskiville. "Some of them camped out a week, a whole week. They're one of the main reasons we're fairly successful."

North Carolina fans would be depressed for days. Duke replaced N.C. State as the team they most wanted to beat. Now the only hope for redemption would be a win over the Blue Devils in the upcoming ACC tournament.

Following the game, the UNC locker room closed quickly. Though Chapel Hill was just 10 minutes down the road from Durham, the team bus was revving its engine minutes after the afternoon game. Sportswriters following the team had the choice of hearing Coach Smith's remarks or trying to elicit a few comments from the disappointed players. Most chose to hear how the players were taking the agony of defeat, an emotion infrequently experienced by UNC basketball players. The locker room was quiet and businesslike, but not overly subdued or morose. The players dressed quickly and responded to questions in matter-of-fact tones. Though the inquisitive media didn't know it yet, any questions prior to the conference tournament would have to be asked quickly. With the university officially on spring break, the team was about to go into deep isolation to concentrate on the ACC tournament. There would be no distractions from the local or national media.

Basketball players at North Carolina are normally sheltered from the media, appearing briefly only after ball games or after an appointment is secured through the UNC sports information office. Once an interview has been granted, the session is usually scheduled 20 to 30 minutes prior to a practice or team meeting and often with another sportswriter present. The presence of an additional writer helps limit the amount of time a journalist has alone with the player and theoretically protects the player from a blatant misquote. With five days off from classes, the players would be off limits to the press.

•   •   •

Dean Smith shunned the weekly ACC call-in teleconference held on Tuesday. Members of the teleconference weren't informed until after sitting through the entire ACC coaches' conference call that Smith had decided not to be available to the media that day. His stated reason, said ACC Service Bureau Director Skeeter Francis, was that he had scheduled an early practice for his team since the university was closed for spring break. A week later, in response to an unfavorable article that pointed out his absence, Smith hoped to set the record straight that he hadn't purposely avoided the teleconference.

"We were having two-a-day practices, and I didn't want to have to schedule an 8 a.m. practice." When a writer jokingly suggested he "hung up" on the teleconference the week before, Smith had a ready alibi. "I didn't hang up. The whole phone system in Chapel Hill went dead. Seriously." But at least two members of the media hook-up who were calling from Chapel Hill on the same system had no problem getting through.

· · ·

The next day, at a UNC press conference, area writers and broadcasters, all with a full supply of questions, got less than 15 minutes to talk to selected players Kevin Madden, Scott Williams, J.R. Reid, and Jeff Lebo. Ranzino Smith was also present, but left early. When Dean Smith arrived, the media was ushered away from the remaining players. Smith fielded questions after remarking that he hadn't called a press conference and didn't expect the large turnout. About a dozen members of the media were present for his remarks.

It is at such impromptu and relatively small gatherings that Smith reveals the most of himself. Though Smith doesn't seek personal publicity, he often relishes a question and answer period to compare notes with what is being said and thought about the program. One writer, Barry Jacobs, the author of the popular *Fan's Guide to ACC Basketball* and a correspondent for *The New York Times*, is clearly a reference point for the coach, who likes to play by the numbers. When the coach (who normally has an astounding memory) is stumped by a question concerning a conference or team statistic, he calls on the astute writer for the answer. Part of Smith's reasoning may be an element of trust. Jacobs has written more in-depth articles on Smith than any other writer. In addition, Jacobs embraces many of the same political and philosophical ideals.

"He's grounded in probabilities, tendencies and historical precedent," Jacobs says. "He uses all three as objective criteria to gain some understanding of truth. In private, I think Dean Smith is the least evasive of the ACC coaches. He doesn't mind confiding things if he thinks they are not going to be repeated. But he's certainly not one to talk about his personal life."

The first question on everybody's mind was not about Smith's private affairs. The press wanted to know if the season finale's loss would greatly affect the team's play in the upcoming tournaments. With the NCAA now taking more than one team from deserving conferences, Smith felt the pressure was relieved.

"I'm not ever concerned about momentum going into the tournament," he said. "We've won eight straight, I think, in '65 and then lost in the first round. We've lost two in a row in '68, I know, after we clinched the championship and then went on a tear and played really well. I would have been concerned if we had lost to Temple and Duke back-to-back. But to come back from the Temple loss and play what I thought were our two best games makes me think we're getting better.

"But the team came together after the Temple game. It's been a couple of years that every game [loss] has been down to the wire. We talked like we got beat by 80. And we felt that way. It was a blowout in my estimation."

It was a number of years since the Tar Heels had been beaten severely by an opponent. The 1986-87 team had lost only four games, and those were by a total of 12 points. To find a game in which the Tar Heels had lost by as many as 17 points, one would have to hunt through the record books back to March 9, 1980, when the team was ambushed by Texas A&M in the first round of the NCAAs. And that one wasn't a blowout — the Aggies needed two overtimes and a slew of deliberate UNC fouls to win, 78–61.

When the coach was asked about Jeff Lebo's play and his lack of scoring in the last few outings he quickly came to the player's rescue. "The funny thing about that is there really is no difference in his play once he gets rid of the ball. In our free-lance [offense] we try to set screens for him. Last year, teams had to contend with Kenny Smith, so Jeff got open more. But he's unselfish. I thought he played very well against Georgia Tech [in Atlanta] and some TV announcer said Lebo had a bad game. And what was he that game? One for five? And those were open shots, but my gosh, we were up 25 with four minutes to play and he kept getting the ball inside and playing good defense. Just having him on the court gives some room for our big people.

"It would look from appearances that we made him get people the ball and not hunt his shot. On the contrary, he's got the green light to go any time on the shot. I don't want him to take it if it isn't there. I differ from a lot of people that way," Smith admitted, philosophically. "We don't like to do what the defense gives us. Those guys [the opposition] are against us out there if we're going to do what they tell us to do, it isn't good for us. That doesn't make a lot of sense. These people say take what the defense gives you in basketball — my gosh, they'll give Buck [Steve Bucknall] the open shot right away. We don't want it."

The questions began centering on the ACC tourney, but Smith still talked in generalities. In speaking of their depth advantage over first-round opponent Wake Forest, Smith was quick to jump on his personal bandwagon against frequent and lengthy television timeouts and his philosophy about teams that play only a limited number of players.

"They're a good shooting team," Smith said, "and they're loose because there's nobody to come in for them. They go 0 for 10, and they're still going to play the same people. LaSalle plays that way. Their five people know they're going to be in the game the whole game. And there's a lot to that in building chemistry." One criticism of the North Carolina program that has surfaced over the years is Smith's policy of removing players quickly for making mistakes. Many players are constantly looking over their shoulders, concerned about playing time. Others become afraid to take normal shots for fear of missing, and thus never get loose or into the flow of the game. Former player Dave Popson was one player who felt the pressure and is comfortable enough to speak about it.

"There is so much competition for playing time," he said a week after he graduated. "If you do mess up, you're coming out. And you know you might not go back in. You have to go out and do the regimented things. There is a lot of pressure to do that for fear of coming out. I always played to please him — so that he would play me more. That was the wrong way to think about it. I should have been playing for the program, for the system.

"I remember when I was a freshman, and we were in Greece. I dribbled across the top of the key and took a jumpshot from the foul line — which was normal to do a couple of months before when I was in high school. The ball went in, but the coach took me out and said, 'You don't take shots like that,' and I didn't go back in for the rest of the game." Popson never really recovered. The highly sought-after prospect hit a mental downslide lasting for years. After graduating, Popson didn't even bother with a tryout with the Detroit Pistons, the NBA team that drafted him. Instead, he went straight to the European league to play for a team based in the Mediterranean.

"But you could suffer on fatigue on the other side," Smith continued on about possible scenarios in playing just five players. All of the assembled writers and broadcasters began to smile, knowing what was coming next. "Of course, with TV timeouts that shouldn't be a factor. They're so long, and they sit down and rest — it's a wonder they don't put out a pillow and let the guy lie down for five minutes." It's easy for a program like UNC to want to exploit its deep bench. With more and more parity in collegiate basketball, the edge of having high-quality reserves on the bench is that much more advantageous.

One writer asked Smith how the conference would do as a whole in the NCAAs.

"It's a guess," he said. "Two years ago, the Big 10, I thought, was a very good conference, and none of them made the top 16. And then everyone said the Big 10 was a bad conference. Well — they weren't. There's just that one game thing and you're out. I imagine we should do well." But first things first. Smith turned the conference back to the task at hand with a brief look at what the Tar Heels had accomplished to date.

"Our main goal was to get into the NCAA tournament," Smith continued. "And I wasn't sure we had that goal. Think of all the close games we won, though — that could have gone either way — Illinois, Syracuse, Fordham. But then in February, I thought we were going to make the NCAA tournament. That was our number-one goal. Our number-two goal was to do well in it, but we'd certainly like to add the ACC tournament. We haven't won an ACC tournament, I've been reminded by everybody, for five years.

"Last year's team wanted very much to win the ACC tournament. And they tried very hard. State plays poorly against Duke and Wake and then plays super [against UNC]." As an aside, he asked if both had been overtime wins. Then he recalled that Lennie Wirtz had been involved as an official in the semifinal game between N.C. State and Wake Forest. Smith's body language and facial expression implied what he thought of Wirtz's expertise.

It was no secret, at least among the media who followed North Carolina, that Smith and Wirtz didn't get along. Over the years, Wirtz had given Smith more grief than any official regularly working UNC games. Wirtz, a sales rep out of Florida, is small compared to the giants he controls during a game, but his size is not reflected in his attitude on court. And it is probably his officiating manner that disturbs Smith more than any questionable or missed calls. Smith dislikes Wirtz so much he has gone out of his way to state his feelings.

"After 17 years of marriage," Smith had said after a particularly trying conference game in 1987, "you'd think they would give us a divorce." Wirtz, when later informed of Smith's comment, said that he wouldn't mind if the divorce were granted if he could have the house.

Because of the feelings between the two, the number of UNC games Wirtz has officiated has dropped significantly. Beginning in the 1984–85 season, when Wirtz officiated in eight UNC games, the number has decreased each year. Fred Barakat, the ACC supervisor of officials and one of only two such directors in the country, has found himself in the role of marital counselor for the two. Before a writer can talk to any of the conference officials, he must obtain permission from Barakat, who can then forewarn the referee. Officials can then be ready to ward off any controversial questions that might stir up the coaches or the fans.

• • •

The Tar Heels were a third of the way home. They had won the regular season, realizing one of their preseason goals. Still, it was only one more step on a quest for the national championship. The next step would be to win the ACC tournament. It had been a long time since UNC had brought the tournament trophy back to Chapel Hill.

V.
OVERTIME

Thursday, March 10, was ACC tournament acclimation day — the day the majority of the fans, players, coaches, broadcasters, sportswriters, and ticket scalpers roll into town. By nightfall, the entire region would be counting the hours left until the beginning of perhaps the most exciting nonstop three-day event in collegiate basketball. It may have been the last ACC tournament in Greensboro. The powers that be were talking about moving to a larger site and foregoing the Greensboro Coliseum. Further discussion would have to wait. The tournament was only a day away.

The coliseum was humming with activity by mid-morning. Photographers tested their equipment, focusing on the various teams as they took the floor for a semi-public practice. Determined by seeding and Friday's game lineup, each school was scheduled for an hour practice to be followed by an interview period. Only a handful of schools, those farthest away from Greensboro and not-so-distant Wake Forest, chose to use their allotted time. Virginia, N.C. State, and North Carolina all declined to use the coliseum for final tune-ups.

"Dean never practices here before the tournament," said Lefty Driesell. "He didn't practice before the tournament in Maryland last year, either. Hell, I can't remember the last time he used one before the ACCs."

Driesell and Dick Vitale, ESPN's analyst, filled in for the Tar Heels admirably. Grabbing a loose basketball, the not-so-dynamic duo entertained the assembled media and photographers with a few games of one-on-one and a free-throw shooting contest. The two former coaches looked like anything but basketball players, but the accompanying comments and verbal challenges were priceless. Vitale told everyone that there was no way Driesell would take the head coaching job at James Madison University as had been speculated the day before tournament. "I have a better chance of growing hair than you have of going to James Madison," stated the nearly bald ESPN analyst.

"How do you know that, Vitale? No one ever heard of Davidson before I went there," Driesell countered. "You hadn't heard of it. Shut up and shoot." Driesell, representing the ACC as a former Duke player, won both

171

games easily.

"What the heck," Vitale said. "He was on scholarship, and I was only a walk-on [at Seton Hall]."

At the start of the next season, on October 15, 1988, Duke graduate Charles "Lefty" Driesell would be coaching the JMU Dukes in Harrisonburg. Dick Vitale, by virtue of winning a bet made over the air that Larry Brown wouldn't stay in Kansas, would narrowly avoid "walking on" the Jayhawks' gym floor to scrub the hardwood.

UNC 83, WAKE FOREST 62

The longest day of the tournament — four games within 12 hours — was Friday, March 11. By the end of the day four teams would be en route home, disappointed at losing out on two more days of competition. Three of the losers — Virginia, Wake Forest, and Clemson — eliminated themselves from an automatic NCAA tournament bid. Georgia Tech, surprised by a Maryland rout in the day's only upset, would regroup before NCAA action. The winning teams quietly celebrated, knowing that another battle was just hours away.

UNC had the easiest go of it. The top-seeded Tar Heels knocked off the Deacons in the first game and earned the right to relax the rest of the day. They owed a round of applause to Ranzino Smith for the victory.

The senior had struggled in the last few games as he was removed from the starting lineup and relegated to a substitute role. Though he'd briefly quit the team in anger, Ranzino regained his composure over his coach's late-season adjustment and refused to respond publicly about his demotion. Whatever his emotions, he channeled them into a flurry of firepower against the Deacons. Entering the game with North Carolina down 18–11, he set off a scoring spurt rivaling his MVP performance against Syracuse in the season opener. Ranzino tallied a hat trick of three-pointers and scored seven additional points to lead a 21–1 rally. He scored eight of those points in a span of 1:19. After the game, neither Ranzino nor his coach made much of his performance.

"The coaches decided to go with a big lineup," Ranzino said, following the company line. "I can't worry about that. It doesn't matter if I play a minute or 40 minutes. I try to be ready at all times, and I think I'm ready at all times."

Coach Smith took his senior's play matter-of-factly. "Certainly Ranzino can shoot it. Actually, we put him in there today to give somebody a rest. He hasn't really shot it well this year — and his defense has improved — but we'd rather have that size in there." Interesting. The guard covering Smith most of the game was Cal Boyd, who was listed at the same height as

Ranzino. Size couldn't have been too big a factor. After Ranzino replaced Kevin Madden at the beginning of the run, Coach Smith inserted 6–0 King Rice for Jeff Lebo. The Deacons retreated into a zone and Ranzino scored 13 points.

Another highlight of the first half was a technical foul on Lebo. Referee George Toliver called a foul on the Tar Heel point guard and Lebo uncharacteristically responded with an audible "worst call I've seen in my damn life." Though many feel the young man has led only a charmed life, the resulting Deacon foul shot chipped a point off the halftime lead. Even more detrimental was the fact that Lebo would catch some flak from his coach for the use of such an inappropriate word. UNC prides itself on abstaining from profanity — though various invectives do occasionally reach the ears of press row and beyond.

Lou Bello, one of the most colorful men ever to wear a black-and-white striped shirt, remembered an instance with a player back in the mid-'60s. "You'll never hear Dean curse. In fact, I've only heard one of his players curse in all the years I refereed. Bob Lewis at Virginia Tech in a Christmas tournament up there cursed another official. He cursed George Towner. He cursed him bad. Lewis said 'fuck you' under the basket. Dean didn't hear it, didn't know it. 'T!'" screamed Bello, mimicking his former colleague while forming a T with his hands. "Dean couldn't believe it. He said, 'What's the technical for?' and Towner told him it was for cursing."

"At halftime, [UNC] assistant coach Kenny Rosen came into our dressing room and said, 'Coach is a little upset. Lewis said he didn't curse the official.' Well, he lied to Coach Smith because he knew that cursing wasn't permitted." That a player would risk lying to his coach to cover the use of an obscenity shows how strongly Smith feels about such lapses in discipline.

There was no such lack of discipline in the second half of the Wake Forest game in Greensboro. The team's intensity remained high for the rest of the contest. The ball frequently found its way inside the Deacon defense in the second half, giving J.R. Reid and Scott Williams enough room to score 41 points between them. On defense, the Tar Heels played some of their best of the season, as Carolina ran away with its first-round game, 83–62.

•   •   •

In other action, Maryland upset Georgia Tech, 84–67, N.C. State survived Clemson, 79–72, and Duke beat Virginia, 60–48.

The Terps and their coach, Bob Wade, wished they had more time to savor their big win over the Yellow Jackets. With another game scheduled against UNC only 20 hours away, Wade was reluctant to get too excited. "Any time you win in the ACC tournament, it is important. A game of this magnitude really feels great, and a win means a lot to our kids. But with Carolina coming up ... it's back to business."

Wade was asked if the win over nationally ranked Tech assured his team of an NCAA tournament bid. "I think we're in, but I'm no politician." Keith Gatlin, the Terp senior who led the way for his team scoring 25 points, felt they needed to win the championship to ensure a bid. "We know if we win the whole thing we'll go. That's what we're here for and that's why we packed for three days."

The Terps had all the incentive they needed even without the fact that Carolina had beaten them in the season's two previous outings. "The first two games with North Carolina were embarrassing," Wade said. "They did everything they wanted to to our basketball team." Would they do it again the following day?

UNC 74, MARYLAND 64

Everything seemed to be on schedule for a rematch between North Carolina and Duke. Only a couple of games stood in the way — a couple of ACC tournament games. UNC faced Maryland in what most likely would result in a win. The second game, the Duke–N.C. State matchup, would be more interesting, according to most of the fans. As long as UNC won, the final would be a guaranteed classic. Even avowed Tar Heel haters wanted to see the Terrapins lose. Only those from Maryland wanted an upset in the first game and they were disappointed. North Carolina was regaining the momentum it had lost in its regular season finish at Duke. The Tar Heels rung the register with a 10-point victory, 74–64.

"I thought we did so many nice things," Smith said after downing a Coke and smoking a couple of Kent Golden Lights. "Overall, we got the shots we wanted. Defensively, I thought we were active. Our concentration level has been good the last two weeks. We're playing our best basketball now."

Maybe so. Maryland didn't help support this case, however. The slow-down game that Wade devised only managed to put the brakes on his own team's offense, as the Terps shot 36 percent from the floor. Friday's 25-point hero, Keith Gatlin, was held to six points by UNC's designated defensive specialist, Steve Bucknall. The Maryland inside game was also held in check. Forward Derrick Lewis and freshman center Brian Williams each scored 14 points, but together were limited to half that many rebounds.

On offense, UNC unveiled a new weapon. Bucknall, an adequate shooter at best, delivered two of three three-pointers. King Rice also got into the action, canning three field goals and three free throws. "King Rice came in and gave us a lift," Smith said. "Generally, that's Ranzino's place, but with their quickness, Ranzino is not a point guard and so we wanted to have a little bit better ball-handling."

It paid off. The Tar Heels limited themselves to nine turnovers, with only two coming from their guards. They would need to hold on to the ball against the winner of the Duke–N.C. State game. Though no players wanted to go on record as saying they hoped to meet Duke, many a face betrayed that desire during postgame locker room comments. A third match with the Blue Devils was definitely on their minds. A game against the Wolfpack would give them a chance to revenge last year's upset, but to a man they were praying for a Duke–North Carolina finale.

Ask and ye shall receive. In one of the best games of the tournament, Duke squeezed a victory out of State senior Charles Shackleford's hands, 73–71, when "the Shack" couldn't control a teammate's pass in the final seconds of the game. The stage was set for another Blue and White showdown.

● ● ●

Derrick Lewis, the senior center for Maryland, left the tournament on a sour note. In some parting lines aimed at ACC officials, he complained that there was a double standard in conference officiating. "The refs read the papers, too. They know who the superstars are. Right now, the big man is J.R., and he's the one getting the breaks." He went on to say that the same preferential treatment had been given to his former teammate, the late Len Bias. "The best can get away with more than the rest," Lewis said, relinquishing frustration. "I saw it with Lenny. He could hack away and they wouldn't call things on him the way they would on anybody else.

"Reid gets away with murder. If you look at Reid wrong, it's a foul. And he gets away with more walking than anybody I've ever seen."

The referees may let the future superstar get away with murder, but one of J.R.'s teammates wouldn't let him get away with anything. That evening at Slug's At The Pines, a popular Chapel Hill restaurant, Steve Bucknall and Reid left a postgame meal well before the final course to mix it up in the parking lot. The two had decided to physically settle their differences after a Reid practical joke misfired. The fire took place in Bucknall's mouth. Minutes earlier, when Bucknall left the table to use the restroom, Reid seized the opportunity to plunge his teammate's fork into the flame of a candle, heating the end of the utensil. When Bucknall returned and began eating, he got burned.

Durham's WTVD television station was the first to break the story, two days following the incident, but the majority of the team's fans didn't hear about it until the next week. A customer had contacted Ron Savage, the station's sports director, and told him of the scuffle in the parking lot. The customer, who declined to be identified, had been asked not to discuss the incident. The customer said he was unsure whether the request came from a team representative or a member of the restaurant staff.

When asked to comment on the altercation, Dean Smith, the head of the household, said it was a family affair. "Our policy has always been that anything that happens on the team — that's why our practices are closed — I never comment on anything that has to do with our players. I call it team dynamics. We're family and it stays there."

(The incident didn't have a positive effect on the two "siblings." The next day in the ACC finals, Reid and Bucknall scored four and seven points, respectively.)

•   •   •

The lead story of the Sunday *Greensboro News & Record* shocked thousands of North Carolina fans in town for the tournament. The article and accompanying sidebars took up over two and a half pages in the front section of the newspaper.

Below a headline "Dean Dome funding cast shadow at UNC–CH: Center's donors rank as favored few," ran an article claiming a polarization between mainstream UNC fans and what sports writer Wilt Browning described as the "Spectating Elite."

"The Spectating Elite, about one-fourth of the UNC Educational Foundation's total membership, includes 2,700 families and represents an approach to athletic fund-raising so new that, as far as can be determined, it is unique in North Carolina, if not the nation.

"Together the Spectating Elite underwrote the $36 million construction cost of Smith Center and its adjacent structure, the Maurice J. Kourey Natatorium, through the foundation, UNC–Chapel Hill's athletics support organization. In the process they bought the rights *forever* to season tickets in basketball's Taj Mahal, to the exclusion of virtually all others except students and members of the faculty."

Browning concluded that the house that Dean Smith built was in reality a house built for and by the Spectating Elite. The article reported that the Educational Foundation has the rights to 9,400 seats of the 21,444 total, and all but 1,400 of the total have been reserved solely for donors to the Smith Center. The 1,400 go to athletic supporters who have endowed athletic scholarships through the foundation at values beginning at $50,000. There is a waiting list, but realistically little chance of purchasing a season ticket.

Browning said that the Spectating Elite has caused the formation of another entire class: "longtime university supporters who now are figuratively on the outside looking in." He cited the case of Paul Schenck Jr., a 40-year member of the Educational Foundation who has given more than $15,000 to the non-profit organization. At the time of the article, Schenck owned foundation membership priority number 937, and, according to the foundation's own point system, is listed among the top 10 percent in generosity and long-term giving. His donations entitle him to watch basketball games from his living room. Though he continues to support the foundation at an annual clip of around $500, the article went on to say, "Schenck's hurting runs deep."

A former manager of the UNC basketball team, Schenck also worried about the state of affairs at his alma mater. "I'm concerned about the direction athletics is going at Carolina and everywhere else. It's getting too big, not just at Carolina, but athletics as a whole is getting out of hand. When they schedule games the way they do for the benefit of television, they do it for the almighty dollar and nothing else."

Obviously, a larger basketball facility can provide more seats in addition to a few more almighty dollars. Three major groups benefited from the move from 10,000-seat Carmichael Auditorium to the 21,444-seat Smith Center. The article stated that the Educational Foundation's seating rose from 3,200 to 9,400. Faculty numbers increased from 2,800 to 4,800, and the student seating increased from 3,000 to 6,500. The remaining seats (around 800) are set aside for athletic department use. In the move, the students lost their courtside seats. They now sit in the end zone and in the upper deck.

Interestingly enough, the students were never consulted in the Smith Center undertaking, according to Moyer Smith, who reflected on the subject a month later. "We couldn't have built the building if we had students all around the court," said Smith, the man who directs the incorporated Educational Foundation. "There is a way the students could have done that, but the administration was not interested in pursuing it. I don't think the student body was ever approached. That's a shame, I think we'd have been better off if we had asked the students to participate. Through the power of the student fees, they have enormous economic potential at their hands." They never got the chance to exercise their clout. The powers that be — the Spectating Elite — already held tight control.

DUKE 65, UNC 61

Maybe Jim Valvano was right when he said winning the regular-season championship was meaningless. For the second straight year, North Carolina came up a basket or two short in the ACC championship game. This time around it cost the team much more than another tournament banner. By virtue of a 65–61 loss, the title gave Duke a first-round NCAA tournament game in the Smith Center and eventually a trip to the Final Four representing the Eastern Region. It was the route the Tar Heels had desperately wanted to take. Instead, UNC reeled from its sixth-straight conference championship loss, and found their journey toward Kansas City taking a western detour. "We are very disappointed," Coach Smith said after the devastating loss. "We put a good bit of emotion into this game, for the first time in a long time. We really wanted to win it."

In the recent past, Smith had prepared his teams specifically for eventual play in the NCAAs. The ACC tournament was for fun. The team didn't want to expend too much emotion on the conference title in case it should lose. In 1988, Smith threw such caution to the wind. With fans and foes clamoring for a championship, Smith and his team decided to let it all hang out against Duke. The Blue Devils had beaten them twice already, but the winner of the third clash would come away with all the marbles. The Tar Heels wanted a victory more than ever before, with the possible exception of the NCAA title game against Georgetown in 1982. This time around, however, Fred Brown, the Hoya who literally threw away that game, wasn't on the floor to assure victory.

The 1988 ACC championship game went down to the wire. But the last eleven minutes and forty-eight seconds decided the game. In that time span, the Tar Heels scored only *one* field goal. A combination of Duke defense and UNC cold shooting shut down their attack. To their credit, the team channelled its remaining energies into a solid defensive effort. The Blue Devils were also stymied on offense for the better part of the period. In fact, UNC held Duke to a measly 31 percent average from the floor in the second half, but it wasn't enough. North Carolina countered with a pitiful 28 percent.

North Carolina out-rebounded, out-blocked, and out-stole its opponent. The Tar Heels fouled less, made more three-pointers, and connected on more free throws. Somehow it wasn't enough. Duke made up the imbalance with three more field goals. Tournament MVP Danny Ferry provided the difference in the game. His three-pointer, and a conversion after a teammate's missed free throw, decided the outcome.

The Blue Devils were ACC champs.

"Beating Carolina at all is a feat," Duke's Kevin Strickland said later. "We defied all odds by beating them three times this year. In fact, at the beginning of the season to think we'd beat Carolina once this year would be defying all odds." So much for the odds. Numbers did determine the outcome, but they didn't tell the whole story. The tournament winner could just as easily have been determined with a roll of the dice.

"It was a great championship game," Duke coach Mike Krzyzewski said. "Both teams —Carolina and Duke — left it all out there. Outside of a few breaks for us, they could be the champions." A few breaks were the difference in a lifetime for Ranzino Smith.

The senior sat at his locker after the game for what seemed like another lifetime. He had played in his last ACC tournament game. The majority of them had been wins, but he had never experienced the thrill of cutting down the nets. He never would. "All I know is, I'll go out into the world knowing I never won an ACC championship," Smith said while tears streamed down his face. "I'll never, ever know what it feels like."

Hundreds of students back in Durham would know what it felt like to win. Within two hours of the final buzzer, T-shirts celebrating the ACC championship (including the final score) went on sale in the Bryan Center Lobby Shop on the Duke campus.

Shirtmakers in Chapel Hill stayed closed. Johnny T-Shirt, a local custom shirtmaker and distributor of university artifacts and souvenirs, was still embroiled in a high-stakes legal battle with the University of North Carolina concerning the use of the school's logo and royalty payments. UNC had sued the incorporated business and its two owners, Chuck and Mike Helpingstine, for $1.5 million in July 1987. (In 1985-86 UNC had earned less than $90,000 in royalties for the use of its logo.) The small business refused to bow to the powerful state university. Popular opinion and the facts weighed in favor of Johnny T-Shirt. The North Carolina attorney general represented the university. It might be years before the case was settled.

• • •

UNC and Duke each placed two players on the ACC all-tournament team. The ballots, as usual, were picked up from the attending sportswriters prior to the outcome of the final game. The need for quickly determining the all-tournament team weakened the chances of an accurate representation. Instead, the team occasionally represented an all-star team of sorts, with members' regular-season play considered in the selection. J.R. Reid and Scott Williams, neither of whom scored in double figures in the final game, represented the Tar Heels. Danny Ferry and Robert Brickey shone for the Blue Devils. Charles Shackleford rounded out the first team. Jeff Lebo was named to the second all-tournament team.

That evening, the NCAA tournament committee, chaired by Arnie Ferrin, announced which teams had been invited to the big dance. Of the 64 contestants, the ACC received five bids. Should the teams advance no further than the first round, the conference and its teams would realize more than $1 million in tournament earnings.

North Carolina, by virtue of the ACC tournament loss, would travel west to Salt Lake City, Utah, to meet North Texas State. Maryland was to face California-Santa Barbara in the Southeast. N.C. State would take on Murray State in the Midwest, and both Duke and Georgia Tech would remain in the East.

UNC fans possessing NCAA ticket books for the opening round of tournament action in the Smith Center had to decide whether to attend and cheer for close rival Duke or sell out and make the journey to Utah. Thousands of Tar Heel fans had bought the tickets expecting to see their team on their home floor. Many of the NCAA tournament ticket buyers had never seen the Tar Heels in the Smith Center. The disappointment was a brisk slap in the face.

•   •   •

The next day, Coach Mike Krzyzewski publicly apologized for a faux pas he had committed immediately following the ACC tournament final. In his exuberance, Coach "K" had forgotten the coaching ritual of shaking the opponent's hand following the game.

"I thought, 'you dumb Polack,'" he said. "I went and shook his hand and I apologized publicly. I regret him [Dean Smith] just waiting there. It's not that what I did was so awful. It should have been in the proper order."

Krzyzewski said he had felt his respect for Smith deepen after looking at a videotape of the moments following the game. "I saw him on the tape going out and looking for individual [Duke] players to congratulate. I saw Ranzino Smith and Kevin Madden looking for players. They had to go out of their way to find them — they didn't have to do that. They're a class act all the way." The Duke coach must have missed a videotape of the 1987 ACC Tournament Final. After that game, a 68–67 UNC loss to N.C. State, a frustrated Dean Smith had left the floor in different spirits. A national television cameraman following Smith as he left the floor transmitted a revealing shot of the disgruntled coach storming off the court. As Smith crossed in front of the cameraman, he reached up to place his hand across the lens of the camera. Thousands of basketball fans saw a side of Smith's personality rarely displayed. But in 1988, Smith masked similar disappointment behind a solid display of sportsmanship.

While Coach "K" was voicing kudos for class, down the road at N.C. State, Coach Jim Valvano was exhibiting a lack of it. He spoke of his concern about the officiating in the recent tournament. "After a win, everything's fine," Coach "V" said. "I'm saying that when the referees were fair, the game was fair. But when you lose, I watch every single call."

Valvano was concerned about the no-call that ended State's chances in the tournament semifinal against Duke. But with the NCAA tournament beginning in just days, his tune changed quickly. "Really guys, I do think the referees are doing a marvelous job. And the ones in Lincoln, Nebraska [the site of the Wolfpack first-round game], I'm sure, are going to do a great job. But I can just see the headlines tomorrow, 'Valvano rips refs.' Holy cow, no, I love them all. Don't forget, my father was a ref."

•   •   •

The AP final Top 20 basketball poll that week placed Duke fifth, North Carolina seventh, and N.C. State 14th. All of the five teams that had held the top spot during the season — Syracuse, North Carolina, Kentucky, Arizona, and Temple — finished within the Top 10. Eleven teams had stayed in the Top 20 for the entire season.

•   •   •

That Wednesday, Dean Smith was selected ACC Coach of the Year by the Atlantic Coast Sports Writers Association. It was the seventh time in 27 years that the conference sports journalists had honored the coach. It was the first time since 1979.

Smith beat out Jim Valvano for the accolade by a single vote, 39–38. Mike Krzyzewski of Duke received only seven votes. The coach of the ACC champions would have to be content with the use of the Dean Dome for a springboard into the NCAAs as his reward.

The day before, J.R. Reid had been named a first-team AP All-American. He was the only sophomore selected for the honor. The ACSWA didn't feel, however, that Reid was the best the conference had to offer. Danny Ferry of Duke was voted the 1988 ACC Player of the Year, receiving 90 of 125 votes. Reid tallied a mere 25. Both Reid and Ferry were later named to the U.S. Basketball Writers Association All-America team.

UNC 83, NORTH TEXAS STATE 65

The game against North Texas State's Mean Green in the opening round of the NCAA West Regional helped the Tar Heels return to their winning ways. But it did so with mixed blessings. North Carolina was able to revive its inside game with a strong 29-point contribution from J.R. Reid and 20 rebounds between Reid and Scott Williams. But the Tar Heels' nemesis, the turnover, continued to haunt the team. Another blast from the not-so-distant past was the return of a sharpshooting Ranzino Smith. Still unsettled in his new role of substitute offensive guard, Smith jumped at the chance to put 15 points on the board in 22 minutes of playing time.

The Tar Heel guard play was changing, even in the first round of NCAA tournament action, when guard play is so critical. Jeff Lebo was still the dominant point guard, but King Rice spent more time in the game as both a substitute and as a complement to Lebo. Kevin Madden started at the number-two guard spot, but rotated in and out of the game in both front-court/back-court positions. Smith's job in the guard rotation was to spark the offense. But though all four could score, the main obligation for the guards, as is always the case at UNC, was to get the ball inside.

The Mean Green cooperated with North Carolina's inside attack. Instead of sandwiching Reid with a front man and weak-side help, a strategy some teams had proved successful, North Texas State decided to play behind Reid. "They chose to play J.R. straight-up," said Coach Smith, who must have been smiling inside. "We're not accustomed to that. When a team does do it, we'll go to J.R. and see what happens." The results were more than pleasing to Reid, his team, and his coach.

"Our philosophy is that if we get the ball inside, good things will happen," Reid related. "We knew we had bigger guys than they did and it worked for us." It didn't hurt that getting the ball inside meant getting it into either the All-American's hands or the capable ones belonging to Williams. Reid enjoyed the additional freedom, letting the ball fly from as far as 15 feet. "The jumpers I had around the free-throw line are the shots I take out of our offense, or secondary break," Reid explained to a writer who asked if he was extending his range. "All of our big men are allowed to take that shot. Most people think of me as a power player, but I can hit that shot if nobody is checking me."

It's interesting to note that the sophomore All-American referred to his outside shots as ones that are "allowed." At North Carolina, most shots are approved in practice before the players are given the okay to use them during a game. With the exception of layups and short jumpers, a player must have the coaching staff's seal of approval before launching a three-point attempt or a sophisticated jump hook. The players' shots are charted throughout preseason and early season practices. When the time is right, the shot is allowed to become incorporated into the offense. Of late, both Williams and Steve Bucknall had been *allowed* to add the three-pointer to their repertoire and Pete Chilcutt was permitted to add a jump hook. Though the coaching staff encouraged the hesitant King Rice to shoot when open, it shuddered collectively whenever he shot from more than 12 feet. The freshman's shots continued to improve, however, and he would be counted on to assume the point guard duties on a more permanent basis in the years to come.

Also contributing to the lopsided 83–65 win was the failure of the Eagles to hit their shots. North Texas State, appearing in the NCAAs for the first time, succumbed to the opening-night shakes and were out of the game in the first few minutes. "Their experience and the jitters caught us early," Eagles head coach Jimmy Gales said after the game. "We missed a couple, two, three layups and never could get going offensively. Of course, North Carolina's defense probably had a lot to do with that." It did. UNC's height advantage and strong defensive fundamentals made a major difference.

The Tar Heels could have enjoyed the opening-round victory more if they had closed out the game the way they had started it. Instead, the company lost points with its coach by throwing the ball away often in the closing minutes. "We played terrible in the last 10 minutes," Smith said. "That's why I don't feel so happy now. Between now and Saturday, Jeff Lebo and King Rice have to be the ball-handlers I think they are for us to have a chance. I did want to play King Rice more in the second half today because he's supposed to be a better ball-handler. Notice I said supposed to be. When we get into our closed practice tomorrow, we need to improve our heads."

When the Tar Heels got to practice the following day they were too busy to think about the mistakes they had made against the Mean Green. With only one day to prepare for second-round action, Smith was about to demonstrate why he is one of the master coaches of all time.

UNC 123, LOYOLA MARYMOUNT 97

With a stunning 119–115 upset of 13th-ranked Wyoming the day before, 15th-ranked Loyola Marymount was making believers out of the country's media and fans. Curry Kirkpatrick, *Sports Illustrated*'s flamboyant sportswriter, wrote of his enamoredness with the team, and the likelihood of the transfer-laden, highfalutin' Lions advancing all the way into the regional finals to take on Arizona. Even CBS color analyst Tom Heinsohn declared the team the latest Cinderella at the NCAA ball.

Dean Smith loved it.

The higher-seeded Tar Heels were becoming the popular underdog. It would make Smith's job that much easier. The Lions' tenth seeding in the West and 15th-ranking was considered well below where most basketball experts now thought they should be. Smith was quick to voice his opinion and add to the media blitz. "They are a vastly underrated team by those coaches and writers who voted this season," he said. "If I would have had a chance to see them more, I would have voted them among the top three teams in the nation." Smith went on to paint a picture of Loyola brilliance, pointing out that since Coach Paul Westhead had settled on his current lineup, the Lions had won 25 straight games, the longest winning streak in the nation. Smith also took the opportunity to complain that UNC, by virtue of its seeding, shouldn't have to meet such a tough team so early in the NCAAs. Smith, who normally doesn't place much stock in the rankings when it comes to his team, was always quick to use UNC's low position in the polls whenever possible to motivate his players. The chance to do so didn't happen very often.

The day before, Loyola Marymount had indeed looked potent in its game against a talented Wyoming team. Averaging over 110 points per game, Loyola raced to its first-round victory and a new NCAA tournament scoring record in perhaps the greatest first-round matchup in the history of the tournament. While UNC had retired to the hotel after the day's first game, Dean Smith had made a point of watching the second game from the stands, something he rarely does. With only a day between games, Smith would prepare for whichever team emerged victorious the night before practice. But with the unexpected Loyola win, there was little time to prepare for such an upbeat and radical style of play. Still, Smith relished the prospect. A challenge, any challenge, is what makes the game interesting for the college game's most accomplished tactician. And though the challenge of the entire year to date had been tough enough to gain the coach his seventh ACC Coach of the Year award, finding a quick solution to beat the Lions looked doubtful.

Smith pulled out all the stops. Doug Moe, head coach of the Denver Nuggets, was in town and available for consultation. In addition to making his former coach and benefactor laugh and loosen up, Moe was able to provide some possible ways to offset the reckless offense the Lions used. Moe's teams run a similar offense and he probably knew some tactics to employ.

After planning his strategies, Smith exercised another seldom-used trick to get his players' attention. He made the team watch the previous day's Loyola Marymount–Wyoming game on videotape to demonstrate his concern about the game. Usually, Smith is content to ready his team by working on execution and self-improvement. Not against the Lions. "Normally, we don't show players films of our opponents," Smith said. "We try to get our team ready for what we want to do. But in this case, we will show them some tape so they won't be too shocked when they see it live and in person. They need to know what to expect and to set themselves up properly on both offense and defense." His message was received.

"Coach Smith was very worried about their team," said Steve Bucknall, the team's designated defenseman. "I knew that when he showed us a tape of them. I couldn't believe it." Jeff Lebo, the team's floor leader, noticed the difference in the coach as well. "He was really worried about how we would react to them. We knew they were good just by the way he spoke of them. I've never seen him (pause) — he seemed a little extra nervous."

Excited probably, nervous unlikely. Smith knew his team could beat Loyola. There were gaping holes in the Lions' defense. Their full-court pressure would force many turnovers from the careless UNC ball-handlers, but the Tar Heel discipline could take full advantage of the overplaying Lions. If North Carolina was to win, Smith would have to motivate his players to keep their heads and utilize the fundamentals he had taught them. "The real key is to prevent them [Loyola] from getting the offensive board," Smith said. "If we can hold them to 15 or less, then we will have a chance of controlling them." Many felt that Loyola's frenetic defensive pace, an offshoot of Smith's own run-and-jump "scramble" defense, would control the contest. With the Lions' stated goal of putting up a shot every seven seconds, the game could turn out to be the most up-tempo game the Tar Heels had played in all year. How would the Tar Heels handle the fast pace? Smith answered the question with another.

"Do we take the easy layup, or do we make them play defense?" he asked. "Certainly, any coach doesn't want to pass up an easy shot, but that's what they want you to do to get into their tempo. It's a decision our players and staff will have to make as the game progresses." It was a decision Smith had already made and one the team would emphatically support the next afternoon.

* * *

Actually, Smith had used the "hidden videotape" trick as a motivator a year earlier. Prior to playing Notre Dame in their regional semifinal matchup, Smith had pulled out a cassette of the Tar Heels regular-season loss to the Irish in South Bend, Indiana. "The fact that they beat us and they had that big celebration with Digger kissing the crowd — we watched it right before we went to play them in the Meadowlands," said Dave Popson, a senior on the team at the time. "Coach showed it to us and it was like throwing a log on the fire. And in my freshman year, he showed us a tape of Maryland beating us real bad up there in College Park. That made us hungry."

Despite all of the hoopla surrounding Loyola, Coach Paul Westhead, and the thousands of newly recruited fans, a few basketball aficionados weren't convinced that the Lions were the greatest act under one roof since Barnum and Bailey. Prior to Saturday's much-publicized matchup, a reporter asked Michigan coach Bill Frieder who was going to win the game.

"The Master," replied Frieder.

The omnipotent being Frieder referred to was Dean Smith. The Michigan coach knew basketball and he knew firsthand how well the UNC coach could transmit his coaching knowledge. The only time Michigan and North Carolina had met in a basketball game had been a year earlier, in a similar situation. In 1987, Smith's team had defeated Frieder's Wolverines, 109–97, to gain a berth in the regional semifinals against Notre Dame. Frieder fully expected the two teams to meet again on the road to Kansas City. They would, but not before North Carolina stunned the basketball world.

Setting two new NCAA tournament scoring records, the Tar Heels beat the Lions at their own game, 123–97. In what had to be their best 40-minute game of the season, the Tar Heels added another chapter to the all-time NCAA ledger by setting the record for the most points in a game by a single team and by compiling the best field goal percentage (79 percent) in a game.

The Tar Heels played like a team possessed. North Carolina blew by the speeding Lions with an assortment of backdoor plays, layups, alley-oops, and dunks. When they weren't beating the Loyola full-court press, they calmly toyed with the Lions' half-court offense. Smith and company had done their homework, even if it was done at the last minute. The Tar Heels took advantage of every situation they faced and seemed able to score at will. Jeff Lebo attributed the win to preparation and execution.

"We watched the way they played defense," he said, "and they don't help out. Coach said a lot of backdoor plays would be open, but I didn't know they would be that open." They were. UNC capitalized on 10 backdoor plays throughout the game.

"We play a denial defense, and North Carolina countered by backcutting," Loyola coach Westhead said. "Backdoor cuts hurt us deeply. The turning point was the backdoor cuts and our inability to make enough baskets to stay in the hunt." The hunt was more like the overzealous buffalo shoots that took place a hundred years ago in the Great Plains. The Tar Heels kept firing at will, pausing only to reload with fresh troops. A steady rotation of players kept pace with the run-and-gun Loyola team. It was too much for the Lions, said Loyola forward Mike Yoest. "Carolina's bench — whew, I thought it would never end. Everyone that came in seemingly was 6–7, 6–8 and 240 pounds. I was really surprised they kept pace with us."

It took the Tar Heels just under ten minutes to amass a 13-point lead. By intermission, North Carolina led 65–40. Smith didn't let up. At halftime, he told his team a 25-point margin wasn't enough against Loyola. His charges responded by increasing the winning margin by a point. Ranzino Smith led the way, scoring 27 points on 11 of 14 field goals in just 18 minutes of playing time. (It would turn out to be his swan song. In his final two games, the outgoing senior wouldn't hit double figures. It didn't matter; the 6–1 senior had contributed greatly to a combined effort against a strong Loyola Marymount team.)

But the game belonged to the other Smith from North Carolina. Rising to the challenge with a gleam in his eye, the brilliant coach had masterminded the correct strategy and demonstrated his talents to the national audience. The team reflected his leadership, and in this case, it had never shone brighter.

•   •   •

Unbeknownst to the North Carolina followers, Jeff Lebo had played the Loyola Marymount game with a borderline fatigue fracture in his left ankle. It hadn't affected his performance as far as his numbers were concerned. The junior point guard had scored 19 points, including three of four three-point attempts, and had seven assists in 33 minutes of action. More importantly, he had directed his team past a talented squad to the NCAA western regionals. Lebo had informed team doctors of the injury the previous Friday and then played the game Saturday in pain.

An injury to one of UNC's starters is nothing new around NCAA tourney time. Actually, the fact that the team had entered the 1988 playoffs without an injured player was something of a relief. In the past few years, the Tar Heels had limped into NCAA action. In 1976, point guard Phil Ford was injured prior to the first round of the NCAA tournament. The following year Tommy LaGarde missed the Final Four while both Ford and Walter Davis played with nagging injuries. Mike O'Koren went down in 1978 just prior to the NCAAs. James Worthy was lost for the entire season in 1980. A year later, Matt Doherty missed nine games. In 1984, Kenny Smith injured his wrist and missed eight games. The team finished 28–3, but lost in the second round in the tournament. The next year, Steve Hale went down in NCAA second-round action. Hale also suffered a collapsed lung the following season, Joe Wolf hurt his ankle, and Warren Martin limped through 1986 postseason play.

A week earlier, Dean Smith had been happy to make it to the NCAAs in very good health, other than the usual bumps and bruises. But Lebo, his coach, and the team weren't too concerned. It would take a more serious injury to keep the talented "gamer" off the playing floor in Seattle the following Friday evening.

•   •   •

On Tuesday of the following week, a press conference was called in Chapel Hill. "Rick [Brewer, Carolina's SID] thought we should hold a press conference," Coach Smith said. "That's why I'm here, so, whatever questions you all have..." It wasn't the first time Coach Smith had felt self-conscious facing a large turnout for a press conference. His uncomfortable feelings were sincere, yet unnecessary. The reporters and television crews wanted to be there, as the public demanded to know everything they could about the program. No one thought the coach was pretentious for summoning the media as a group, rather than speaking individually with 30 or 40 writers and broadcasters. Still, despite his humble approach, the coach would have been hurt if the turnout was light.

"We're happy to be going somewhere," Smith said. "I'm glad I'm not playing golf today. Our only concern right now is Michigan." The coach went on to describe the Wolverines as a quick and experienced team, listing all of their major players and their strengths. He also began to play up the matchup between Terry Mills and J.R. Reid in an obvious attempt to light the competitive fires in his sophomore sensation. "Did you guys get this out west?" Smith asked the attending writers. "I didn't realize Mills is comparing himself to J.R. — you know they were two that were highly thought of — but he [Mills] says he always outplays him [Reid]. I hope he doesn't when we go out there on Friday." Smith's intent was twofold. First, to let the writers know that they should play up Mills' words. And secondly, to reinforce the challenge made by Mills to Reid. The '88 Tar Heels played better when the challenge was greater. Mills' words would look good in newsprint on the locker room wall. The two teams wouldn't suffer for want of reading or hearing about each other.

"In the NCAAs we used to play teams that you didn't know a lot about and they didn't know a lot about you — that's the way it used to be. Now, we have so many tapes of Michigan I can't even get through them. And I'm sure the same is true of North Carolina because North Carolina and Michigan are on TV so often."

Actually, in a syndicated sports listing that named the most frequently televised teams on CBS, NBC, ABC, ESPN, USA, or FNN/Score networks, Michigan didn't make the grade. Of the ten schools represented, North Carolina led the field with 16 national appearances. Syracuse and Georgetown were next with 12, followed closely by Kentucky, Villanova, and DePaul with 10. ACC companions Duke and Georgia Tech had entered the national airwaves nine times. Indiana, then the reigning national champion, was tenth with seven scheduled showings.

Regardless, Coach Smith armed himself with videotape of the Wolverines. He wasn't sure if he would repeat his tactic of showing videotape of UNC's opponents to the team, however.

"We're trying to get what we want done for this game and we may show them a couple of plays that we want to stop. They [the Tar Heels] know how good [Michigan guard Glen] Rice and [forward Gary] Grant would be. If they know that then we don't have to scare them by showing them a tape."

Smith went on to outline some of his thoughts about Michigan and its players. In the course of discussing how the Wolverine guards would play the Tar Heels, Smith casually mentioned that Lebo was injured. It was the first knowledge anyone outside of the program had received of his ailment.

"And let me say this," Smith said, almost as an aside. "Lebo couldn't work out yesterday. He has a very sore ankle bordering on a fatigue fracture in the ankle. Today we're going to have him play one out of 10 plays and then see if it gets worse tomorrow. It's where the fibula attaches to the ankle.

"I'm keeping my fingers crossed that he will be all right. He played with pain over the weekend — the doctors said it won't hurt him, but it is painful. It won't hurt his future."

The injury might not affect Lebo's future, but his play in the next game would be crucial to any Tar Heel success. With the news of the team's handicap, the Wolverines were surely licking their lips in anticipation of a wounded opponent. Hours later, the spirits of the UNC floor leader would be boosted, however. With its first pep rally of the decade, hundreds of the North Carolina rank and file showed their appreciation for the efforts of their team.

* * *

Weeks before, Scott Beckley, a sophomore at UNC, had approached Dean Smith on behalf of a new organization, Carolina Fever, a pep group formed to generate student spirit on campus. Though the Tar Heels are known far and wide for their basketball prowess and their fans number in the hundreds of thousands throughout the country, the attitude of many of the on-campus fans is complacent.

The thunderous din once generated by the students at the resonant Carmichael Auditorium had given way to polite applause and an occasional outburst in the plush and muted Smith Center. With the team's interest in mind, Carolina Fever had approached Smith and his program about holding a pep rally for the team. Originally the idea was to give the team a boisterous sendoff before the ACC tournament in Greensboro, but with the students leaving on spring break, the plan was postponed.

"Besides, we wanted to do it like it should be done at Carolina," Beckley said. "We got the pep band, the cheerleaders, and we reserved the Great Hall in the Student Union. I cleared everything with Coach Smith and he said he'd try to come and speak to us." Unbeknownst to those who patiently waited for the coach and his team that night, Smith had informed the media earlier in the day that he had attended his last pep rally many years ago. "We had them [pep rallies] back in '67, '68, and '69 out on the South Building steps and the whole place was crowded," Smith said. "In a way it was nice, but then one year, '72, they had a hundred people there — and that does more damage than it does good. So let's quit pep rallies.

"Four of our players even have a three-hour class tonight, but the teacher is going to let them miss 30 minutes to go to Great Hall. I have a talk show to go to so I don't have to go to another pep rally." Conveniently, Smith had the excuse of taping his radio show to offer as an excuse to the hundreds who jammed the Great Hall to hear him and see the team. Considering that the radio show was rescheduled anyway to allow the team to catch a plane the following night for Seattle, it wouldn't have been too much trouble to attend the rally.

Regardless, the sendoff was only a mixed success. Out of the thousands of students who claim allegiance to the Tar Heels, less than 300 attended the rally. At least those who did manage to be present were full of school spirit.

While the students (many of high school age or younger), a few television cameramen, and a handful of university workers waited for the team to arrive, the UNC band played through its entire repertoire of fight songs in an effort to pump some enthusiasm into the crowd. It worked. Inside the packed room, a room far too small to house such an event, the frenzy built to an explosion as the team made its entrance down a staircase led by the cheerleading squad. The team members were introduced individually to allow each member of the team to receive a generous round of applause. Assistant coach Bill Guthridge thanked the crowd for the team and its absent headmaster. And then Jeff Lebo took the microphone. The crowd voiced its pleasure with many of them holding up both arms in the referee's signal for a three-pointer, one aspect of the popular player's game. Many females in the audience nearly swooned at the sight of the boyishly handsome point guard.

"I wish we could pack you all up and take you along to Seattle," Lebo said, causing a hundred sighs from the girls present. "I wish I could go with you," senior Laura Drum gasped to a friend.

Ranzino Smith spoke next. It was interesting to see the senior, normally a well-composed spokesman for the team, clearly rattled by the mob of adoring fans. "Good evening, everyone," he said in a delivery rivaling a first-time speaker in a freshman speech class. "You are the best fans in America. (Applause) And, ah, I just want to say, ah, thanks to you all on behalf of the team. (Applause) We'll do the best that we can." After some prompting from nearby David May, Smith, reduced to a caricature of the tongue-tied student athlete, concluded with, "We're going up there to win."

It was refreshing to see the members of one of America's best college basketball programs let their youth betray their experience in public. Away from the fishbowl existence and program protection they are forced to live with after accepting a UNC scholarship, the players resemble most 18- and 19-year-olds. The seriousness of the program and the forced humility often overshadow the importance of being allowed to appreciate their exalted status.

One man's glory is not always the same as another's. While those assembled for the pep rally placed the Tar Heel team upon a pedestal, a dozen other North Carolina students in a lounge just outside the Great Hall were content to watch Vanna White turn vowels on a 50-inch color television.

•   •   •

The next day, while the team was en route to Seattle, the sports desk of the Turner Broadcasting System was busy speculating about one of the North Carolina players during halftime of the Chicago Bulls–Philadelphia 76ers game. Journalist Roy Johnson of the *Atlanta Journal-Constitution* was a guest on the program. Rumors were flourishing as to who would declare hardship and join the next crop of NBA draftees. The decision to declare must be made 45 days prior to the draft, so most players would need to decide soon. The question put to Johnson was why collegiate players would opt to leave school early.

"The contributing factor is money — pure and simple," Johnson said. "The lure of the lucrative contract in the 17 years since the NBA instituted the draft is often too tantalizing for the young kids to ignore. It's a calculated risk that could either set a player for life financially or place him in a bind he'd never recover from.

"Junior center Pervis Ellison from Louisville was considered college basketball's premier man — but that was before J.R. Reid came along. Only a sophomore, Reid has established himself as college basketball's low-post land baron. He owns everything in the paint. He'd be a number-two lottery pick, or maybe even number one ahead of Danny Manning of Kansas."

It would just be a matter of time before Reid would reveal his decision. Months had passed since the issue had threatened to disrupt the team's harmony. Reid's parents had set the record straight earlier, saying their son would remain in a North Carolina uniform until he received his education. If the lure of having a millionaire in the family could be safely resisted for a year or two by Reid and his parents, the team's stock would continue to rise over the summer. If Reid took the money and ran, the program would still be a contender, but not the odds-on favorite to win it all in 1989.

• • •

There would be no sympathy vote for Carolina's Jeff Lebo and his tender appendage. The Wolverines announced that they too had ailments to elicit the public's concern. Forward Glen Rice, the Big 10's leading scorer that season, had injured his ankle in practice the day before. Guard Rumeal Robinson added to Michigan's woes by suffering stomach cramps in the morning. Both players practiced in the Wolverines' workout at Seattle's Kingdome with Rice dunking a couple to dispel any belief of a serious injury, but the trainers would be working overtime to curb any lingering effects.

"If Glen's not 100 percent healthy, we're in trouble," head coach Bill Frieder said. "But he's good with injuries." A week earlier, Rice had proved the coach's point. Reaching into a dishwasher to extract a drinking glass, Rice had broken it in his shooting hand. The resulting cut required six stitches to close. It hadn't affected his play against Michigan's NCAA second-round opponent, Florida, however. In that game, Rice had poured in 39 points. Frieder may have been stoking the competitive fires, anyway. Coaches have been known to play up controversies and injuries to ensure better performances from both the injured player and his teammates. The game was very important to the Michigan coach. His thoughts were on the game the two teams had played the year before, even though he attempted to downplay its importance to the media.

"We really haven't discussed the game in Charlotte much or played on it," Frieder said. "Oh, we showed them the film, but just as a learning thing. Last year, we were defending J.R. with [6–8] Mark Hughes. We had a guard on one of their 6–10 guys and [6–7] Glen Rice guarding another 6–10 guy, which made us overly matched at every position. Now, we can go more size by size. We've got more of it. And although no one player can guard J.R. for 40 minutes, we can change defenses and defenders on him."

Stopping Reid is usually an opponents' biggest worry. If any single player would have a good chance it would be the Wolverines' Terry Mills. Mills and Reid were not strangers to each other, even though they had never faced each other in collegiate play. While Reid was busy gaining the nation's respect and adoration during his freshman year, Mills, another highly sought prep All-American, had sat out the 1986-87 season under Proposition 48. The two first met during high school on the asphalt of heated summer battles in basketball camp. The rivalry had been renewed again in July 1987, in the U.S. Olympic Festival on the hardwood floor of the Smith Center in Chapel Hill.

Mills and his squad from the North had routed Reid and the South team in the gold-medal finale. Still, both players told the press there were no overly competitive feelings toward each other. "I had the better team at the festival," Mills said. "And I got a lot of backside help on defense against J.R." Reid went on to describe any comparison between Mills and himself as somewhat like apples and oranges. "Terry's not a true post player," Reid said, trying to dismiss any excess media attention focused on the matchup. "He's more of a finesse forward. He's quick around the basket and has a nice touch."

The other matchup getting the attention of the fans and the coaches alike was the guard play of both teams. Frieder possessed the quicker backcourt in All-American Gary Grant and another resuscitated Prop 48 casualty, Rumeal Robinson. Compared to the methodical play of North Carolina's backcourt of Jeff Lebo and Kevin Madden, many hoop fans thought the Wolverines would blow past the Tar Heels. To fight that notion, Frieder quickly pointed out his concerns.

"With Lebo, Madden, and Ranzino Smith, they have a quality backcourt," he said. "What they lack in quickness, they make up for in great intelligence. Lebo really knows what to do with the basketball. He pinpoints his passes, shoots well in transition. And we must prevent three-point shooting by their guards. They really hurt us with that last year. We can't leave Lebo and Smith to help out with their big guys — just can't do it and expect to win."

With Lebo only practicing for 10 minutes in the week preceding the Friday night game, Frieder's worries might have been in vain. Freshman King Rice had performed well in his previous start for Lebo, when both Lebo and Ranzino were sidelined in January against Fordham, and had continued to improve in limited relief at point guard, but against a team like Michigan the young guard would have been out of his element in a 40-minute game. The Tar Heels' chances hinged on the well-being of its chief floor asset.

UNC 78, MICHIGAN 69

Michigan head coach Loy Vaught felt his pack of Wolverines would devour the Tar Heels in the semifinal of the NCAA West Regionals. "We're deeper talentwise," Vaught said the day before, raising the eyebrows of the reporters who followed the talent-laden Tar Heel team. "What I mean is, individually, we're more talented. And our depth is also a big asset for us. We can come in with four big guys, while they basically just have J.R. and Scott Williams." Despite his huffing and puffing, the Wolverines turned out to be much meeker beasts in nylon clothing. Contrary to Vaught's prediction, it was North Carolina's bench that made the difference in the game. UNC reserves outscored their Michigan counterparts 19–1 in a 78–69 win to gain a shot at another pack of hungry beasts, the Arizona Wildcats.

"This team keeps surprising me," Dean Smith said of his wild-animal tamers. "They've amazed me by the way they've improved and the way they compete. We showed the ability to hang in there when things didn't look so good." After clipping the wings of the North Texas State Eagles, Carolina was not expected to dine on Loyola Lions or Michigan Wolverines. Smith's teams are always respected, but if there was ever a year to knock them out of action, it was during a so-called rebuilding year.

In the first half against Michigan, UNC played as if it finally realized that it was playing in an NCAA regional semifinal. The Wolverines started howling at the beginning of the game, employing a full-court press and forcing bad shots from the nervous Tar Heels. On the downside, Scott Williams had a shot blocked, Jeff Lebo, Ranzino Smith, and J.R. Reid all missed jump shots, and King Rice threw up an airball. The good news was that all nine regulars saw action and got some rest; Michigan's starters were tired, and All-American Gary Grant had to sit down with two early fouls.

"Our depth is nine deep and we play those people," Smith said after Rick Fox and Ranzino Smith made early contributions. "I think that could have been a factor, particularly at the four and five spots — our big people. We were trying to keep moving without the ball, and their big guys aren't used to playing so many active people." While Michigan's inside attack was worn down physically by the constant influx of fresh Tar Heels, sophomore guard Rumeal Robinson and forward Glen Rice swished jumpers to keep the game even. After 13 lead changes, UNC led 31–30 at the end of the first half. The second half, as usual, would determine the outcome.

"Coach Smith gave us a great pep talk at halftime," Reid said, remembering his source of inspiration. "He told us this was a once-in-a-lifetime opportunity and that we had to be more patient." More patient to North Carolina means looking to work the ball inside to Reid or Williams, and for the Tar Heel big men to avoid forcing their shots. Reid, who was two of eight in the first period, began producing in the second. His 18 points, combined with Williams' 19, doubled the output from their Michigan counterparts.

On defense, North Carolina was able to shut down the Wolverine inside game while not giving up the easy foul. In the end, it may have been Michigan's propensity to foul that made the difference. UNC went to the line and made 21 of 30 attempts. The Wolverines could only manage nine points from the charity stripe. Still, the Tar Heels could have just as easily lost the game at the free-throw line. In the critical last two minutes, with the game still undecided, they missed five bonus shots, including the front end of three one-and-ones. On three of those occasions, Reid made up for the misses. Twice he crashed the offensive board and came away with the ball. And with the Tar Heels holding a four-point lead with a little over a minute to play, Reid missed the front end of a one-and-one opportunity only to steal the ball back from the rebounding Grant.

With a combination of luck and heads-up play, Carolina had proven its number seven national ranking. The inexperienced and overachieving team had advanced past the "sweet sixteen" into the round of eight. Their fans were hoping the bubble wouldn't burst too quickly.

Despite the morale-building and confidence-swelling the victory over Michigan had brought to the young Tar Heels, the regional semifinal game had extracted its toll. A hobbled Jeff Lebo proved he could play with pain by logging 33 minutes against All-American Gary Grant. He did so with considerable rest during the preceding week. One day's rest before taking the floor again might not be enough time to maintain his high threshold of pain. More importantly, the team had suffered two other setbacks in the game. Scott Williams popped his shoulder out due to Michigan's tough inside play. He recovered enough to complete 28 minutes, but he would be needed to go the distance against the highest-ranked team still in contention. And last, but definitely not the least of Carolina's woes, was a re-injury to Steve Bucknall's toe. Bucknall, the Tar Heel designated defender, would need to slow down Arizona's top cat, All-American Sean Elliott.

Considering the Wildcats' assets and the Tar Heel liabilities, it was little surprise North Carolina was made a six-point underdog. Again, the underdog role was where Smith wanted his team — but this time the role was for real. With such considerable handicaps, the odds should have been greater. Even the UNC program, an outfit that never conceded a game until the buzzer sounded, knew it would take a super effort to win. Whatever luck was present in the Michigan game would be needed again — in spades. When UNC players were asked before the Arizona final what they needed to do to beat the Wildcats, their reply was "to play a near perfect game."

"We've had three good wins," Lebo said at Saturday's press conference. "We have great respect for Arizona and we have nothing to lose going out there. If we play well and lose, we'll be happy. We'll give it all we have." Lebo's assessment of the problem North Carolina faced was relaxed and matter-of-fact. The point guard was one of only a handful of Tar Heels who had experienced the thrill of being in a regional final as both the favorite and the underdog. As a freshman, Lebo played through the season as a member of a top-ranked team. The 1986-87 team was expected to win every time out. Consequently, each game was an emotional and physical struggle to keep from losing.

His current team was a different shade of Carolina blue. True to form, Smith's Tar Heels were greatly respected and still a national contender each time they took to the hardwood. But a weight had been lifted from the shoulders of the young team in 1988. Gone was the confident expectation that North Carolina should win every game. The team's inexperience and lack of consistency had brought back an element of unknowing. The wins were appreciated a little bit more and the losses were taken a little easier by the players and those who followed the team. The team no longer played to escape without a loss, but competed to win.

•   •   •

Back in Chapel Hill, another ex-Tar Heel was also in competition to win. While the Tar Heels were plying their trade in the spacious Seattle Kingdome, the Dean Dome was host to yet another basketball tournament. The North Carolina high school championships for boys and girls were scheduled on the UNC campus. One championship, the boys 2A basketball title, held special significance. Sitting at the opposite end of the bench from where he had sat years before, James Daye, a member of the 1986 UNC basketball team, coached the Lexington High School team to a state title over Pender, 91-71.

Like the inexperienced 1987-88 Tar Heel squad, the Lexington Jackets were not expected to advance so far in postseason play. But, unlike UNC, the end result would prove to be different. In both their sectional and regional final, the Jackets met the previous year's state champion, Salisbury, a team that had returned the majority of its championship lineup. The Jackets had accepted the challenge and defeated them twice. Coach Daye said that he enjoyed coming back to Chapel Hill for such a momentous occasion. Carrying on the North Carolina "coaching" tradition of unselfish praise, Daye was quick to recognize his players' contributions.

"This was really something for the kids," he said. "As a coach, I took the back seat, but it is something that the kids will never forget." Daye, a walk-on who had earned a scholarship just as Dean Smith had at Kansas years ago, had already mastered two aspects of his former coach's traits — winning and public self-effacement.

ARIZONA 70, UNC 52

The nation's best team took on the nation's best program Sunday, and the better team won. Arizona, 35-2, advanced to the Final Four with a 70–52 victory over the Tar Heels. The loss signaled the sixth consecutive year North Carolina failed to clinch a regional championship and a trip to the "big dance." For Dean Smith, a man with seven regional championships under his belt, the most by any coach in the game today, getting an invitation to the exclusive party was becoming harder and harder.

One of the problems was due to such success. With the team's constant national exposure and Smith's own philosophy of sharing his knowledge with other coaches, there are few surprises about his teams' abilities or his coaching strategies. Any weaknesses have been exposed long before tournament play begins. Of course, there is still the matter of defeating his team. It doesn't matter if you know everything Smith will throw at you if you can't stop it. Few teams, even better ones, get the best of North Carolina over long periods of time. The numbers don't usually add up in favor of the opposition. The Wildcats were a different story.

Based on 1988 NCAA tournament performance, the Wildcats were statistically the better team. Smith had crunched the numbers before the game and come up with Arizona as the probable winner. "If we played a series, Arizona would probably beat us seven out of 10," he said. The game didn't start out with such a clear-cut advantage.

The Tar Heels fell behind early as the Wildcats scored the game's first five points, but they quickly rallied with a nine-point run of their own. Steve Kerr scored the Wildcats' only point during the run at the free-throw line. It was a vintage UNC pressure defense that forced the balanced Wildcat attack to hesitate. Arizona countered with a zone, forcing North Carolina to shoot jumpers instead of J.R. Reid hook shots. Had the Tar Heels hit their outside shots the game might have broken open in the first half. Instead, they were cold from three-point range and unable to effectively penetrate the paint.

Throughout the first half, Jeff Lebo directed traffic while assisting Kevin Madden and Ranzino Smith in their attempts to score. But Madden and Smith were one for nine before Smith hit a three-pointer to give North Carolina a one-point lead late in the first half. The Tar Heels had an excellent chance to run their lead up to five points when Kerr was called for an intentional foul with 33 seconds remaining in the half. The Arizona guard had been a step late in a foolish attempt to stop a Rick Fox layup from behind. But Fox could only hit one free throw and Carolina squandered its chance for a last-second basket by muffing a Four Corners play. The half ended with UNC holding a two-point lead, 28–26. It wouldn't be nearly enough.

Both coaches wanted to change their strategies at halftime. Smith wanted to get the ball into the hands of Reid — to let him determine the outcome and keep up the pressure defense. Lute Olson wanted to attack North Carolina's defense, regain the lead, and then spread out his offense to allow Elliott more freedom to play one-on-one. Both teams were successful in their changes. But while Arizona began to score inside, getting 18 second-half points from 6–7, 242-pound center Tom Tolbert, the Tar Heels' first-half cold spell got icy. The lead changed hands six times before a Tolbert three-point play gave the Wildcats a working lead they would never relinquish.

Reid scored on a thunderous dunk with 9:21 to play to cut the Wildcat lead to five points at 51–46. The brief storm was over as quickly as it started, though. Over the next seven and a half minutes, North Carolina missed eight straight field goal attempts. Everyone on the floor for UNC tried to make a jump shot. Madden, Reid, Smith, and Lebo all missed from within their normal shooting range. "We all had some very good shots out there," Lebo said after the game. "We had a couple jump shots at the foul line. We had a couple three-point jump shots that we normally hit and some inside shots that normally go in for us. Sometimes they just don't go in."

"For Jeff's sake," Dean Smith interjected, "he is playing with that fatigue fracture that could have changed his shot in the second half. We do want to protect him on that by all means." Regardless of the reason, the missed Tar Heel shots eliminated their chance of getting back into the game.

At the other end of the court, the Wildcats turned to Elliott and Tolbert to provide a one-two punch that worked the lead up to nine points. It was Elliott, the eventual regional tournament MVP, who finally took control of the game and guaranteed his team an outing to Kansas City. UNC's Reid, used to taking control of a game instead of watching, knew the damage Elliott was creating. "In the second half, Elliott would go one-on-one, and we would have to step up to help out. He would then make excellent passes," said Reid.

Lebo agreed. "He's hard to cover one-on-one and what makes him so good is he can shoot the ball. You have to honor his jump shot, and when you get up on him, he can blow by you." Steve Bucknall had held Elliott in check in the first half. With Bucknall unable to continue effectively, due to his injury, the task was split between the North Carolina guards and forward Rick Fox. But no one could keep Elliott from taking the game to the Tar Heels.

Eventually, Coach Smith went to his last-chance, rapid-change, offense/defense platoon. Ranzino Smith went in for King Rice in offensive situations and went out for defensive purposes. Madden replaced Williams. Williams replaced Madden. But no substitution could stop Arizona once it began to sense victory. The defense that had propelled the Tar Heels into the regional finals wasn't sharp. In a game-long parade to the foul line, the Wildcats stepped forward and delivered on 23 of 28 attempts. When a frustrated Madden committed an intentional foul with only a minute to play and his team down by 12, Smith threw in the towel. With a show of compassion for his gutsy overachieving team, Smith pulled his remaining starters and replaced them with the seldom-seen practice players.

With the game and the season ten seconds from conclusion, sophomore Jeff Denny paid one more tribute to Dean Smith and the UNC tradition. In true Carolina fashion, Denny took one last charge to end the 1988 quest for a trip to the Final Four.

• • •

The season had been over for only a few minutes when the next began. Tar Heel Network color analyst Jim Heavner, in a postgame interview with UNC Athletic Director John Swofford, started the earliest preseason hype in the history of sports. Mentioning that he wished the two teams could meet again with all of the players on the floor as seniors in what Heavner had described as a dream game, he speculated that the difference between the two teams might not have been talent so much as it was experience. "That bodes extremely well, I think — and I'm going to start that business of looking forward to next year — because the Tar Heels bring so much talent back."

Swofford was quick to agree. "We do have reason to look forward to next year with great anticipation, with Ranzino being the only player on this year's team that won't be back next year. Certainly, you hate this loss, particularly for Ranzino, but the other guys will have another chance."

In the locker room, Ranzino Smith was not thinking about next year. The Chapel Hill native had exhausted four years of solid effort to get to the Final Four. The years of disappointment were written all over the senior's face, but he was unable to experience his anguish in solitude. Throngs of reporters and broadcasters were there, asking the whys and why nots that are so painful in postgame losses. Smith fought back the urge to release his pent-up emotions and bravely answered the questions thrown at him without regard to his feelings.

Woody Durham, the voice of the Tar Heel Sports Network and a longtime fan of the program, was caught between his job and his feelings. With microphone in hand, the renowned North Carolina sportscaster betrayed his emotions to the network audience, a situation many fellow sports journalists identified with. "I'm holding a microphone right now," Durham whispered, "and I almost feel like it's an invasion of privacy to put a microphone right now in front of Ranzino Smith, the only senior on this team."

The network picked up Ranzino in mid-sentence as he tried to describe how he felt. "It really hurts inside," Smith said, his voice cracking. "My college basketball career is over and I never got a chance to go to the Final Four. It hurts bad to come this far and lose ..."

Durham mercifully cut off the locker room report. "That pretty well summarizes things," he intoned dramatically, "and as we said during the closing stages of the game — there ain't nothing that feels any better than winning at this level, and there ain't nothing that hurts any worse than losing at this level."

The broadcast, and the Tar Heel season, ended.

VI.
POSTGAME

The team, cheerleaders, band, and assorted supporters arrived back on campus via a chartered bus. Few UNC fans were on hand to greet the team. In fact, there was no postseason celebration at all. It didn't matter that the squad had overachieved continually all season, compiling a 27–7 record and representing the university nobly before losing in the West Regional finals. It didn't matter that the returning team would probably be the nation's top-ranked team in just a matter of months. For, despite the accomplishments, nothing less than another NCAA championship trophy is considered acceptable for the only college basketball team that could be called "America's team."

The next day, March 28, was business as usual. Dean Smith, before leaving for the Final Four and the accompanying National Coaches Association convention in Kansas City, began to conduct individual postseason interviews with his players. Only two would be turning in their gear, Ranzino Smith and Joe Jenkins. Both seniors were called into the inner chambers to express parting thoughts. Jenkins, a practice player who had joined the glamorous program for his senior year, was treated like a four-year recruit.

"Coach asked me if I could think of anything that might help the program in the future," Jenkins said later, on a bright warm afternoon in the pit, a courtyard of sorts in the heart of the UNC campus. "He does that every year. I can't think of anything that could've been done better, though."

The rest of the team were given assignments for the summer. Each player knew just what parts of his game to work on and further develop. Each player knew that he still represented North Carolina and needed to be aware of such responsibility.

• • •

Hosted by the Voice of the Tar Heels, Woody Durham, and originating in Chapel Hill, the ACC Hotline radio program had hoped to feature Carolina in its Final Four final edition. With guest Billy Packer via telephone from Kansas City, Tuesday's show dealt mainly with call-in questions about the Blue Devils' chances in Kansas City. Still, callers couldn't resist asking Packer about the Tar Heel's season-ending game with Arizona.

"UNC got beat by a better team," Packer said. "I think Carolina is a year away from being a really outstanding team." It pacified UNC listeners. The CBS color analyst then went on to point out an interesting statement by Dean Smith. Packer said he would have to discuss it with Smith this summer. "It was Dean's comment where he said, 'We don't take what the defense gives us, we work until we get what we want against the defense.' I spent a lot of time analyzing that statement. One thing has been apparent in both the Michigan and Arizona games. Teams play Carolina not to take certain shots, particularly shots by J.R. [Reid] at the foul line. In my estimation, he is very capable of making those shots.

In essence, Packer was questioning Smith's control over himself, his players, and the team's shot selection. In his book entitled *Hoops! Confessions of a College Basketball Analyst,* Packer had written, "Dean normally has things buttoned up so tight there is little or no opportunity for mistake. Even when things don't go well for him, he responds with control. Only once over many years did I see him lose control, and in a way it was nice to see that happen, to know that he's human. It was back in 1975.

"Wake Forest was playing Carolina in Chapel Hill. Marvin "Skeeter" Francis, an ACC administrative official, was in charge of calling the television timeouts during the game. Skeeter was also a former sports information director at Wake Forest. During the broadcast, Skeeter didn't control when television timeouts were called. He simply followed the established procedure (timeouts are usually called at 16, 12, 10, and 8 minutes left in the period), and Dean certainly would have recognized that if he hadn't been emotionally involved in the game. When the game ended and Wake Forest had won, Dean really jumped on Skeeter. As the postgame press conference began, Dean essentially accused Skeeter of using television timeouts to help Wake Forest win the game. In more than 20 years of watching Dean Smith, it was the only time I've seen him respond emotionally rather than logically."

Packer also gave his predictions for the 1988 champion. "I like Arizona ... I can't see Kansas winning both games out here." He was to be proved wrong twice.

•   •   •

Two years earlier, *The Chapel Hill Newspaper* sports department had run a story about Dean Smith accepting a part in a *Miami Vice* episode. The April 1 piece had caused many an excited telephone call to the three-man staff from local readers failing to pick up the obvious hint of an April Fools' joke. Officials with the program hadn't voiced a formal complaint, but off-the-record comments had indicated that while the article "might be" funny, it was immature for an established daily newspaper to involve itself with such a prank. Though many readers looked for a similar story to appear in 1988, the new sports staff decided to avoid risking the wrath of those without a sense of humor.

•   •   •

With Duke's loss to eventual national champion Kansas, the final tabulation of ACC winnings was complete as far as NCAA monies were concerned. Actually, the tally could have been completed immediately following the regional finals, as all of the Final Four teams earn the same amount from the NCAA till. Considering that the NCAA expected to rake in over $66 million from the 64-team extravaganza called "March Madness," the five conference schools did their fair share of business. All eight league members benefited from the approximate $3.25 million, but Duke and North Carolina would pocket the most change.

After applying the ACC formula for division of wealth (all schools entered in the tournament get to keep all first-round money and 70 percent from that point forward), the Blue Devils saw take-home pay of $801,660 from a check of $926,660.

According to Martina Kendricks, a UNC business manager, Carolina received approximately $735,000 out of about $923,000. North Carolina ran up NCAA tournament expenses of $200,000, including two chartered plane rides for $147,000. (The corporation should look into purchasing its own jet.)

In addition to NCAA monies, each conference school would get an eighth of the remaining 30 percent each tournament school gave to the ACC annual TV income pool. There's more. The NCAA gave each participating school expense money totaling $3,300 per day plus airfare for any days the team took part in the tournament. Discount a few grand for any additional expenses and North Carolina added another million to its $4 million projected basketball revenue. After subtracting overhead for the year, four months of basketball had netted the UNC athletic department about $4 million — a profit of roughly $33,000 per day.

•   •   •

The UNC Educational Foundation held its annual meeting April 9 in the Smith Center. In less than an hour, the foundation officers, two coaches, UNC's chancellor, and the newly appointed chancellor-elect all spoke to the group made up of approximately 750 members and their families. Not all made the trip specifically for the meeting. In addition to the assembly and box luncheon, the day, promotionally named 'Super Saturday,' showcased a spring Blue-White football scrimmage, a North Carolina baseball game against Virginia, a women's tennis match, a state collegiate track meet, and a round of the Tar Heel Invitational golf tournament.

Many were meeting the new chancellor and new football coach for the first time. But in spite of a standing ovation for the chancellor-elect, Dean Smith was obviously the popular favorite among the noted speakers. Smith acknowledged his sunburned face and explained that he had been practicing his golf game to compete against the two chancellors in the coming week. "I hadn't played since October 15, so I snuck off this week and played, thanks to some friends I stayed with [in Florida]. I should have been out recruiting, but I had tried that before about six years ago trying to get Danny Manning — but that didn't work out.

"We are happy for our graduate Larry Brown, our former player, former coach. Incidentally, UCLA has called me many times in the past," he said in reference to Kansas' NCAA championship and to Brown's day-old announcement that he had turned down UCLA to stay with the Jayhawks. (Brown would later accept a head coaching job with the San Antonio Spurs as the highest-paid professional coach.) The audience was expecting Smith to say that he had been offered the job. "And I got a call this time ... and they said, 'What about Larry,'" he continued to nervous laughter. "Anyway it's nice that they called again. Of course, they called quite a few people around here." The crowd erupted with more laughter to the reference to area coaches Jim Valvano and Mike Krzyzewski. They were relieved that their coach hadn't been lured away.

Smith entertained the crowd for a few more moments and then opened the floor to questions. He did so because he had been "given a sabbatical" from his yearly duty of speaking at Educational Foundation meetings throughout the region. The "chore" of making the rounds for the faithful is an obligation many Division I coaches experience annually. With a new Tar Heel football coach on board, Smith could take a break from speaking and let the newest addition entertain the athletic supporters.

The first question posed to the coach was to the point. Already, next year was on the minds of the moneyed alumni. They wanted to know if Smith had recruited another outside shooting guard, the position that had kept the outgoing team from the Final Four and one that graduating guard Ranzino Smith had filled intermittently. Smith, who refuses to discuss recruiting, eschewed his normal "we don't talk about recruiting at Carolina" that is *de rigeur* for members of the media. Instead, he did a smooth song and dance around the question to appease the questioner, whom he knew by name. The coach went on to mention many prospects who had ended up with North Carolina as their second choice. They had chosen to attend other schools, something that hasn't happened often over the years. "And as Eddie Fogler [a former assistant coach at UNC and now the head coach at Wichita State] once said, 'They must see playing time and they must be close to home,'" Smith offered as an excuse. Why he used Fogler's reasoning is a mystery. Smith never guarantees playing time and long-distance recruiting is the norm for UNC. Out of the expected returning players for 1988-89, the top seven are from out of state, with three starters from California, the Bahamas, and Great Britain. Within minutes Smith casually mentioned that one of his coaches was in Europe to scout a player (most likely Henrik Rodl in Germany). The Educational Foundation members were in effect treated to a mild version of doublespeak.

Smith then took the opportunity to mention that his two seniors would graduate, and that over the last 10 years the graduation percentage was 100 percent, with the exception of Michael Jordan and James Worthy, who came back later and finished their degrees. He didn't mention the other players who hadn't graduated within four years, but took longer, during the last decade.

"I should tell you that we [the basketball program] are happy with this season, although I'm never happy at this meeting unless we've won our last game," Smith admitted. "I'm still amazed at how many people follow this program so closely." Smith went on to talk about people he had spoken to in Florida and a three-page letter he had received from an alumnus who talked in depth about the past season. Smith said that he couldn't believe the people didn't have other things to do. "One thing is nice, though. At least when *you* walk out of here after a loss, it doesn't ruin the next day — it does mine." (Of course, stating it doesn't make it so. Most North Carolina fans do suffer after a Tar Heel loss.) Though the expectations of his fans are unrealistic and much too lofty, it's unlikely that it will change as long as the living legend coaches in the center that bears his name.

•   •   •

Speaking of living legends, Michael Jordan, the country's most visible basketball superstar, but just one of many former North Carolina All-Americans, reached an agreement with the Chicago Bulls of the NBA on an eight-year contract worth $28 million. The contract, described in the *Chicago Tribune* on April 8, will pay Jordan an average yearly salary of $3.5 million, more than any professional basketball player has ever been paid. What "Air" Jordan receives from the Bulls isn't half of what he makes, by a long shot. The numbers he records in the basketball history books are incredible. The numbers compiled in his bank books are even more impressive, making him the world's highest-paid team athlete. Jordan had been in the fourth year of a seven-year contract with the Bulls that was worth between $6.2 million plus incentives. But that represented only a fifth of his total net income.

"And that percentage is diminishing all the time," says his agent, David Falk of Washington-based Proserv Inc. "The number of his endorsements is staggering. From the national and regional stalwarts like Coca-Cola, McDonalds, Nike, and Chevrolet, Wilson, McGregor, Johnson and Johnson, to his own line of watches and a stake in his family's auto parts business — Michael Jordan's endorsement is money in the bank."

In spite of the temptations of extravagance, the young multimillionaire has maintained an unaffected attitude toward his success. Even now, Michael Jordan reflects the program that helped mold his basketball talent. Though his playing style is "in-your-face," he is one of the first to speak highly of his teammates and opponents while downplaying his own talents. He was more pleased with the Defensive Player of the Year honors he received than being named the game's MVP. He also speaks out against excesses, especially the use of drugs, pro basketball's greatest threat.

Michael Jordan doesn't belong to the Chicago Bulls and their supporters. He, like the collegiate program he played for, belongs to the country. Like a handful of superstars who are known internationally on a single-name basis — Reggie, Chrissie and Martina, Magic, and Arnie — Jordan has been added to the list. And even with such notoriety, he hasn't forgotten his beginnings. To this day he wears his UNC practice shorts underneath his Bulls' uniform to remind him from whence he came.

•   •   •

A young man many had hoped might be the next Michael Jordan, UNC signee Kenny Williams, headed the 1988 AP men's all-state high school basketball team for North Carolina. It was no surprise. Earlier, Williams had earned the AP Player of the Year award in North Carolina, Parade All-American status, and had been named a member of the McDonald's All-Star Classic team. The 6–9, 220-pound senior was considered by many collegiate scouts as one of the top 10 high school players in the country.

Williams would add even more depth to a team that returned eight of its top nine players — if he played. The biggest question mark concerning the young prospect was his eligibility. His first attempts at the Scholastic Aptitude Test (SAT) yielded less than the 700 score required by the NCAA. Williams, who had transferred to Virginia's Fork Union Military Academy

as a junior to improve his grades, had said he had gotten over the require-
ment on his third try. He was mistaken. Adding to the youngster's woes was
his failure to graduate with his high school class.

Coach Smith spoke to the recruit about sitting out his freshman year to
concentrate on academics, but Williams said he'd rather "make a go of it
right off the bat" and forego a redshirt season. Whether or not he would ride
the pine in a business suit or a blue and white uniform wouldn't be
determined for months. (In mid-June the signee had not yet applied for
admission. Smith would later ask the prospect to apply elsewhere. Williams
eventually enrolled in a junior college in Kansas.)

•   •   •

The same week, the 1988 version of the ACC All-Stars announced an
eight-game basketball exhibition season around North Carolina. UNC
seniors Ranzino Smith and Joe Jenkins would both log some time and pick
up sporting goods and a few dollars to spend until graduation. As their
amateur days were over and the Olympics out of the question, both were free
to become "professional" in terms of accepting payment for play.

The money received for each game wasn't much, compared to what
some of the all-stars would later command in the professional ranks, but for
walk-on Jenkins and even Smith, it might be the only time they would be
hired to play basketball and receive payment for it. The majority of the
performers over the years had been bona fide all-stars, and only North
Carolina seemed to squeeze a few also-rans and managers into the barnstorming tour. For the players leaving the close protection of the UNC
program, it was the first of many doors that their association with Dean
Smith would open. Jenkins would add his year of experience to his resume
and pursue a position in business. Ranzino Smith would look for a
professional basketball team.

•   •   •

Granville Towers, the privately owned dormitories where many of the
Tar Heel basketball players live during the school year, was the site that
Thursday night of an unusual basketball game. Two hours before midnight,
a full-court game began among a few daring individuals. Late-night hoops
are a way of life on almost any campus in the Tar Heel state, but normally
the participants are clothed. At this contest, the ten men played the game
wearing only their high-topped basketball shoes.

The game didn't seem to upset the assembled crowd of a hundred coeds
and a few other men, but at least one resident was offended enough to call
the police to halt the action. Public Safety Officer Woody Sands Minton

filed a report the next day that was later picked up and published by the Chapel Hill bureau of the *Durham Morning Herald.* His report was succinct:

"A group of about 10 nude males were playing basketball at Granville. They had attracted the attention of 100 or so coeds with varying focuses of attention. The suspects ran upon the approach of the police car. The coeds booed. No suspects were caught."

One coed, who preferred not to be identified, later remarked that she couldn't remember if any of the school's varsity basketball team were involved in the game. "You know," she giggled, "I didn't even see their faces."

• • •

Another graduate of the program made headlines that week. Brad Daugherty, a former All-America center at North Carolina, scored a career-high 44 points in a resounding Cleveland Cavalier victory over the Boston Celtics, 120–109. The NBA All-Star had become an integral part of his club's success in only his second year in uniform. Though not a spectacular player like a Michael Jordan or James Worthy, Daugherty makes his impact known in a less demonstrative fashion. Though a consistent scorer at North Carolina, the seven-footer was accused of not "having what it takes" to play in the NBA. Foregoing the popular slam dunk, Daugherty had been content to softly lay the ball off the glass during his collegiate days. For his gentleness, many fans didn't believe he should have been the top pick in the 1986 NBA draft.

His skeptics were wrong. Another former company man, Kenny Smith, followed in Daugherty's footsteps a year later when he too was named to the NBA All-Rookie team.

• • •

Retirement dinners are always the same; only those being honored change. The UNC basketball program, via its annual basketball banquet on April 18, released two more graduates into the world of life after North Carolina. Joe Jenkins, a walk-on, represented a student athlete poised and ready to enter corporate America. Ranzino Smith withdrew into the past, unsure of what the future held for him.

UNC honored its seniors with a cozy prime-rib dinner for around 500. Not to worry, the banquet was budgeted into basketball expenses for $28,000 and some of the invitees would pay for the privilege of attending. Over the years, the banquet had been held at various hotels and fine restaurants. With the building of the Smith Center and the adjoining annex in 1986, the postseason meal has been held in the Skipper Bowles Hall. The well-attended affair is a good chance to see the program in a different, semi-relaxed atmosphere, even though the voice of Woody Durham, the Tar Heel Network play-by-play announcer turned master of ceremonies, added a note of professionalism to the event. The two-hour presentation of awards is also videotaped, adding a bit of stiffness to the players' and coachs' remarks.

Like the basketball program itself, there are few surprises or spontaneous comments. The same coaches have presented the banquet for so long that frequent attendees can recite the spiels by heart, minus the current award recipient's name. As the attending faithful know all the latest statistics on every player, seldom does one receive a tribute that isn't already known. Even Rick Brewer's dramatic announcement of the recently named invitees to the Olympic tryouts [Lebo, Reid, and Williams] was expected. No matter.

Those who attend the banquet aren't there to be surprised. They come to honor the team and to send off the seniors who have given so much of themselves to the program. They come expecting to see watery-eyed young men attempt to put into words what words so inadequately express. The emotion that is suppressed by the team in the heat of competition is allowed in farewell. Saying goodbye to their number-one basketball program and their number-two father is no easy task.

"First I would like to thank Coach Smith and the coaching staff for giving me the opportunity to have the best year of my life," Joe Jenkins said in his farewell remarks. "There are a million kids who play basketball in their back yards that wish they could be here." Jenkins experienced a highly emotional year. On New Year's Day his mother passed away after a long illness. A year with the Tar Heel varsity team had gone a long way in easing his recovery. His remarks were serious, sincere, and humorous.

"When I joined the program in September, I didn't know what to do or say," he continued. "They told me to be at the gym at 3:15 and be ready to run. I was out on the floor stretching with the other walk-ons and Harley Dartt [the Carolina strength and fitness coach] comes out and screams at me. I'm shaking in my boots and he says, 'Don't you know better than to walk on the court with black-soled running shoes?' So I said to myself, 'Who is this guy?' — I'd never seen him before and he scared me to death. I'll never forget that day as I thought I had ruined my chances to make the team.

"Two weeks ago I was playing basketball with Jeff [Lebo] on the court and Harley walks out and starts shooting some and he's wearing black-soled running shoes. (Laughter.) I could have shot him."

After more laughter, Jenkins thanked Marc Davis, the head basketball trainer, for repairing his injuries sustained in practice. ("I was the designated punching bag for J.R. this year and he bruised me daily.") and the cheerleaders for their support. ("If I didn't say that I would be in the doghouse.") Jenkins, like his teammate Jeff Lebo, dated one of the varsity cheerleaders.

His remarks became more serious as he concluded. "My biggest reward this year was how happy and proud my family was. I leave here happy," he continued as his voice began to crack, "because when you do something for someone else it's the best feeling in the world."

Ranzino Smith, who spoke next, would also leave the crowd with tears in their eyes — but for a different reason. Though obviously sincere in his comments, Smith displayed a reluctance to leave both the program and the podium. "Joe [Jenkins] had an advantage as he had his list of people to thank and I don't, so bear with me and I'll try to do the best I can," he offered. The crowd couldn't help but inwardly smile to the point of tears as Smith then meandered through a 20-minute impromptu confession that rivaled the all-time lengthy farewell. It was painful to watch and listen as the senior stared down at the podium reliving the good and bad moments spent with the team. Still, no one could interrupt such a heartfelt rambling. Like Kenny Smith, who had spoken last at the banquet a year earlier, Ranzino Smith ended his remarks with what has become an ongoing prophecy. "I know that you (pointing to members of the team) will go all the way next year."

•   •   •

Seniors Joe Jenkins and Ranzino Smith would pick up diplomas in less than a month. They would always be a part of the large North Carolina family and welcome to visit at any time, but they would have to live and work elsewhere. Like all parents who one day encourage their children to move out and make a life for themselves, Smith and company had served their purpose. The experiences each graduate enjoyed would last a lifetime. The knowledge they gained was even more rewarding. Their basketball skills would eventually rust and fade away, but the memories of exciting moments on the hardwood floor would, like a good fish tale, shine brighter and receive more polish with each passing year. And the fundamentals of teamwork, practice, and hard work would prove invaluable throughout their lives.

Next year's team looked like another in the long line of strong North Carolina teams that vied for the right to be called the best college basketball team in the nation. Perhaps they would fulfill the prophecy. Perhaps they wouldn't. Regardless, they would follow Coach Dean Smith's corporate line.

ACKNOWLEDGMENTS

A great many people helped make this book possible through words, actions, or deeds. Among them are Woody Durham, Billy Packer, Dick Vitale, Hugh Morton, Kip Coons, Bill Brill, John Feinstein, Charles Mann, Eddy Landreth, Paul Ensslin, Skip Foreman, Rick Bonnell, Jim Heavner, Jim Furlong, Al Featherstone, Art Chansky, Keith Drum, Frank Dacenzo, Dwayne Ballen, Don Holstrom, Lillian Lee, Dr. Hank Nichols, Lennie Wirtz, Lee Roberts, James Surowiecki, Scott Smith, Merle Thorpe, Rick Willenzik, Elliott Warnock, Tom "Dulaney" Slonaker, Johnny Phelps, Dan Collins, Tessa Smith, Darcy Williamsen, Bryan Liptzin, Diane Smith, Lea Campbell, Ken Bentz, Arlene Leveille, Robert Crawford, Saul Brenner, Ed Ibarguen, and the many sports photographers at *The Chapel Hill Newspaper* who contributed photographs. Their time, insights, anecdotes, musings, reminiscences, and suggestions were appreciated.

A special thanks to: Charles "Lefty" Driesell, for his thoughts; Barry Jacobs, for statistical help and for providing a sounding board throughout the year; Lou Bello, for friendship and enough stories to fill another book; Marvin "Skeeter" Francis, for providing access to the ACC tournament and the conference record books; Garry Glaub, for helping me fine-tune my work and cross-check the facts; my dad, Jim Holstrom, for wading through countless rewrites to "nit-pick" for errors; Dr. Louis Rubin, for working my book into his busy schedule; and Arnie Hanson, publisher, and Jim Donovan, editor, for taking on this project and making it work.

My thanks to the many sports information directors and their staffs for providing access to their programs, players, coaches, and games during the 1987-88 season. They, like the schools they represent, are all first-class.

Many former UNC players helped provide insights into the overall basketball program including: Brad Daugherty, Dave Popson, Dennis Wuycik, Joe Wolf, Warren Martin, Matt Doherty, Michael Jordan, Sam Perkins, James Worthy, Doug Moe, Billy Cunningham, Buzz Peterson, Kenny Smith, James Daye, and Phil Ford. All of the 1987-88 squad were consistently accessible during and immediately following the season, but a special thanks to Jeff Lebo, Steve Bucknall, Kevin Madden, Ranzino Smith, and Pete Chilcutt for their input. To the rest of the players, former players, managers, trainers, and administrative officials, including Athletic Director John Swofford and Educational Foundation Vice President Moyer Smith, who took the time to answer questions about themselves and the country's best basketball program — many thanks.

Coaches Bill Guthridge and Roy Williams were instrumental in describing the personal side of the UNC family and its father. And executive secretary Linda Woods, who always did her best to relay messages and appointment times with the staff, your help was appreciated.

Finally, a sincere thanks to Dean Smith. I knew going into this project that he was a special coach. After spending a year exploring his program, I came away further convinced of his gifts of teaching and understanding. Smith is human. He has faults. But Dean Smith is also a man who cares deeply about his profession and the people who surround him. If I were a talented high school basketball player, I could think of no better coach to play for. He is the dean of college coaching.

NORTH CAROLINA FINAL BASKETBALL STATISTICS 1987-88

Record: 27–7; ACC: 11–3

Opponent	Result	Score	Location	Date	Attendance
Syracuse	W	96-93 OT	N-Springfield, MA	Nov. 21	9,128*
So. California	W	82-77	N-Richmond, VA	Nov. 27	9,171*
Richmond	W	87-76	N-Richmond, VA	Nov. 28	9,171*
Stetson	W	86-74	Home	Dec. 3	18,732*
Vanderbilt	L	76-78	Nashville, TN	Dec. 5	15,626*
SMU	W	90-74	Home	Dec. 12	21,004*
The Citadel	W	98-74	N-Charlotte, NC	Dec. 17	11,031
Illinois	W	85-74	Champaign, IL	Dec. 19	16,712*
Nevado-Reno	W	115-91	Reno, NV	Dec. 30	11,200*
UCLA	W	80-73	Los Angeles, CA	Jan. 2	12,544*
Fordham	W	76-67 OT	N-Greensboro, NC	Jan. 6	11,689
La Salle	W	96-82	Home	Jan. 9	12,480*
Maryland	W	71-65	College Park, MD	Jan. 14	14,500*
Virginia	W	87-62	Home	Jan. 16	20,822*
Duke	L	69-70	Home	Jan. 21	21,444*
N.C. State	W	77-73	Raleigh, NC	Jan 24	12,400*
Wake Forest	L	80-83	Greensboro, NC	Jan. 28	14,500*
Georgia Tech	W	73-71	Home	Jan. 30	21,444*
Clemson	W	88-64	Clemson, SC	Feb. 4	9,508*
N.C. State	W	75-73 OT	Home	Feb. 11	21,444*
Virginia	W	64-58	Charlottesville, VA	Feb. 14	8,200*
Wake Forest	W	80-62	Home	Feb. 17	21,444*
Maryland	W	74-73	Home	Feb. 20	21,444*
Temple	L	66-83	Home	Feb. 21	21,444*
Clemson	W	88-52	Home	Feb. 28	21,444*
Georgia Tech	W	97-80	Atlanta, GA	Mar. 2	16,400*
Duke	L	96-81	Durham, NC	Mar. 6	8,564*
Wake Forest	W	83-62	N-Greensboro, NC	Mar. 11	16,500*
Maryland	W	74-64	N-Greensboro, NC	Mar. 12	16,500*
Duke	L	61-65	N-Greensboro, NC	Mar. 13	16,500*
North Texas State	W	83-65	N-Salt Lake City, UT	Mar. 17	12,514
Loyola Marymount	W	123-97	N-Salt Lake City, UT	Mar. 19	14,062
Michigan	W	78-69	N-Seattle, WA	Mar. 25	23,229
Arizona	L	52-70	N-Seattle, WA	Mar. 27	22,470

* Sellout

PLAYER STATISTICS

PLAYER	G	FIELD GOALS M-A	PCT	FREE THROWS M-A	PCT	REB	AVE	A	TO	S	PF-D	PTS	AVE	MINS
Steve Bucknall	33	108-219	49.3	75-94	79.8	137	4.2	124	70	33	66-2	300	9.1	960
Pete Chilcutt	34	66-117	56.4	36-51	70.6	110	3.2	43	41	10	32-0	168	4.9	573
Jeff Denny	16	7-13	53.8	2-5	40.0	10	0.6	6	5	0	2-0	16	1.0	47
Doug Elstun	12	1-4	25.0	2-2	100.0	0	0.0	0	2	0	1-0	4	0.3	16
Rick Fox	34	59-94	62.8	15-30	50.0	63	1.9	32	41	26	68-1	136	4.0	371
Rodney Hyatt	13	3-11	27.3	3-6	50.0	1	0.1	4	3	1	0-0	10	0.8	20
Joe Jenkins	15	7-11	63.6	0-0	00.0	12	0.8	4	3	2	3-0	14	0.9	48
Jeff Lebo	33	120-275	43.6	86-98	87.8	87	2.6	159	76	34	66-0	404	12.2	1115
Kevin Madden	32	107-186	57.5	41-60	68.3	90	2.8	51	45	25	40-1	274	8.6	720
David May	15	1-2	50.0	2-5	40.0	8	0.5	1	3	1	3-0	4	0.3	27
J.R. Reid	33	222-366	60.7	151-222	68.0	293	8.9	57	127	39	113-2	595	18.0	1042
King Rice	34	22-56	39.3	24-30	80.0	26	0.8	55	38	21	20-0	70	2.1	352
Ranzino Smith	31	128-255	50.2	52-58	89.7	50	1.6	40	45	15	38-0	362	11.7	642
Scott Williams	34	162-283	57.2	107-159	67.3	217	6.4	42	80	45	122-9	434	12.8	900
UNC Totals	34	1013-1892	53.5	596-820	72.7	1175	34.6	618	581	252	574-15	2791	82.1	6833
OPP Totals	34	939-2063	45.5	417-605	68.9	1043	30.7	490	536	260	687-21	2490	73.2	—

(Deadball Rebounds: UNC 109, Opp 88)

THREE-POINT FIELD GOALS: Lebo 78-168, 46.4; Smith 54-133, 40.6; Madden 19-41, 46.3; Bucknall 9-19, 47.4; Williams 3-7, 42.9; Fox 3-9, 33.3; Rice 2-12, 16.7; Hyatt 1-3, 33.3; Chilcutt 0-1, 00.0 UNC Totals 169-393, 43.0; OPP Totals 195-519, 37.6.

BLOCKED SHOTS: Williams 43, Reid 38, Chilcutt 10, Fox 5, Madden 5, Bucknall 2, Lebo 1, Smith 1.

INDEX